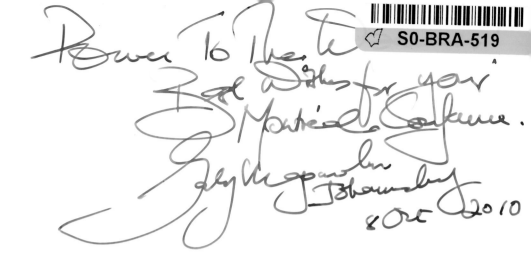

To Nana, for her enduring love and support
To my children who give meaning to my life
And to the memory of my parents

hidden histories series

Published in this series

GABY MAGOMOLA
Robben Island to Wall Street

hidden histories series

Unisa Press
Pretoria

© 2009 University of South Africa
First edition, first impression

ISBN 978-1-86888-570-1

Published by Unisa Press
University of South Africa
P O Box 392, 0003 UNISA

Book Designer: Lubabalo Qabaka
Cover photograph: Meggs Reddy
Editor: Lynne Southey
Typesetting: Marlé Oelofse
Indexer: Hannalie Knoetze
Printer: Harry's Printers

Contents

Acknowledgements

I know for sure that there is a reason why I and everyone for that matter, exist. As I travel throughout our country, I am constantly reminded by many strange people who stop me to enquire what I am doing lately. Very many have told me that I was part of the reason they were driven to complete their tertiary education particularly in business studies. Some have risen to be leaders either in government or strategic sectors of our economy. This book is the result of their inspirational messages which I have received over the years and I would like it seen as my way of saying thank you.

I am deeply indebted to my wife Nana who consistently insisted that I should chronicle my experiences. This book should have been published earlier but for the intervention of one Mike Nicol, who felt a need to re-organise the text to emphasise my hazardous business journey and the bridgehead constructed during those difficult days. Thanks Mike for your sterling structural editing. I was also privileged to secure the assistance of Sindiwe Magona, one of our country's eminent writers, who read my text and provided editorial advice. Thanks Sisi, I will forever value those cold days I spent with you in Wynberg, Cape Town.

I offer my overwhelming gratitude to my sister Semakaleng for giving her time generously and the contribution of her incredible memories. My personal assistant, Eukelia Dube, went beyond the call of duty in wading through mountains of paper, organising, retrieving materials and typing the manuscript endless times. Thank you for your patience and understanding.

During the last three years, I have had numerous people advising me and I would like to thank some of them for bearing with me. Chris Ball, thanks for reading the text but more importantly, thank you for standing by me when it counted most. Justice Richard Goldstone a long-standing friend, I feel deeply indebted for taking time off your duties at Harvard Law School to read the script and comment on it. Barbara Wood, editor-in-chief of PMR was helpful and gave impetus to our early efforts. My friends Leslie Mampe and Khehla Mthembu's contribution in strengthening the text are highly appreciated. Both did not spare me with their constructive criticism.

I would also like to thank the many people quoted in this book for generously allowing me to repeat their words and this includes former President Nelson Mandela, Dr Neville Alexander, and Dr Aubrey Nchaupe with whom I travelled on that memorable trip back to Robben Island in 1994. I also give appreciation to my Bekkersdal-Randfontein friends – Archie Jacobs, Sam Thabapelo, Joe Seremane, Bruster Nchoe and Moss Mokotong who have shared their confidences, time and great memories with me. My indebtedness is conveyed to those too numerous to mention who gave time, advice and support in preparation of this book.

To Jabu Mabuza, CEO of Tsogo Sun and Professor Louis Molamu of my alma mater, the University of South Africa (UNISA); my gratitude to both of you for having your organisations collaborate on the production of this work. I am particularly grateful to the enthusiastic support I received from the UNISA Press production and editorial team. Special mention goes to Melita Mhlwa and Kea Kgarebe, graphic artist Lubabalo Qabaka and last but not least, Lindsey Morton and Tshego Sehlodimela.

Finally, thanks to my children for their wonder and support; it has made the effort worth the time for me. After the writing of this book they have all said to me, 'You know, dad, we knew you as just dad before, but now we know the man, Gaby Magomola.'

Foreword by Dr Richard Maponya

My Journey: Robben Island to Wall Street is a self-narrated memoir by Gaby Magomola, who explores his experiences of the world that shaped the man he is today – a father, husband, grandfather, business pioneer and a mentor to many. This book spans his life from his birth in the minefields of the West Rand, and his childhood in post-World War II apartheid-zealous South Africa. Taking broad lyrical strides across major epochs in the history of his country, Gaby takes us on a journey through the harsh realities of his imprisonment in some of South Africa's maximum security prisons including the infamous Robben Island.

At sixteen, after the loss of his mother, Gaby dropped out of school to work as a factory hand in Krugersdorp by posing as a Coloured person to escape the legal limitations imposed on Africans. During the 1960s, South Africa was in the grip of various uprisings leading to the Sharpeville massacre. This led to the arrest and incarceration of various leaders and activists of the day, including the young Gaby. He completed his high school education in prison where he had the opportunity to interact with influential struggle stalwarts and extraordinary men like Dr Nelson Mandela.

A wide range of events are aptly captured in this brave book – vivid descriptions of his life as a young man, his involvement in the struggle for the liberation of his country and his adult life as a businessman in the new South Africa. I enjoyed sharing his journey to various places which had shaped his life: from a tiny Bekkersdal township, to Robben Island, then moving on to Mabopane outside Pretoria, followed by a swift relocation over to the United States to carve a brilliant career as a banker and then, thankfully for us, back to Johannesburg.

This true account is a significant contribution to documenting life in Apartheid South Africa. In looking wider than the inside of Robben Island, as one of South Africa's most symbolic centres of incarceration during the dark days of Apartheid, Gaby elevates his personal story to a life-affirming tale of courage and hope for all generations.

In overcoming historical injustices and dealing with a painful personal history in a courageous manner, Gaby tells a gripping story which will serve to encourage a new generation of business leaders. He generously shares his life strategies which led to his survival within and triumph over a business world that was hostile to black people. He endured a harsh prison life at the tender age of nineteen and then navigated the steep climb from a casual labourer to a global career in banking. On his return as South Africa's foremost black banker, Magomola made a pioneering effort to empower emerging businesspeople and set up new business ventures – some of these during the height of apartheid in the 1980s. Such highlights form the lifeblood of a bold and enduring narrative.

I personally got to know Gaby more closely as my business partner in the 1990s; his undying spirit of enterprise was an inspiration to all of us. Those who were detained with him on Robben Island speak highly of his fearless encounters with his captors as well as the music he provided with his trumpet. With his determined effort at raising the morale, Gaby, with his 'horn', was virtually the Island's Pied Piper, and was the first political prisoner allowed to keep a musical instrument. In the same manner as his music stirred hearts, I believe this book will serve to inspire generations to come.

Dr Richard Maponya

Chairman and CEO
The Maponya Group
Johannesburg, September 2009

Part 1

1994

Robben Island revisited

In July 1994 I was invited by Zinzi Khulu to narrate a documentary she was producing of five well-known ex-political prisoners who returned to Robben Island to reminisce about what it was like almost thirty years before when they were incarcerated there. This assignment required that I go to the island ahead of everyone to investigate the environment and make some impressions which I would use during the interviews.

The day before our reunion I journeyed on my own with the documentary crew by ferryboat to the once-too-familiar intimacy of Robben Island. It had been twenty-six years since I was released from the island to return to life on the mainland of South Africa.

The water changed into a clear turquoise as we approached the tranquil beauty of what appears to be an idyllic island paradise. I heard the breakers thunder against the rocky coast. My eyes watered involuntarily as we approached the cream, sandy shores. My saline saturated mouth felt heavy with numerous words that I couldn't utter all at once. With trembling lips, I felt an unfamiliar anxiety, accompanied by the whispers of the ghosts I thought I had put to rest two decades before. I wavered at the possibility of the past being revoked.

Robben Island still possessed that dark, ominous, foreboding atmosphere of a fortress. I shuddered and clasped the railing of the ferry in remembrance. Seals splashed and squealed their welcome to bring me back to the present. I heard the soothing sounds of nature accompanied by the inhabitant seagulls and colonies of penguins.

We alighted on the dock under the bright blue sunshine of the western coast of South Africa. From where I stood, I could see Table Mountain shielding the receding city of Cape Town from the harsh gales of the sea, to which we were totally exposed. I remembered the agony of being able to see the mainland, the island so positioned as if to taunt us with real life just ten kilometres away. We could look at the mainland and remember soft gentle voices and smells of females, which always brought a gentle breeze inside my heart, especially when I thought of my mother's generous kindness. For the better part of my imprisonment, I hardly heard the sounds or saw the innocence of playing children. With time, or it was just my mind adjusting to the reality that we faced, some male shapes and mannerisms began to resemble those of females.

Robben Island nights are cold and eerie and this one night was no different. Alone, I slept surrounded by the phantom spirits of those who had died on the island. That night I'm convinced I saw their faces, I know I felt their presence. Never had I ever slept by myself, or on a bed, on Robben Island. In a cell there would be sixty to seventy people, always.

The un-claustrophobic guest house echoed with vacant lifelessness. I was petrified of the utter loneliness. With wide eyes, I sat and heard every creak and stir of the pitch-black night outside. I had a spectral dream vision of one of us, the Randfontein/Bekkersdal group, Simon Fana Khuboni – known as Ganja, who was the first casualty we witnessed in early 1964. He resembled me, everyone used to say. As I stared at the ceiling all alone, I saw his smooth, pleasant face smiling upon me. Or was it a reflection of my own young face? It could also have been the swinging shadows playing with the light.

I surfaced from the dreams at the sound of the all-familiar foghorn bellowing its warning to approaching sea traffic. Its volume intensified with the thickening of the mist. I started every time I heard that long, haunting sound. It echoed and dragged back to vivid life every hopeless moment of those five years I spent on the island. Not able to withstand the torture, I jumped out of bed, afraid the past twenty-six years since my release were just a dream that would soon evaporate. During my incarceration, every time that foghorn sounded, I was reminded of the fact that there was no escape from the cruel trap, the torture, and most of all the crawling passage of time. For the duration of that night I paced, unable to exorcise the haunting memories. I danced to every bellow of the foghorn, until the mist started to rise, bringing the yellow morning sun.

After a sleepless night on my own on Robben Island, fellow former inmates arrived. First was Dr Nchaupe Aubrey Mokoape, a community-based physician with a big laugh. We hugged and shook hands, already anticipating laughter. We shook our heads, 'Ei, no' and swallowed hard before we began to speak. The foghorn welcomed him, he laughed in remembrance. In the daylight it was less audible, just a background annoyance against the hive of life on the island. We laughed even louder when we remembered that sound, emanating from a living benevolent building where it was encased. On the way to the quarry we used to stare at it hoping to catch its watchful eyes. In the daylight, it was a white two-storey building with red lines running around its circumference. Its roof was painted in sinister red shiny blinding enamel paint.

President Nelson Rolihlahla Mandela soon arrived. In our presence was a man who has surpassed mortal distinction, who had spent much longer than any of us in this hell-hole. He was also on one of his early visits to the island after being incarcerated for eighteen years, before he and others were unceremoniously transferred to Pollsmoor Prison, a maximum-security prison on the outskirts of Cape Town, in 1982. We remembered how friends would just vanish with no warning, bonds broken without reason. We would find out later that the men were moved, charged, fast-tracked through a trial and executed by hanging, what was called *intambo*.

Dr Neville Alexander, a prominent academic and struggle veteran, joined us. We remembered in his words, 'how we learned to suffer: how we had to fight from within ourselves; and how we were able to use the untimely opportunity to gain deep self-knowledge, to grow intellectually, to learn from others and to study further as many of us eventually did.'

Deputy Chief Justice of South Africa, Dikgang Moseneke remembered how he had to reassure his anguished parents on their first visit. Their love could not comprehend such a bleak future for their young son. At fifteen years of age, he was the youngest prisoner ever sent to the island. He told them he was young, he would make it. This was an optimistic prophecy which did come true, if only ten years later.

We were told, during the visit, that the island museum was being prepared to be opened to the public. It was heart-warming to know that our presence there would not be forgotten; knowing that after such a long time others cared to share and know our journey in spirit. I could imagine the eager, questioning human faces of those who would visit and wondered if they would find the answers that had (and still do) eluded me during my confinement on the island.

We drove on the paved roads, surrounded by lush green vegetation on sand that offers protection and sustenance to the roaming wild ostriches, and *bontebokke,* the agile antelope. We toured that former colony of lepers, pausing at the cemetery, their skewed weathered grey gravestones the only witnesses to their lives. With them were fresher stones, symbolic monuments that we put down to remember those we knew who had succumbed to the brutality of our captors and the system; anonymous heroes, whose identities are not in historical records. (I couldn't distinguish which stone it was that we had laid for our friend Ganja). I had heard some of their echoing screams of agony that I will never forget. During our incarceration, our own mortality was always at stake, so that we learned to look inwardly, instead of just seeing the walls, the double steel doors with heavy keys, the bars on the windows, the high meshed steel re-enforcements and barbed razor-sharp wire. We heard the sounds of seagulls and our own songs instead of the clanging keys, the moans of the suffering that we couldn't soothe. We felt beyond the humiliation, the constant counting of our heads – when we woke up, at meals, when we went to *span*, when we returned, when we ate, when we slept. Being called by a number, the degradation of the daily stripping and anal searches, the food rations – we had the same meal of *motoho* for six years – the uniforms, the back-breaking hard labour, the ice cold gales ravaging our scantily-clothed emaciated bodies with sickness and death.

We passed the fenced-in secluded small cottage where the banished Africanist leader, Robert Sobukwe, was held in solitary confinement.

During his detention, he was allowed visits by National Party officials to persuade him to apologise in exchange for his release. He refused to trade his ideals for freedom. The five of us stood under the blistering sun at the quarry remembering with laughter our ideological quarrels that diminished when faced with the damp, windy, wintry nights of the Western Cape Coast, when the gales threatened to blow the roofs off our makeshift barracks into pieces. We remembered the *Ou Tronk*, part of which was also an isolation hospital for the tuberculosis-stricken. We laughed at how the windows were re-inforced with wire mesh so that we couldn't even smuggle in old stolen newspapers to break our isolation from the world beyond.

We sang when we remembered digging the limestone quarry. Aubrey led us, '*Unzima lo mthwalo*' (This burden is heavy), our imaginary hammers and picks poised in the air while we toiled, like other slaves must have done before us. Singing those songs, we remembered how the hum of our voices in unison raised hairs to give us the courage to persevere. Even the warders were not immune to the hypnotic rhythm of our war cries; they would shift and smile widely, for they believed that our effervescent energetic songs increased productivity. We could curse them in isiXhosa without them knowing for they didn't understand any African language.

'Remember?!' we said simultaneously, 'Fatima, my love', one of the songs we sang in response to our yearning for female company.

We laughed and looked at our hands, remembering the oozing, bloody blisters we had on our palms with no means to soothe (forget heal) them. We coughed for suddenly our throats were dry. As we reminisced we patted shoulders, leaning on others who knew. I know they remembered. We wiped the dust from our eyes. We removed our spectacles to clear the mist. We wiped the sweat off our brows with surreptitious handkerchiefs.

We looked and listened to Nelson Mandela. With noble dignity he towered over us in stature and in spirit. He stood with his back straight, his strong eyes contemplative. His disciplined face did not betray what he must have been thinking or feeling. With a playful smile on his lips, he remembered with us his very first day on the island. We punctuated his memories with laughter, '*Eh, he. Eh, he, he. Eh he he* …' The tears in our eyes were of laughter. I experienced only part of his pain, and in my heart I know I was fortunate to have been sent to that place. My life would have been different in so many ways had I not witnessed this desolate island shape the lives of black men.

The apartheid government's evil intent to crush our individual spirit and extended community was reversed. I am still amazed at how we were able to overcome this shattering experience. How the very same tools of destruction we had to endure served as the catalyst that enabled us to transcend our own traditional prejudices of ethnicity, race, political ideology and social class – prejudices evident in our society.

Our shared destiny transformed us into a staunch brotherhood regardless of where we had been before Robben Island. I remember scholars and academics, debating with members of the Poqo uprising, rural men from the small villages in the Eastern Cape and Pondoland who were proud of being *amaqaba*, and publicly pronounced they had never entered a church. They had a profound conviction in their cause that shook my very core. Whereas we were banished to be silenced, to be forgotten, the island became brighter, a beacon to the shame of the system of apartheid.

We can still breathe, though most of us are plagued by health problems we acquired on Robben Island. Many of us have suffered from cataracts and other eye complications from the glare and powder of the quarries, ear problems from the blasting, asthma from the dust, wheezing chests from all the dust in our lungs resulting in various forms of cancers. The toll of the toil of Robben Island remains evident in the death it caused for many of our brothers. In 1978, Robert Sobukwe died of throat cancer. He had by then been confined to a small African township outside of Kimberley after his release. It is not just those of us who were on Robben Island who can claim to have suffered more than others. Many across the political spectrum lost their lives for liberation.

A few days later, after that cathartic journey, we returned to our separate lives. Mine is in the mushrooming city of Johannesburg where I live with my wife and youngest daughter, Naledi, now at university.

Thabo, my eldest, is married to Mosima and the proud father of four lovely girls: Thuto, Boitumelo, Botshelo and Gomolemo. It is to him that I have handed over the baton. Our daughter, Amara (Dineo) has gone to America to study at a university in Memphis, Tennessee. My wife is Director-General of the Northwest Provincial Government.

I carry Robben Island in me; it is etched in my soul for eternity.

As I put my thoughts down on paper, many years after my release from Robben Island, I hear an announcement of the death of ex-President P. W. Botha. Sadly, it is one of the few times in my life that I am tempted to celebrate the passing of a person. In 1966 during my incarceration, I felt a similar sentiment after the assassination of ex-Prime Minister H.F. Verwoerd, the man credited with the introduction of apartheid. It is extraordinary that it is particularly in the case of these individuals and their ilk that I have been filled with so inhuman an emotion. I am unable to explain why I felt this except to say that even Satanism cannot but bring the very worst in us. But this is something one has to resist as otherwise one descends to the level where the devil stands. In which case then, can one claim to be any better; standing side by side with him and perhaps holding his hand?

Perhaps, my mind tells me, this is a foreshadowing – it marks the final death of the apartheid era, which P. W. represented and defended.

This man presided over my life and was indirectly instrumental not only in the destruction of my own family life; not only in my own incarceration and that of my colleagues, but in taking this country of ours back many years. Then I remind myself that maybe he has already been punished enough. I remind myself that he lived long enough to suffer the humiliation of seeing democracy unveil and all he stood for held up, for the whole world to see, as the evil it was. He has suffered enough, for truth always prevails. And, I am consoled – and do not celebrate. Instead, I ask myself, 'One of the *few times*? Gaby, when is the last time you ever celebrated when a human being died?' I have to laugh at myself sometimes.

But the fact is that both the evocative and poignant trip to Robben Island and the death of P. W. Botha signalled a beginning to this book although my account is less about jail cells, the pain of separation and the agony of isolation and torture than it is about my childhood and the extraordinary sweep of circumstances that propelled me from dusty Tshepe Street in Bekkersdal into the national resistance movement and then via Robben Island to Wall Street, New York, and, finally in 1982, back to South Africa.

It is in 1982 that I wish to begin my story because the last twenty-eight years reflect my commitment to this country and my struggle to force a bridgehead in the white business laager. Had I not gone through the hardships of Robben Island I might not have persevered.

I might have given up and returned to the United States where life was somewhat easier for a black professional. But then, the island is etched on my soul, and the island does not let you give up. What it proves, if proof is needed in these times when black professionals abound in all enterprises, is that success is hinged on determination. Some might call this determination a bloody-minded intention to defy prejudice and to demonstrate ability and integrity. What the island taught me is that with the right attitude anything and everything is possible.

A1: (top) Neville Alexander who served 10 years on the Island and I on a nostalgic trip back, 1994

A2: (left) Nelson Mandela, Dr Aubrey Nchaupe, Gaby Magomola and Deputy Chief Justice Dikgang Moseneke on the historic visit to Robben Island in 1994

A3: Receiving Dr Aubrey Nchaupe in the memorable journey back to Robben Island, July 1994

A4: 40 years later, the Robben Island Museum is celebrated. With me is Ahmed Kathrada, who served 26 years with President Mandela, and Judge Dikgang Moseneke, 10 years

Part 2

1982–1990

2

To Vilakazi Street, Soweto

Elsewhere is always a difficult country. I left South Africa in August 1976 for the United States on a Fulbright scholarship to study for a Masters in Business Administration at Ball State University in the Midwest. I can remember flying out of Jan Smuts Airport on that cold winter's evening wondering when I would return. I was not going into exile, I was not emigrating, although my wife, Nana, and our children would join me. We would set up a house and call it home. For years we would do the things that the people of our new country did. We would raise our children, and acquire a circle of friends. I would go off each day to further my career. We would eat out, go to the theatre, to movies, we would buy the trappings of a north American lifestyle. But there was always a hole in my heart. Always the feeling that I was only partly living. Until in 1982 I returned with my family to the land of my birth.

But it was not an easy re-entry, it was not without trepidation. Our furniture and our car were in a container heading for South Africa which implied an intention, yet we decided to return via Europe and a two-week holiday, almost as if we were reluctant to face the future. So we travelled from New York to Rome for two days, and then spent four days in Paris.

Our final stopover was London, where we spent a weekend with our friends of long standing, Johnny and Edith Moema. Often our conversations were of what was happening back home.

And then the day dawned – we flew out of Heathrow for Johannesburg. Our landing could not have been easier. We found that Citibank had arranged for us to be housed in a premier hotel in Johannesburg on the lower end of Hillbrow, The Johannesburger, one of the international hotels that had the legal status to accommodate Africans, Coloureds and Asians – 'non-whites'. We occupied one of the penthouses. It had two bedrooms, and a large lounge overlooking the skyline of

Johannesburg. Hillbrow was not what it is today. Then it was not just a good place, it was prestigious, the preserve (in terms of the Group Areas Act) of white citizens. For the few months we were in that hotel, we were the only black residents among a large group of expatriate Europeans: Germans, Italians on contract, or those who had decided to make Johannesburg their home. This was worrying to us and we felt alienated from those close to us, particularly our families. How would we, thus accorded this privilege, be viewed by the rest of the community? From a practical standpoint, however, the options were limited and we thought we would utilise the space to pull ourselves together. Of great convenience though, was that we were also given access to use the hotel for meals.

The next days we reserved for meeting our relatives, most of whom we hadn't seen in a long time. Nana's parents were still alive and she was looking forward to spending time with them and for them to spend time with their grandchildren. We knew that, in the nature of things, these would most probably be their last days, making the sharing all the more important. A number of our friends and relatives came to meet us at the hotel. Without exception, all were overwhelmed by the red carpet treatment extended to us and a curiosity about us arose, induced by the unusual circumstances. We did not, however, allow this to alienate our extended family and friends, and Nana and I had decided to play things down. On occasion, we would go out to our old house in Mabopane, where my sister lived, or to nearby Ga-Rankuwa to visit Nana's sister, Doris, and her family.

A few days after our arrival, I reported to the bank's offices in Johannesburg to meet the American resident head, Tim Wood, to receive my briefing. Once again, I was assured by management that they would do their best to ensure a smooth transition for my family and me. Cautiously optimistic, I was quite excited to be home, a feeling that was not shared by my wife. I was looking forward to serving a purpose, to playing a meaningful role and, in particular, to growing my career by using the knowledge I had acquired abroad. I was particularly looking forward to raising the awareness of young black professionals to banking as an alternative career.

That had always been one of my objectives and I knew that in order to do that effectively, I would have to not only succeed but excel in what I was doing.

I joined a fellow black African banker, Jethro Mbau, who had been with Citibank for a while and had made some good strides. I was encouraged by the way Jet seemed at home with both the white colleagues and clients alike. My initial impressions were not reassuring though. The work environment was not that much different from what I had left back at head office. All menial positions were left to black employees and just a trickle of Africans occupied clerical positions. Not much had changed since I had left the country, I quietly observed.

Nana and I were aware that our stay in The Johannesburger was transitory. We had to find a more permanent place and that was a task that we tackled as soon as we could. Two years prior to our return, I had purchased a piece of land in one of the new suburbs of Soweto, which had been designated for the new upwardly mobile township residents. Curiously named Prestige Park, it was adjacent to the old township of Diepkloof. All I needed was to obtain a mortgage to finance the construction of the house we had begun to plan.

The bank tried to get us suitable housing, somewhere in the suburbs of Johannesburg. More importantly, there was the question of where our children would go to school.

Their return to South Africa was both dramatic and traumatic because we had moved them out of their comfort zone in a relatively free society where they were accustomed to venturing anywhere they wanted. The one thing that Nana and I had agreed on was that the children would receive the utmost priority in whatever decisions we took. We found that language was also a problem, because the variety of languages spoken in a South African township was an entirely new experience for them, coming as they did, from an English-dominated environment.

Since their kindergarten days, back in Indiana, no matter how much we tried to drown them in Sesotho in our household, no sooner had we left for work in the morning, than they defaulted to English as spoken in the USA.

After numerous failed attempts to secure us suitable housing, the bank came back to us and said, 'Sorry, the government won't allow you to live anywhere else but in Soweto.' The best I could be offered was a two-bedroomed apartment in a block of newly built flats on Vilakazi Street in Orlando West in Soweto. This newly-built housing complex was a joint effort of USA companies to house their senior employees who were slowly rising through the ranks. I remember going there and being told, 'We'll give you the first one which is the largest and nicest. From your lounge you can see Mr Mandela's house (although he was still a political prisoner) and Bishop Tutu's house is just around the corner.'

Grudgingly, we accepted our new residence in a highly polluted neighbourhood with badly designed streets with no pedestrian sidewalks. Mind you, this was truly one of the best Soweto could offer at the time and the authorities felt proud to showcase this complex to tourists and other dignitaries. Little did I know, then, just how famous Vilakazi Street would become perhaps a decade or so later. After all, it is probably the only street anywhere in the world where two Nobel Peace Laureates lived, President Nelson Mandela and Archbishop Desmond Tutu.

During those days, schools for black children in the country were in constant turmoil and memories of the 1976 slaughter of scores of children still lingered. The simmering tensions were exacerbated by the inferior Bantu Education and growing expectations of change.

The solution for us became the American International School, which was in the process of development for the USA expatriate community in the greater

Johannesburg metro. Situated in the suburb of Morningside, the first classes were to commence in September of 1982.

Nana and I were fortunate to participate as co-founders of the school, which was housed in a private residence before it moved to a properly constructed structure with suitably equipped classrooms.

Our children made history as inaugural learners of what later grew to be a flourishing institution. That was a comfort to us because they didn't have to make a big adjustment as far as the curriculum was concerned. The environment at the school was nurturing, intellectually challenging, and had a low teacher-student ratio.

My son rose to the occasion and his poem, aptly titled, 'The eagle has landed' was deemed most appropriate by the principal to be published in that school's first yearbook.

Despite the awkward transport logistics, this institution was one single morale booster and sustained the confidence of my kids who were confused by the sharp turn of circumstances for them. We had known that it was going to be difficult to explain the complexities of racial laws that excluded the majority of citizens from freedom of association to them.

Though, socially, we were extremely happy to be with family and relatives, the adjustment to the repressive apartheid conditions and the palpable political tension was a huge challenge. We had to learn, once again, to deal with all those hostile elements around us. The government of the day had made a habit of conducting aggressive cross-border military raids into neighbouring countries resulting in the deaths of several South African exiles. Other exiles were abducted and assassinated from the neighbouring countries that include Lesotho, Zimbabwe, Botswana and Angola, which was also occupied by South African armed forces.

Inside the country, the Security Police were abducting and assassinating activists, among them one of my mentors and English literature teacher on Robben Island, attorney Griffiths Mxenge, who was assassinated on November 19, 1981. Later, his wife Victoria Mxenge, also an attorney, was herself murdered by security police, in cold blood, just outside of Durban.

Despite this, the armed struggle was gaining momentum with more daring and symbolic attacks such as the bombings of the Voortrekkerhoogte military base in Pretoria and the Koeberg nuclear power plant near Cape Town.

Meanwhile, Nelson Mandela had been transferred from Robben Island to Pollsmoor Prison, resulting in the beginning of the worldwide 'Free Mandela' campaign.

By the end of 1984, the Internal Security Act 74 of 1982 was enacted, which provided for the banning of people and publications, and prohibited people from attending any kind of meetings. Violation of this act would result in house arrests, indefinite detentions and solitary confinement for detainees, coupled with mysterious deaths.

Later on, some changes started to manifest themselves, particularly in the area of improved housing. One of the most noticeable interventions in those sombre repressive days were the efforts of the Urban Foundation, a non-governmental organisation which had embarked on a campaign, with private companies, to construct decent new homes for black people. For the first time since the forced removals of the late fifties and early sixties, there was limited ownership of houses in urban areas for black people, through the concept of 99-year leases. Our people were feeling a sense of ownership and were getting titles to homes for the first time.

The consequence of that was that three elite suburbs were built; don't ask why they ended up with such curious names: Selection Park in Pimville, Prestige Park in Diepkloof and Beverley Hills in Orlando.

This is where prominent professional and business people such as my friend Bobby Makwetla and the well-known soccer maestro turned businessman, Kaizer Motaung, lived. I remember a reception party organised by attorney Ratha Mokgoatlheng, now a Supreme Court judge, at his architect-designed home in Orlando West. It was attended by several high profile professionals, and I could not help but admire the tenacity of this suppressed lot. These were people brought up mainly in the townships who had scaled immeasurable heights without the advantage I had been privileged with. Soweto was truly a place of major contradictions.

We did, however, note that in some parts of the white community of South Africa, there was a growing gravitation towards change and integration, led by the likes of Dr Jan Steyn, Head of the Urban Foundation. Courageous visionaries like Dr Beyers Naude, who was very vocal, were viewed as extreme leftists – a terrorist threat in the eyes of the government which rejected him. Ironically, Dr Naude was an Afrikaner Pastor of the NGK – a church, which condoned the doctrine of apartheid. Dr Naude turned against State-sponsored dogma and worked with progressive forces seeking to transform the country.

There was a white middle ground, 'liberals', who were concerned and I think they could read the future. The End Conscription Campaign (ECC) was also launched by whites who opposed conscription and were willing to face prison for their convictions.

It is no exaggeration to state that organisations such as the Black Sash, NUSAS and Helen Suzman's Progressive Party were a thorn in the flesh for the ruling party with its apartheid dogma.

At the bank, I was trying hard to adjust. Working in that environment was never quite comfortable, no matter how much I tried. The social divide among races in South Africa was a yawning gap and, forever, one had to play catch-up, itself a game short on comfort. That I was forced, by law, to live in the segregated township of Soweto with the attendant problems of overcrowding; rampant crime; unpaved roads, and a generally dysfunctional maintenance system were a major disincentive and my productivity could not but be affected. I could not, under the circumstances, compete equally with my empowered white colleagues who not only had a wide choice of residence but did not have to deal with bussing their kids to far-off schools or worry about any of the myriad preoccupations which beset township dwellers on a daily basis.

I recall, for example, the instance when my secretary, who was an immigrant Irish lady, submitted a home loan application for my approval. She wanted to upgrade to a suburb I could only dream about.

The irony of it all was that the bank made such privileges available to all employees, but my choices were almost non-existent, prescribed as they were by the government – to my unending, designed disadvantage. I would often listen with envy and resentment as my colleagues casually shared their weekend social engagements, activities such as golf, tennis and other similar pursuits in their fancy northern suburbs – all things out of my reach.

I worked in the Corporate Lending Division, which served large corporations and constituted the bulk of the income of the bank.

My interaction with clients was somewhat different to what I had experienced in other markets, particularly in the USA. I almost always needed to explain myself to new clients. That was understandable, in part, because I represented the unpredictable. Many refused to accept me as a native South African, partly because I had grown some accent, but perhaps more so because of my eloquence in selling our product. However, once I had won their confidence, I was able to conduct business with them in a mutually satisfying way. I made friends with many of them and I could often sense their empathy once they got to know me closely. These spontaneous human reactions allowed me to grow and understand the depth of human nature in different ways. It became clear to me that people are attracted to each other not always because of their hue but perhaps, and more importantly, because of common likes and dislikes.

The architecture of apartheid had the inherent failing in its design that it overlooked or failed to understand that key element in human nature and hence was bound to buckle under its weight.

The discoveries I allude to above reassured me that my career would grow, even in this country, notwithstanding my unique circumstances. I'd given myself five years to gain local experience and, thereafter, my family and I would either move back to the USA or seek opportunities some other place abroad. I was particularly looking at the growth markets of the Middle East for the next phase of my career. Having briefly lived in Greece during my training, I had developed a strong desire to work in those emerging markets, notwithstanding the cultural challenges that were glaringly self-evident.

Though we had returned to South Africa with our eyes wide open and knew it was not going to be easy, in reality, the experience was quite overwhelming.

My wife was going through all of that under major protest and it took a lot of convincing for her to accept that we should continue to live in South Africa. Part of the reason was that women were limited and severely discriminated against by both African customs and the government.

Nana, as a black woman in America, knew she could grow to be the best she could be within certain confines. The barriers back home were much higher for women in general, black or white. She encountered obstacles in finding employment.

On several occasions, Nana had noticed that every time she applied for positions, as she made the phone call, the secretaries would laugh at her for pursuing positions for which she was qualified.

Before giving up though, she decided to go to the Nurses Teaching College at Baragwanath Hospital personally, to apply for a position as a Sister tutor, a goal she had had even before we left South Africa. She already had a BSc degree and had worked as a nursing sister here and in the USA. She felt she could make a significant contribution in mentoring young nursing students.

It was most distressing for her when she was told, in her face, that there were no positions for tutors available to someone with her qualifications. They felt that she should first work in a South African hospital and gain the experience. Hadn't she? Though she always resented bedside nursing, she still went to explore a possible opening in the wards. After relating her visit to the Nurses College, she asked for application forms. One of the matrons said to her, 'We cannot give you this post without an application letter.'

Nana said, 'But I'm here.'

The woman gave Nana a piece of paper to write her application, which she duly completed and included her qualifications. The secretary, who happened to be white, seemed excited and exclaimed: 'Wow! Mrs Magomola is truly well-equipped to assist us by sharing her unique experiences. She may even teach us a few things.'

Unexpectedly, the African matron held a contrary viewpoint! She quickly turned to Nana and with biting sarcasm remarked, 'Maybe, we can teach *her* a few things.' Without warning she then asked her what *I* do for a living.

Nana mentioned that I was a banker.

'Yes, we will consider your application, but our first priority is to give positions to people who are needy. And then we will consider the likes of you,' said the matron, with a sneer.

My wife knew the door had been slammed in her face. It was most likely that she was never going to re-enter the hospital environment as a nurse. She knew right there that she had to explore other options. She promptly applied and was accepted by the University of the Witwatersrand to study medicine.

There were, however, severe logistical problems that confronted us. One of these was that we lived in the narrow confines of Soweto and the children had to travel to Morningside, forty kilometres away, for school. In the mornings, I had to drop them off way in the north, and then drive back through the city to do my day's work. At two o'clock the school came out, and I had to take a break from work, drive to Morningside, fetch the children and keep them with me until the end of my work day at five o'clock, to return home. That was our routine while Nana was at Wits Medical School. Faced with those challenges, after six months, Nana had to drop out of the university to take some time off to manage our home affairs.

Our life on Vilakazi Street was more stable. At the time, we didn't know that the street was going to gain international fame because of two of its eminent citizens. Although Mr Mandela was still incarcerated, Archbishop Desmond Tutu lived some three hundred yards from where we lived. Bishop Tutu's son, Trevor, and Trevor's wife, Zanele, were our neighbours in the same apartment block. We went out to visit the Archbishop occasionally, for dinner, or just to go out with Trevor for a cup of tea. Pretty much like us, Trevor had just returned from the UK – where the Tutu children were raised and he was experiencing adjustment problems of his own. The last time I had seen Bishop Tutu before this was in 1958, when he was my English teacher in Munsieville Junior High School.

Now Trevor was travelling extensively, globally and also in South Africa; but he was always willing to host us. Later, he and his wife were blessed with a daughter, Palesa, who was baptised by the Bishop at St Paul's Anglican Church, in Jabavu, Soweto. Nana and I were honoured by Trevor and Zanele as Palesa's godparents.

One of our new friends, Cyprian Mahlaba, helped us to find our feet by introducing us to his circle of friends. Cyprian was a school inspector and a man of great intellect and charisma. This was of great help to us as we knew very few people in the neighbourhood. Cyprian's wife, Muntu, was an administrative clerk at Citibank. We grew to be good friends with the Mahlabas and later their son and our daughter ended up studying at Langston University in Oklahoma together.

Sadly, Cyprian passed on prematurely, and didn't live to see his eldest daughter, Busi, become a prominent editor of a popular women's magazine.

In the township we made friends easily and we visited for drinks and lunches. Nana developed her own circle of friends, including the late Thando, Gigi Mbere's wife, who introduced Nana to other professional women who are up to this day her best friends – the Thabang Women's Club.

However, while some were excited about meeting South Africans who had lived abroad, learning about the things we had accomplished and acquired in America, there were those who were judgemental, especially regarding the fact that our children, who had African names, couldn't speak Sesotho.

'They think they're white,' some scoffed. Others told us that it was shameful to have children who couldn't even communicate with their ancestors or relatives who couldn't speak English.

Under that magnifying glass, our children's gregarious attitude was also seen as being forward and disrespectful – in the African custom context – where there is a distinct strict line between adults and children with the children mostly seen but seldom heard. The children, however, seemed to take things in stride their and enjoyed their assimilation and the curiosity they created. Other children would call out, 'Here's Thabo, and he's from America. Hey, Thabo, speak.' His strong American accent provided many funny moments in the street.

We were surprised to find out how much our values had altered. When we lived in the United States our transformation had been gradual, we had assimilated parts of their way of doing things, so to speak. This naturally earned us severe criticism from many and we had to take that in our stride. For example, a husband who takes care of children was a strange experience to many of our friends and neighbours whom we had left behind.

I remember distinctly how, when Nana's friends came to visit, they would find me happily vacuuming the house or washing the dishes, they would almost faint. They couldn't understand that. Our Sunday mornings were often interrupted by friends, some arriving a bit too early for our comfort – not an uncommon a practice in our neighbourhoods. We had been divorced from that lifestyle for far too long and had adopted different ways. Our friends would just open the gate and before we even answered, they would already be in the bedroom, 'Gaby, Nana! Are you guys still asleep?' Others would arrive with their long playing records and boxes of drinks to share with us. 'Gaby, I have the beer, I've got a couple of LPs. What have you got from America, now? Can we hear the latest Miles Davis?'

And, of course, that's what people do here at home, it's common practice. Our cultural expansion had made us forget the carefree township lifestyle and we had to quickly re-adjust to the dictates of the day. We found some parts of this a bit disruptive but we were home and understood that's how things get done here.

Having lived in a foreign culture for as long as we had, we had learned new habits. Our African culture requires one to greet or acknowledge anyone you come into contact with. We had unlearned this and people noticed. One of Nana's colleagues told her to do something about it because everybody at work had a problem with what they thought was an uncaring attitude. Nana didn't understand what it was she was doing so wrong, until her colleague told her she doesn't greet people when she meets them. From then onwards, she had to remember to greet everyone, starting from the guard at the gate.

On the positive side, we received lots of hospitality everywhere we went. It rubbed on to our family members. My brother Malefetsa used to go to any shebeen and people would buy him booze because of his association with me. My brother would boast: 'I'm Fets, Gaby's brother!'

People would ask, 'Which Gaby, the one in the newspapers?'

One of the people who had encouraged me to return to South Africa was Johann Rupert, Chairman of the Rembrandt Group and son of the well-known philanthropic businessman, Dr Anton Rupert of the Rembrandt Group. Johann had worked in New York and took an interest in those South Africans living in the city.

I was introduced to him by Brian Gule, the entrepreneur who can arguably be credited as the architect of the black hair care industry in South Africa in the 1980s. After his return from abroad, Brian came to settle in Johannesburg with his American wife. Johann assisted him in opening a glamorous hair salon in the city centre of Johannesburg. Many of the fashionable people at the time used to go Brian's 'Black Wave' Salon in the Carlton Centre for his famous and somewhat revolutionary and innovative black hairstyles and imported hair products.

There was very little nightlife of any scale in Johannesburg with the restrictions on where, when, how and with whom to entertain. However, what was available was purely South African, which we enjoyed very much, especially the theatre, which had a heavy political bias though it usually was told with humour. It was great to be immersed back into our complex and rich culture. There were shebeens like 'Irene's' in Orlando and 'Rowena's' in Rockville – taverns where you would meet people from across the spectrum of the community.

I credit my two friends, both physicians at the famous Baragwanath Hospital, who initiated me into these shebeens. Peter Mabe, now deceased, drove me from my hotel at the Carlton to Irene's in Orlando and later we met Gigi Mbere at the famed Rowena's Tavern.

These establishments remained the mainstay of social life in our townships; it is within these trappings that intellectuals could be found in deep conversation with underworld diamond smugglers or young university students. The loud debates that competed with the trendy music were mind blowing. They ranged from inspiration to utter frustration. Township legends of police raids, fights, cunning evasions of road-blocks, feuds, the everyday racism we encountered were shared over whisky and laughter. It is there that I met advertising and intellectual executives such as Madala Mphahlele, attorneys, teachers, politicians and other professionals engrossed in fiery debates. These are people who could have lived anywhere in the sprawling suburbs of Johannesburg, but were restricted to Soweto by apartheid. What was encouraging was that there was a movement; you could sense that this frustration was reaching a boiling point. People were talking about *when* freedom would come rather than *if*. And there was also, at that stage, a build-up of expectation that Mr Mandela and other political prisoners would soon be released; and that would signal ultimate freedom, the end of apartheid.

My friend, Gigi Mbere, moved his surgery into a Johannesburg downtown office tower. This was quite an historical move at the time considering black people weren't allowed to do business inside city limits. Besides the surgery, he was also a lecturer at Wits University, teaching young students gynaecology at Baragwanath Hospital. Gigi was very kind in ensuring that my adjustment was smooth. He, along with David Msiza and Winston Mosiako, were wonderful to us.

Winston, whom I had first met in 1980, resided in one of those fancy suburbs, Selection Park, in Pimville. He drove a BMW and was a known IT junkie who had had a meteoric rise at IBM. Not far from Winston lived someone with whom we became friends and, later, business partners.

Letepe Maisela was, at the time, along with his partner, Reul Khoza, running a very successful marketing research company, which counted some blue chip clients in its portfolio.

There was a rising trend in black consumer spending and firms like theirs, rooted in the community, were highly successful at identifying consumer trends. Their major clients turned out to be large companies who were confounded by so-called black consumer behavioural patterns which were rising rapidly, partly due to the pace of urbanisation. Letepe's wife, Tiny, was a childhood friend of Nana's and they had children about my kids' ages. This also helped tremendously to network us with other similar families in Soweto and to enlarge the circle of people we could relate to. Tiny's generous spirit of giving and sharing helped greatly with this process. In her, my kids found another mother and they spent many fun moments with their friends, Lerumo and Vuyi.

Leslie Mampe, one of IBM's new rising executives, was our neighbour on Vilakazi Street and possessed a passion for winning arguments. He had built himself two masterpiece residences on the same piece of land and named them Les 1 and 2. Les is a big, tall man with a profound knowledge of music, super intelligence and the memory of an elephant. However, behind that big frame lies a man I've always known to be willing to give and to share. As a result, loud and boisterous Les, who hated losing any argument, was loved by everyone.

I still get to socialise with him and we reminisce about our youth in the (to us) famous Madubulaville Township, where I attended elementary school.

Time seemed to roll by very quickly and by July 1983 our house in Diepkloof was completed for us to move in. We had built a face brick house with four bedrooms and a swimming pool. Diepkloof Extension was a place of distinction by South African township standards. The names of the residents spoke for themselves.

Dr Nthato Motlana, the well-known physician who had become a fierce political activist and a leading member of the Committee of Ten (in Soweto), an important civil rights movement, had moved into a house just around the corner. Behind his house lived Gibson Thula, another reputable businessman, and then, just two blocks behind lived Winnie Madikizela-Mandela with her daughters. Across from them lived a famous political businessman who was also the chairman of the famous soccer club (Moroka Swallows), Jack Sello. Judge Seun Moshidi's double-storied residence was right across from us; I could see his house from my lounge.

And behind him was a physician known as KG Mokgatle. Don Ncube, who was one of the directors at Anglo American, lived a block away from us. Further down the road from us lived Reverend Njongonkulu Ndungane, one of my fellow inmates on Robben Island. Njongo rose to succeed Desmond Tutu as Archbishop of the Anglican Church in South Africa. All those neighbourhood friendships have endured over the years though some, like Jack, Peter, Madala and Nthato, have passed on to the next world. It was the crème de la crème of African black society that lived in Diepkloof Extension. One of our neighbours, Dr Sam Shabangu, another family physician, later became our business partner.

So we blended in very well and that's probably what I think gave my wife and I a level of comfort – that we were among peers, people we had grown up with who had made huge strides in life and had gained prominence on their own, because of their own achievements, in spite of the tremendous odds they faced. Occasionally, we would meet at each other's homes for dinner and a lot of people used to come out to my house to share what it was like living away from home for such a long time. On one such occasion, a heated argument started between two of my neighbours, who were high profile personalities. Before I knew it, one of them had fallen into our swimming pool while still clasping the remains of a rare single-malt bottle of whisky. Luckily, he was on the medium deep end and was easily rescued.

Similarly, we would be invited to the homes of our neighbours and friends and there meet with other people. The blending in became quick and very effective and, in no time, we felt like we had been home for many years.

Unfortunately, in the middle of 1984, while I was away on a business trip, my mother-in-law, to whom Nana was very close, passed away unexpectedly. I cut short my trip for her funeral. My friend Winston, one of the rising stars at IBM whom I'd met years earlier when we were still contemplating repatriation, came to fetch me from the airport. Almost all our close friends came over to help and comfort us despite the three hour journey and poor road conditions in the countryside. Such was the friendship we had created in a short period – we had arrived home.

One of my concerns, though, was that we seemed not to be breaking through the wall of apartheid which prevented people from making friends across the colour line. We could not count anyone among our new friends who was not black. This was in stark contrast to our lifestyle in the United States, where we had a wider network of friends, irrespective of race or colour. I also noticed something really strange; if I ran into a white colleague downtown, either on the sidewalk or in a store, they almost invariably would turn away and create a brick wall between us.

I checked this phenomenon with many people I knew, and this attitude was confirmed by some of my colleagues.

It was as though they feared being seen mixing and embracing black people in public! Apartheid permeated every fabric of society and had created invisible barriers which seemed embedded in people's subconscious. Another weird feature of life was in sports; as an enthusiastic boxing fan, I was intrigued by the racial division, where we had a black champion and a white champion – in all divisions. I suppose, as a contact sport, it was unthinkable to see a black guy knock down a white champ; that was South Africa then.

B1: Flanked by Nana and Ali Mokoka, a colleague at First National Bank, shortly after my return from the USA

B2(a): USA Ambassador Dan Perkins came to visit me at The African Bank's Offices in 1988. Perkins was first African-American head of mission in South Africa

B2(b): African Business Cover Picture (Gaby Magomola, A new man, A new direction)

B2(c): The FABCOS delegation to Ulundi, KwaZulu-Natal, to visit Chief Mangosuthu Buthelezi and his officials. On my immediate left is Jabu Mabuza, CE of FABCOS and on my immediate right is Chief Buthelezi followed by James Ngcoya, President of the National Taxi Association. Joas Mogale is on the far right of the middle row

Caught in the middle

Black businesses are caught in a serious dilemma by the nationalisation issue. On the one hand, they are fully aware of the economic folly of such a move; on the other, they see it as a tool to create a fairer distribution of wealth.

The *FM* could find no black business leader who would willingly come out unequivocally in favour of immediate privatisation — a move that has proved to have been universally successful. But black leaders appear to have a more realistic approach to the problem of redistribution than, say, the unions (see "Sharing SA's wealth.")

Lot Ndlovu, chairman of the Johannesburg branch of the Black Management Forum, says his organisation is against nationalisation in principle, but believes it has its uses.

"Sectors of the economy could be nationalised for an interim period until the black community has been uplifted." He concedes that such a move could regrettably lead to a further exodus of skilled managers and workers, but adds that "if these people aren't committed to the future of the country, it might be good riddance."

Once blacks are well-off enough to play a meaningful role in the economy and, only then, would privatisation of some sectors be appropriate, he says. "The State isn't a wealth creator, so companies should be returned to the private sector once the inequities of the past have been alleviated."

Mashudu Ramano, the executive director of the Association of Black Accountants, agrees that whatever the merits of privatisation, it should be put on hold.

"Privatisation should not just be an end in itself or something that must be done because Margaret Thatcher and others have successfully denationalised certain sectors of the economy. It should be seen to be addressing the gross disparities of income and wealth distribution. If privatisation is going to bolster the current imbalance in the distribution of wealth and resources, then it has

more for black advancement in the past, there wouldn't be any talk of nationalisation. "Liberty Life has made a start with its R100m foundation, but why only now? It can't be coincidental that it's come after talk of nationalisation."

This view is backed by former African Bank CE Gaby Magomola, now the chairman of the marketing arm of the Foundation for African Business & Consumer Services. "Blacks aren't prepared to wait for wealth to trickle down through economic growth. Business will have to give serious thought to the question of getting the national income fairly distributed."

He says black businesses have been playing a gentlemen's game and they may have been too muted in their requests. "It took Mandela's nationalisation talk to scare corporations into action."

Business consultant Willie Ramoshaba says corporate SA shouldn't just bury its head in the sand. It should rather help draw up an appropriate agenda with the black community.

Ramoshaba

"The trouble with existing efforts such as the Urban Foundation is that they are white-driven and white-motivated. There was no attempt to negotiate the collective needs of the community."

He says business is very good at uniting when it's under attack, as it was against sanctions, but less so at uniting in finding solutions. "Business was as quiet as a mouse on black advancement before the sanctions threat got them talking."

Black managers do present alternatives to outright nationalisation. Ndlovu says nationalisation doesn't necessarily mean a complete takeover. Some form of partnership with private enterprise could be negotiated.

Sam Motsuenyane, president of the National African Chamber of Commerce, would not comment. But the chamber's newsletter, forwarded by the public affairs director, quotes Motsuenyane as saying that "one alternative is to persuade companies to hive off portions of their productive assets

Magomola

nomic participation and empowerment." Whether companies would be compensated, is not discussed. The chamber is teaming up with the ANC in a joint economic commission that will report to the ANC's National Executive Committee.

Ramoshaba says there needs to be negotiations on the economic future running parallel with those on the political future.

Big business is in the process of setting its own agenda.

The SA Chamber of Business has a task force to investigate redistribution issues that is intended to devise an alternative to nationalisation.

If black managers can be believed, a good selling job on alternatives to nationalisation may take nationalisation off the agenda.
Stephen Cranston

Playing and reffing

The private sector is sharply critical of the Post Office's announcement that it may compete in the fledgling, but potentially very lucrative, electronic message handling business.

At a conference on electronic trading held in Johannesburg earlier this month, the Post Office confirmed it is looking at entering the market in the long term.

Many companies believe such a move would be unfair and could severely disrupt the market for electronic message handling services. They point out that the Post Office already controls the national networks that carry these messages and is responsible for regulating the market.

The Post Office insists that network suppliers such as the UK's British Telecom & Mercury Communications, as well as suppliers in the US, also compete with their customers. It says it will adhere to the same regulations that apply to its clients.

Electronic message handling — which involves the storing and rerouting of computer generated information — is one of the fastest growing sectors of the computer industry. More than 3bn electronic messages are transmitted throughout the world each day and this is expected to rise to 100bn by the end of next year.

These messages comprise electronic mail — person to person communications — and inter-company mail known as electronic data interchange (EDI). The market for EDI services promises to be explosive as companies

B3: Black Business caught in the middle

AND THE ECONOMIC STRATEGY FOR SURVIVAL

"For any emerging nation to stimulate economic growth within its ranks, needs to have its own banks, insurance companies and pension fund management companies which are in the hands of its community. This is an economic strategy for survival. It is supplementary to the political battles fought by our political leaders," he said.

B4: An extract from the Black Leader, 1988, a BMF publication

GABY MAGOMOLA
A CHARISMATIC BANKER

To those who have pinned their financial hopes on Gaby Magomola, he's a dream-maker. To his wife he's a democrat, a true believer in equality. To the Johannesburg community, he's diplomatic, sharp and personable. To *Carolyn Raphaely* he's an interviewer's delight . . .

Right: Gaby's family — Nana, daughter Dineo and son Thabo — are also his closest friends, he says.
Far right: The chief executive in his pinstripe-and-silk-tie banker's uniform.

O N A RECENT Friday night, African Bank chief executive Gaby Magomola finally flopped into his living room at 9.15 pm. It had been a long, hard day and the last straw was being delayed for nearly an hour at a police roadblock in Rosebank. 'We can see you're important,' one of the policemen had said, peering through the window of Magomola's silver Merc 300E, 'but prove it!'

Immaculately dressed in a navy pinstripe suit, Gucci loafers and gold Rolex watch, Gaby had dollars from a recent US business trip in his wallet and an empty gun holster but no photographic proof.

'Use my car-phone, call my home or anyone you like,' said Gaby in his obviously American accent.

Predictably, the policeman was puzzled. 'Well, where do you live?' he asked.

'Bryanston,' was Magomola's easy reply. Then, after a protracted, high-frequency two-way radio debate with headquarters,

he was finally permitted to proceed wearily on his way.

'I guess what really convinced those guys,' laughs Magomola, 'was an invitation they found in my glove box to a dinner at which the state president was to be guest of honour.'

Back in Bryanston, Gaby's wife Nana was patiently entertaining three eager young would-be entrepreneurs, friends-of-friends, who were waiting to ask Gaby's advice about a small business venture they planned to start. A photographer, assigned to shoot Gaby for the London *Sunday Times*, was still due to arrive and *COSMO* was waiting to complete an interview that had been interrupted a week earlier.

Gaby is never off-duty. When he was made chief executive of SA's first and only black-owned financial institution last April, its image was in tatters. Allegations of fraud and foreign exchange contraventions,

hanging over the heads of eight former employees, meant that customer confidence was at an all-time low and that the bank had lost a significant amount of business. Gaby knew only too well that in the wake of the court case a wave of bad publicity for the bank was bound to follow.

Thus his major challenges were, and are, establishing his own credibility and re-establishing that of the bank. To do this, he has opted for a strategy of image promotion as opposed to product promotion, which has catapulted him and Nana rapidly into the public eye.

Now not a week goes by without a TV appearance or mention in the media. Recently a local magazine named him one of South Africa's 'most sought-after dinner guests' along with the likes of Clem Sunter, Denis Worrall, the Australian Consul-General and stockbroker Paul Ferguson.

Unfortunately, Gaby has learnt the hard way that image-building is a full-time job. ➡

132

COSMOPOLITAN, MAY 1988

B5(a): Gaby Magomola, a charismatic banker

GABY MAGOMOLA
A CHARISMATIC BANKER

This has not been an easy lesson for someone who admits to being a loner with no close friends apart from his wife and children, Thabo, 15, and Dineo, 13. Yet accompany him to the Market Theatre, Kippies Jazz Bar – one of his favourite hang-outs – a soccer game, a wedding or a funeral, and inevitably someone will approach him asking for advice, money or both.

'This definitely doesn't happen to Chris Ball,' he says, 'but I'm dealing with a different market, with people who have been denied finance for a long time. I'm seen as some sort of redeemer and all sorts of people come to me with their dreams.' This means that even at home in Bryanston there's a constant stream of visitors.

The Magomolas moved to Bryanston from Sandton in November. They bought their new 10-roomed home, complete with swimming pool and tennis court on an acre of land, because they needed more space for entertaining. They do not have a permit to live in a white area. 'I was a returning son,' says Gaby. 'After all, Sandton municipality gave me the bursary that paid for my BCom Honours.'

Life in the heart of the mink-and-manure belt is a quantum leap from the tiny home where Gaby spent his childhood in the married quarters of the Venterspos gold mine – his father was a miner, his mother a domestic worker. 'That house was about a quarter the size of our tennis court,' he says with a tinge of sadness.

Gaby met his match 17 years ago on a train travelling between Pretoria and Johannesburg. 'I could tell he was trying to pick me up, so I lied to him,' says Nana. 'I told him my name was Sophie and that I was a domestic worker, though I was actually a student nurse.'

'I also lied,' Gaby admits, 'I told her I was a research student on vacation. Meantime, I was working in a garage as a spares-boy.' Only part untrush, since he was studying for a Unisa BCom with the help of an SAIRR bursary.

When they reached Park Station, Nana boarded a bus for Baragwanath. Just as the bus pulled off, Gaby shouted his phone number to her through the window. It took two weeks for her to call him and six months later they were married. 'We had so much to talk about,' she says, 'and we're still talking.'

Initially, Nana had assumed that Gaby was married: 'I thought he was too responsible for a single man. He told me he was caring for his younger brother and sister and owned a house in Pietersburg. I knew a single black man could never get a house.'

The truth was that when Gaby was 12, he had seen his mother die of TB and had taken responsibility for his younger siblings as soon as he was able. To provide them with a roof over their heads, he had found himself a job as a clerk with the Pietersburg municipality in the department that allocat-

ed houses. It didn't take him long to allocate one to himself.

When he was satisfied that his brother and sister were taken care of, he bribed an old coloured woman to say she was his mother so that he could escape influx control and move to the city.

Gaby had dropped out of school in Standard 9 – a victim of the political climate preceding Sharpeville and a good dose of peer-group pressure. For a while, he worked as a casual labourer, doing menial tasks like patching old bags for Delmas

The secret of Gaby and Nana's unusual marriage is complete democracy and mutual respect.

Milling. Eventually, 10 years after leaving school, he enrolled for a matric correspondence course and then his BCom. He obtained both qualifications with a string of distinctions.

'In the early years of our marriage, we'd party on a Friday night till late – but by 4 am Gaby would be up and studying,' says Nana. 'He's a true workaholic.'

During the day, Gaby worked in a number of clerical jobs. For many years he had set his heart on becoming an accountant, but finally decided to try a different tack when none of the eight big white accountancy firms would admit him for articles. 'Employing blacks was not fashionable at the time,' he recalls wryly.

So he applied for and obtained a prestigious Fulbright scholarship to further his studies in the US. The family left South Africa to settle in Muncie, a small Indiana university town, where Gaby enroled for an MBA at Ball State University.

When he finished his MBA, Gaby enrolled for a doctoral programme in business at the University of Illinois. The family had just settled when Citibank, the world's largest bank, tracked him down and asked him to join their international corporate division in New York as a manager. It was too good a chance to miss.

Again the family relocated and the ta-

bles were turned. 'When we moved to New York, I enrolled for a BSc at City University,' says Nana. 'I'd return from the library or the lab at about 9.30 each night and Gaby would have seen to the children and have a hot meal waiting for me.'

Like many American women, Gaby juggled his domestic responsibilities with the responsibilities involved in a demanding job. During office hours he honed his skills in Eurocurrency lending and worked as a loan officer for large companies such as Mitsubishi. But when he got home, it was off with his suit and silk tie – he never wears anything else – and on with the apron.

Clearly on a winning streak at Citibank, Magomola was sent to Europe, London, the Middle East and Greece on numerous training programmes. Then, because South Africa fell into Citibank's European division, he was transferred back here on a four-year assignment.

There was never any question of the Magomolas remaining in South Africa permanently. After eight years away, the decision to return was not easy, but it was carefully calculated: Gaby figured that the assignment would enhance his career prospects when he returned to the States four years down the line.

Nonetheless, even in the short term, exchanging a luxury Roosevelt Island apartment with an unparalleled view of the Manhattan skyline for a Soweto matchbox was not exactly an appealing scenario. Nor was the prospect of returning to the frustrations and indignities of life as a second-class citizen.

As it turned out, instead of a matchbox, the Magomolas built themselves an architect-designed house in Diepkloof Extension and were the first Sowetans to own a swimming pool.

But Nana did not want to come back at all: 'I was in conflict,' she says. 'I knew that being a black professional woman in South Africa was the absolute pits.'

She also knew the move would be problematic for the children. They spoke only American English, no African languages or Afrikaans, and were to all intents and purposes American.

However, the couple are a close team and their unusual marriage is a genuine partnership. 'I'd do anything for him because of the sacrifices he's made for me,' she says, 'so in the end I agreed.'

In 1984, ironically while Gaby was away attending a two-month Citibank training seminar in London, he reversed his earlier decision to return to New York. Given time to re-evaluate his life and with the perspective that distance sometimes offers, he came to the conclusion that despite all earlier misgivings and a guaranteed ascent up Citibank's corporate ladder to the executive suite, his place was in South Africa.

'I felt removed from the community's real needs, and guilty,' he says. 'It started to bother me. Working with white big business and large corporate accounts no longer seemed right for me. I felt I had to share my knowledge and make a contribu- ➡

COSMOPOLITAN, MAY 1988

B5(b): (continued) Gaby Magomola, a charismatic banker

R

d counter-claims

Competition

mpetition looms

Working together . . . Teljoy chairman Theo Rutstein and Afrilink directors Richard Maponya, Jeremy Forword and Gaby Magamola. Also involved in the forming of Afrilink Holdings are Eric Mafuna and Dr Jackie Mphafudi. The partners believe meaningful participation will give Afrilink an edge in selling to big corporates.

B6: Competition looms

33

B7(a): (above) Relishing the forbidden apple – our new house in the northern suburbs of Johannesburg, 1987

B7(b): (right) The beautiful *'One for the Road'*, Naledi

B8: South Africa found Nana's suburban lifestyle completely consuming, giving her front cover celebrity status

3

Crossing the Rubicon

In the middle of all of this, some interesting developments happened. On 2 November 1983, about seventy per cent of the country's eligible voters (that, of course, meant white people only) voted in favour of Prime Minister P.W. Botha's parliamentary reforms. This step was viewed by many as a revolutionary shift away from the right. The outcome was the establishment of a new constitution which gave effect to the establishment of the Tricameral Parliament consisting of three legislative houses (one each) for whites, coloureds and Indians to the exclusion of African people.

On 1 August 1983, the United Democratic Front (UDF), a diversely representative national political movement similar to the Civil Rights Movement of the United States, was launched. Some of our latter day senior politicians formed the nucleus of the UDF and others have since gone into business. Later in the year, a national referendum, by white voters, endorsed the adoption of the Tricameral Parliament. Those were difficult days in South Africa. The government was getting more reckless, more vicious, but watered down its aggressive posture with concessions such as the Tricameral Parliament. Living in Soweto and occasionally dining out in the city created a myriad of problems. Re-entering the township at night became a hazardous undertaking.

Being vigilant against the criminal element was one thing, but dealing with the police was often the more menacing threat.

Often, the police would mount roadblocks and harass us with questions. One night, Nana and I were returning home from an occasion at the Carlton Hotel. I wore a dinner jacket and tie and Nana was in her black evening clothes. The car was flagged down by the police at a roadblock, and after a couple of questions, we were asked why we were dressed up and where we'd come from. It was clearly a way of humiliating us. These were white police constables who, sometimes out of pure malice, would entertain themselves with this sort of harassment. That was something that irritated me, and it gave a sour taste to my new life in Johannesburg. The police, under the guise of maintaining security and order, maimed and killed many civilians as was revealed during the Truth and Reconciliation Commission hearings after the elections of 1994.

Our USA permanent residency status required us to take an annual pilgrimage to that country. In 1985, on our return from the States to comply with Uncle Sam, we found that our children had been missing for half a day and my sister and other relatives who were taking care of them had no idea where they were. Frantic, we phoned neighbours to find out if they knew anything.

Some said that a group of militant youths who called themselves comrades were parading and *toyi-toyiing* in the streets of Diepkloof, forcing every child, including our Thabo and Dineo, to string along in their spirit of protest. I was out of my mind with concern and anger; for while I understood the fierce anger of the youth at the apartheid government I felt they had no right to force their will on other children. Nana and I had dreaded leaving them behind, and our worst nightmare glared at us. Anything could have happened to them.

Our biggest worry was that they had a language difficulty and we worried that since they didn't communicate efficiently in Sesotho, and may not have been able to express themselves appropriately, they might have been found wanting. All that, just because they would not have fully understood the dynamics of the situation.

Our friends and neighbours came to the house and we went out to search for them. Finally, we found them safe and sound at a neighbour's house. Needless to say, those were trying moments for all of us. I began to question whether I had placed my family at unnecessary risk by returning to the country and whether I would live to regret the decision. Radical changes could happen abruptly; it took balancing and keeping alert to negotiate ordinary, everyday life.

Especially as parents of young adults, we had to wrestle with difficult decisions; should we allow these kids to experience living here under the current circumstances or should we be protecting them by returning them to a life they were accustomed to? Would we be guilty of an act of omission or commission by choosing either one or other action? Clearly, this was causing us emotional pain and anger because all of it was so terribly unnecessary.

The years 1985–1992 were extremely difficult times in Soweto and the larger part of the country. The period was characterised by mass protests, student class boycotts, carjackings and the unfortunate internecine warfare in the black townships. Violent vigilante groups had emerged nationwide and they targeted rival activists. The situation was further compounded by the emergence of what was called 'The Third Force'. These faceless groups had initiated a horrific reign of terror by executions, house bombings, outright terror and throwing people out of moving trains. To sow confusion, this so-called black-on-black violence created a semblance of incoherence in the anti-apartheid resistance movement.

And if anybody was suspected of cooperating with the government of the day, whether it was true or not was immaterial, angry crowds charged in, often with tragic results. One such sad instance that is most memorable to me in its horror was when a woman suspected of being a police informer was *necklaced* just outside Johannesburg.

Cameras had captured her prolonged torture and morbid death under a burning tyre around her neck.

In the end, we decided to commit ourselves to remaining in South Africa and find ways in which we could contribute meaningfully. All around us everybody was part of the struggle, in one way or another. While in some areas there was forward movement, there was also an insidious digression into unproductive tactics. Public order was on the decline in most parts of the country. Schools were highly politicised. Militant youngsters agitated and discouraged their peers from attending school and children in private schools, in particular, were vulnerable because there was a sentiment in the community that parents who took their children out of the township were not part of the revolution. In the mornings children commuting to private schools (as did ours), had to wear civilian clothes instead of uniforms or they would be attacked for defying the school boycotts. Upon arriving at school, they had to change into school uniforms and then, on the way back, again change into civilian clothes. Another challenge we faced was the distance between our homes in the township and the schools. We had to wake up at 5:30 in the morning so that by 6:30 we could be at the bus stop with the children.

There, they would either get a ride in a lift club or be driven to school. They came out of school at 3 pm; but it would be 6 pm before they were back at home where they would be watched with vigilance.

The children endured long and hard days. After the abduction referred to earlier, our children found it difficult to socialise on the streets. We found ourselves forced to place restrictions on their movements. Their lives rotated largely around going to school and coming back home. And they would be indoors for the better part of the weekend until Monday. This was arguably one of the most frustrating periods we lived in.

Nana strongly urged me to rethink our continued stay in the country and, for once, I gave that some serious thought. We were helpless and most importantly, we were unable to guarantee the safety of our children. She had her own green card and her employers were willing to place her in any of their American offices.

With the rise of political tensions, rose the negative escalation of the police presence. They continually harassed any black person to uncomfortable levels. The harassment was formally enforced when a partial state of emergency was declared in July 1985. The measures were accompanied by the power to detain any suspicious person. These powers were extended to every member of the police, railways police, prison officials and army members. It became a crime to disclose the identity of any detainee without permission from the Minister of Law and Order. The Commissioner of Police was empowered to impose blanket censorship on press coverage of the state of emergency.

Thousands of people were detained and organisations viewed (by the government) as subversive, were severely restricted or banned outright. The state of emergency continued to be re-imposed annually, with modifications, until 1990.

Meanwhile, overseas, the anti-apartheid struggle continued to mount and the pressure was felt in South Africa. On the night of 15 August 1985, South Africa's President P.W. Botha delivered the infamous Rubicon Speech in Durban. Minister of Foreign Affairs at the time, Pik Botha, had told the world to expect a radical policy shift – but he was wrong. And the expected policy shifts, and the anticipated release of Nelson Mandela, did not materialise.

P.W. Botha disappointed his western allies by refusing to consider immediate and major reforms in the country's apartheid system which, to most people, meant the abolishing of the apartheid system. In a speech that had been preceded by hints that sweeping changes would be announced, Botha told a meeting of his National Party that he would press ahead with reform programmes, which were aimed at consolidating the power his party had, but would not give in to hostile pressure and agitation from abroad, as that would only encourage militants.

After that speech, the rand's value against major currencies weakened to unprecedented levels. You may call it the collapse of a currency!

In his response to the Prime Minister's infamous Rubicon Speech, the President of the ANC, Oliver Tambo, stated that Botha had '… flung an insult in the face of his best friends internationally; telling them, in no uncertain terms, that he has no use for their advice.'

Soon thereafter, one of America's largest banks made an announcement that the bank was going to withdraw from South Africa.

Finally, shareholder pressure exerted on major American corporations had reached peak heights and one of the largest institutions in the USA had succumbed to that pressure. Following that, a number of other institutions, including Citibank, also announced their plans to disinvest from South Africa. This led to a number of foreign companies reacting by adopting progressive employment codes for their operations. It was becoming increasingly obvious that economic sanctions were starting to bite and the economy would not sustain those pressures much longer. Later in 1986, the US congress passed the Comprehensive Anti-Apartheid Act, which imposed fiscal and other sanctions on South Africa.

Calls for Mr Mandela's release from prison continued reverberating with greater intensity around the world. Domestically, there were sporadic marches and calls for the release of all political prisoners. In August 1985, the UDF in Cape Town organised a march to Pollsmoor Prison to demand the release of Nelson Mandela and other political prisoners. Police intervened and tried to disperse the marchers.

The confrontation resulted in bloody clashes where many people lost their lives.

When Citibank decided to disinvest from the country, I knew that something would have to give. The South African assets of Citibank were subsequently bought by a local bank. I decided to quit the bank and joined Barclays Bank and after a short while, was promoted to the position of the Executive Assistant to the CEO, Chris Ball.

This appointment was, historically, unprecedented. It was unheard of in South African banking circles for a black man to work at the very top echelons of a major bank, probably the largest bank in the country at the time, with a huge national network. That sent shock waves throughout the country.

This was, by local standards, no mean feat. By his action, Chris Ball had catapulted me to a level senior enough to create a stir in South Africa's corporate circles. Chris, who was known for his visionary outlook and progressive ideas, commanded great respect. With other business leaders such as Tony Bloom of Premier Milling, Gavin Relly of Anglo American, Chris, a critic of the government, seemed to grasp the inevitable reality of a looming change of regime. What he had just achieved, promoting a black man to such heights, was something that did not go down well in the circles of conservative white South Africa. However, Chris continued to show courage and great acumen, demonstrating unprecedented determination. He challenged the system head on, using his leadership and position of influence in the country.

Once, he came back from one of his meetings with ANC president O. R. Tambo and other top ANC leaders in Lusaka, Zambia and briefed me about his encounters, which awed me and those at the briefing. He made us listen to a tape-recorded session of the proceedings which were dominated by the brilliance of O. R. Tambo, and crowned the event by remarking that he had met senior leaders of the ANC including (former president) Thabo Mbeki and was impressed with the man's political astuteness. 'I am convinced that Thabo will end up president of South Africa,' he remarked, with a visionary's insight.

Chris Ball wanted to change the prevailing mindset inside the bank and, in general, to accept the contribution that black people could make if given the opportunity.

The media quickly responded to catch this development which placed an enormous amount of pressure on me at a time when I was grappling with my new responsibilities. I had been thrust into a position of leadership at a crucial moment in the history of our struggle. Suddenly, I was inundated with dinner requests, speech engagements, television and other media interviews that put me under unprecedented scrutiny. No black man in South Africa had come that far in banking, I was constantly reminded. It was inconceivable at that time in the 1980s that a black person could rise to such a level, particularly at a bank.

In a sense, Chris had taken a very bold move and he must have known that he was not only risking his own career but was risking the reputation of the Bank.

Part of the risk was competition. I reciprocated Chris's faith by making sure that I performed in an exceptionally professional manner.

In some circles I became known to have had an unmerited meteoric rise and I suppose, in the conservative business world of South Africa, I was rising too quickly. The fact that I was academically qualified and had been trained by a reputable international bank and had worked on Wall Street counted for nothing (or very little) in these circles. Therefore was it not amiss of Chris, some argued, to have appointed me into the position? I drove myself because I knew that I had to succeed. One of my early encounters was with a group of senior African business people who called on me to advise on what was to be a milestone business transaction. This group, co-led by Mr Richard Maponya and Gibson Thula, both prominent residents of Soweto, had developed a business plan to buy a Coca Cola bottling plant. Market studies had indicated that the black population was a major consumer of beverages; this was in their view enough reason to seek participation at production level. I proceeded to prepare the case for lending provided Coca Cola was willing to sell them a plant or assist them in establishing a *greenfield de novo* operation.

The consortium was powerful. It also included the veteran physician and political leader Dr Nthato Motlana, Advocate Louis Skweyiya, now a constitutional court judge, Cyril Kobus, who was General Manager of the National Soccer League, Dr Jackie Mphafudi and his father. I was asked to join the group but declined to avoid conflicting interests. Besides, my priority was in my profession and I felt a strong urge to make a visible impact in what I was doing. You can call it passion.

What I had not realised was that we had just stirred the proverbial hornets' nest. Coca Cola promptly sent its International Director Carl Ware to meet the Maponya group and later, one of their directors, Ambassador Don Mchenry, was flown from the USA to hold discussions with my clients. In a heated meeting at the bank's head office in Johannesburg, the Coke directors explained that their company had no plant in South Africa to sell nor could they force any of their franchised bottlers to do so. This response did not go down well with my clients who then flew their principals to Coca Cola's head office in Atlanta, Georgia, where they demanded to meet with the global head of the company. Suffice to say that, in the end, the first black-owned beverage bottling plant, to be known as Kilimanjaro, was successfully purchased from Suncrush which was owned by the Hamilton family in the Eastern Cape. That marked the first large black-owned transaction I had the occasion to help fund at the bank.

A few years later, Kilimanjaro became the second black-owned company to list on the Johannesburg Securities Exchange (JSE) and has since been bought by the Kunene Brothers. The first was Molope Bakeries, a company founded by Mr Molope of Ga-Rankuwa which I helped to recapitalise after I joined The African Bank in 1988. These deals did much to inspire confidence and are without doubt, the first seeds of real economic empowerment for South Africa's black business people.

Prior to these transactions, the JSE had been a closed book for us and this inability to raise large quantums of capital through the exchange was a major delay to black participation in the mainstream of the economy. South Africa's repressive laws had relegated African business people to small retail traders who could only ply their trade in black townships. That was the law. The celebrated Maponya Mall in Soweto, one of the largest in the country today, was totally unthinkable just twenty years ago.

Later, after protracted discussions, we entered into negotiations with the National Soccer League and the upshot was the creation of the First National Bank Soccer Stadium just outside Soweto which boasts a capacity of some ninety thousand spectators. Fittingly so, the 2010 FIFA World Cup Final will be played at this stadium which was made possible by the vision of Chris Ball.

My new position gave me a very quick overview of the entire operations of the bank, which was owned in large part by Barclays Bank of London Plc.

Occasionally, the chairman and other senior executives of Plc would visit South Africa and I would be exposed to people of that calibre. In fact, I got to know the bank's operations in London reasonably well. The continued unrest and political instability prompted many multinational corporations to disinvest from South Africa during the close of the 1980s and after. Citibank, Chase Manhattan, Mobil Petroleum Company and others were some of the notables. Shortly thereafter, Barclays Bank also decided to disinvest and to sell their stock to South African interests. This necessitated a change of name, another process that Chris and I were highly involved in. We commissioned a team of experts to assist in the name change process and in the creation of a brand new corporate image for the bank. Weeks later, the experts presented the new green and yellow tree logo and the new name for the bank, First National Bank. Without warning, a new controversy from totally unexpected sources erupted. Some sections of the white population claimed that the tree branches resembled AK 47 rifles, a potent weapon that was used by Umkhonto or MK, the armed wing of the ANC, while others spotted rabbits among the leaves of the tree logo. Bizarre as it sounded, the lunatic fringe that represented these views found a small credible audience but were clearly trying to place the bank in a negative light.

This did not deter us from completing the essential mission of re-branding the bank, which continues to trade profitably and has made significant strides.

However, my continued stay in Soweto was causing all manner of discomfort to us. First, I had to deal with the distant location of the kids' school. Then there were other social issues to deal with, all my clients and colleagues lived in the suburbs of Johannesburg. After hours, I found myself dislocated from important social networking, which had a marginalising effect on my business relationships. I could not afford this kind of isolation, especially given its impact on my career growth.

Added to that, there was the all-pervasive worsening security situation which had most people in constant fear for their lives. This was real fear and evidence of a lived reality – that of abundant and constant physical assault and plunder. Political confrontation and plain thuggery had become a daily feature of our lives. I was left with no choice but to remove my family to a place of relative safety. The more rational option seemed to be a return to America. After weeks of pondering, we decided to embark on a mission that would prove a major breakthrough, not only for our family but, later, for many others.

4

My suburban bridgehead

In 1986, my family relocated to Wendywood, part of the affluent white suburb of Sandton, north of Johannesburg. This radical move, in defiance of the apartheid government laws, caused a major stir in South Africa. To my recollection, no black family had attempted to challenge the government in the manner we had just done.

I had asked Chris Ball to assist me in relocating my family out of Soweto, after the incident with the children. Of course, my wife was also putting pressure on me, because we had the option of returning to the USA. Moving into Sandton was a huge step for us but a major challenge to the governing authorities. I achieved this by suggesting that the bank (and Chris in particular) purchase the house for me because in terms of the Group Areas Act 36 of 1966, no African was allowed to own property in a white suburb in the country. Chris and I had a long discussion about the undertaking. In the end, we agreed that if I was prepared to take the political risk, the Bank would take the commercial risk. Stated differently it meant, in the worst case scenario, I would go to prison and the bank would forfeit the mortgage investment. There was also the socio-political risk that I could be viewed as a sell-out, deserting the community in Soweto and moving into a so-called white suburb.

In addition, possible abuse and physical attack from the lunatic fringe of reactionary whites, the *verkramptes,* was not a far-fetched fear. These fears loomed large in the decision-making process, considering that, at the time, the attitude of many white South Africans was not fully tested in this regard. Many others had accepted the status quo; their lives were protected and secured by the existence of the discriminatory laws. That the government of the day had been consistently returned to power, with an ever-increasing majority, since 1948 was part evidence of this perception among the majority of the population. There seemed to be some kind of acquiescence by most of the white electorate.

Before embarking on this particular challenge, I had started a consultative process with community elder leaders such as Dr Nthato Motlana and my peers in business, particularly fellow members of the Black Management Forum (BMF), including Don Ncube, then a senior manager at Anglo American and Don Mkwanazi, President of the Black Management Forum and Lot Ndlovu, currently Deputy Chairman of Nedbank and former President of BMF – to name a few. There was consensus that I should take the bold move if I had the courage as this action would help to undermine the Group Areas Act.

'Go for it, Gaby! We have a claim to every square inch of this land,' a friend wrote to me.

The bank's agent approached a real estate company to mount a search for us in the affluent suburb of Sandton, north of Johannesburg.

By then, the bank had agreed to stand as a nominee purchaser. After the repeal of the Group Areas Act, it was agreed that the bank would hand over the house to us. A satisfactory financial arrangement was made.

After intense introspection and discussion, Nana and I decided to make the move. To minimise the impact on the kids' schooling, we targeted the summer holidays. And indeed, come the summer of 1986, the trucks rolled in, and from Soweto to the leafy suburbs of Sandton, they headed. The historic event was widely reported by all major newspapers and some major networks in the United States. It was viewed by many people as a milestone event with far-reaching consequences in South Africa's way of life. We made front page news in almost all newspapers; even the Japanese Broadcasting Corporation flew a crew to South Africa to film this event.

Subsequent to that, I received many calls from people from across the country and beyond the racial divide, congratulating me for having taken the steps that I had taken at the time. Correspondence came from as far as Australia, the UK and Sweden; and while humbled by this, I still felt very insecure for my family. I also lived with the fear of what might come from the Far Right Wing. I had known that this was no small undertaking, but little did I realise the national impact it would have. Shortly after we had settled in, I decided to test the neighbourhood and sent out invitations to the people around my block to come to a house-warming party Nana and I had decided to throw.

One morning at Wendywood supermarket while shopping for the function, two ladies just in front of me were having a conversation. Oblivious of my proximity or who I was, one said to the other: 'Have you heard? Our neighbourhood has been integrated!' The conversation carried on about this black family that had recently returned home from America, headed by the 'famous black banker' who was inviting people to their house-warming party. I choked with mixed emotion at this loose gossip right under my nose, but left the rest to their own devices.

To our pleasant surprise, the majority of the people we had invited showed up.

Many of those who could not make it sent us written apologies and messages, wishing us well. Curiously, some of my neighbours brought their black servants along, presumably to live up to the spirit of an 'integrated neighbourhood' – who knows? Some, it appeared, had come out of sheer curiosity to see who we were.

Others, though, had come with genuine interest and declared that they were not hostile to our move; if anything, they welcomed us into the neighbourhood. And that was demonstrated by the general goodwill that we experienced because, as soon as we had moved in, we received letters, flowers, parcels of this and that and even congratulatory letters from people in the Sandton area for what they thought was a courageous action from First National Bank and my family. But, there were some sceptics who came along as well.

One of my immediate neighbours brought a video camera and seemed to follow every step of what was happening. I also took a curious interest in him and watched him elaborately film a scene where my friend Jiyane Mbere, a UK trained gynaecologist, was mixing a cocktail for his wife. My neighbour stood transfixed at this incident and shook his head incessantly as he walked away.

Later, he confessed that he had never had an opportunity to meet an educated African and apologised for his odd behaviour. His only close exposure to black people, he confided, was to his housekeeper and gardener and their colleagues.

Later that evening, something terrible happened. An unfriendly neighbour had called the police to complain that our party was too noisy. We were surprised by the arrival of the police and, without asking any questions, they fired teargas into the yard and outside to disperse our guests. Ironically, one of the African officers was the most vociferous of the lot. He belligerently confronted my wife to chastise her on having 'all your friends partying here while the madam and her husband were away. Don't you have any respect for your boss?' he barked at my confounded wife.

'Tear gas in Sandton?' That was a great story for the newspapers.

I have always considered that move as one of the riskiest things I have ever undertaken in my life.

Perhaps my greatest fear was the potential backlash from my neighbours who, I thought, would view the assertion of my right as an invasion of their privilege. How dare I? The apprehension I held for the safety of my family was soon dispersed by the warm reception we received. Sooner than I expected, my children started to invite their friends to join them in tennis contests on our floodlit court. Nana and I, over time, watched a phenomenon developing to our sheer delight (and relief, I must add).

Talk about risk: as they say, nothing ventured, nothing gained! What is more, soon after that, a few other African families cautiously moved into Sandton from Soweto, under the nominee model that we had successfully used. While the Group Areas Act stood, such were the subterfuges we had to resort to. But a vital provision was that you had to receive permission from all of your immediate neighbours that they did not object to your moving into their area.

Around that time, a very well known businessman from Soweto, Lucky Michaels, who was a founder of a popular nightclub, Pelican, had moved into the suburb of Fairlands in Northcliff. As if that were not enough, Lucky reportedly moved in with a white woman, something totally forbidden and illegal. Lucky and I started to talk more frequently, to share our anxieties of what might happen. I am told by one of his friends how, shortly after he moved in, he was trimming the perimeter hedge when his neighbour came around to chat.

'By the way,' he told the friendly guy, 'you have new neighbours and they are having a party on Sunday to celebrate their new house. You may want to pop in to say hello to them.' The man agreed and come Sunday he came around and was taken aback to see a predominance of Africans right next door to him. He spotted Lucky in the crowd and asked to be introduced to the new owner. In his characteristic way, Lucky burst into irrepressible laughter and extended his hand to the guy. 'I am your new neighbour buddy, strange as it may seem.'

And the veteran and respected businessman and Soweto racehorse owner, Richard Maponya and his wonderful wife, the late Marina, called us to their beautiful house in Soweto, to check if we were comfortable. Yes, they were also thinking of making a similar move. We shared our experiences and gave them advice on seeking a willing white nominee to buy the house in their stead. About a year later, the Maponyas moved into their new home in Hyde Park. My family went over to welcome them and to help settle them in.

With the passage of time, more people from Soweto started to slowly migrate into the previously whites-only suburbs of Johannesburg, although we remained just a handful in absolute numbers. Eric Mafuna, credited as the founder of the Black Management Forum, moved into Bryanston. My friend Gigi Mbere who had bought his house in Westcliff suburb occasionally called me to obtain reassurance that the government would not confiscate our properties. To the credit of the government not one family was ever moved out.

All of us were cautious and we generally expected a backlash from our new neighbours but perhaps we had underrated their own inner resolve for change. And, needless to say, such a backlash never occurred either – that is, as far as I can remember. The yearning for change from some quarters of the country's white citizens was confirmed to me over and over again in my engagements with them. When the famous American TV network CBS came to film their award-winning '48 Hour' magazine programme during which cameras followed my every move for that length of time, I had occasion to invite some of my neighbours to dinner. One was asked the question, 'What was your reaction to the news that a black family was moving right next to you?' He candidly confessed that, initially, they were worried that property values in the area 'would be slightly adjusted'. That, of course did not happen.

The funny part of all of this was that as the government relented to what was increasingly becoming a common occurrence, black people migrating to Sandton, it also tried to create some semblance of being in control by instituting an amendment to the legislation. The change to the law was that black people could move into a white neighbourhood provided all the immediate neighbours gave written notices of no objection to the move. By that time, I had moved to a larger homestead in Bryanston in 1987.

Our relocation gave us some form of security because the kids were now able to move around, and make friends. Thabo joined the local judo club and went on a European Judo Tour, representing Southern Transvaal, in 1986.

I remember their tour group going to London, Paris, Rome and Greece. The irony of this tour was that the participating kids unanimously voted Thabo the tour captain partly because of the confidence he had developed during our foreign trips and his stay abroad. Once again, our lives turned around and we were beginning to be comfortable in this friendly neighbourhood. What is more, the trip to work became a walk in the park for us; the city was a lot closer to our new residence, not to mention the absence of hostile police. Nana was happy and the children's commute to school was a much simpler undertaking. A new chapter in our lives had just begun and with time, we cultivated a few more friends in Wendywood before moving on to Bryanston.

One of our acquaintances was our family physician. He and his wife invited us to meet a number of their friends and our network continued to expand. Our friendship with them has been of long-standing – some twenty-five years later and Mervyn Wolf continues as our doctor, even administering to our grandchildren when necessary. But despite these breakthroughs, Nana and I felt we could not penetrate the social network of our new neighbourhood. People were friendly and welcoming, yet also distant and unforthcoming.

Around this time, we felt a need to erect my parents' tombstones. Both of them were buried in Bekkersdal and the cemetery there was in a poor state. What strikes you about the Bekkersdal cemetery are the endless rows of unmarked graves – nameless men who died in the nearby gold mines.

What distinguishes these graves are the black wooden crosses at the head of the heaped soil. The grass is normally knee high and often the weeds grow over the graves, in contrast to the nearby cemetery which previously catered only for white residents of the municipality. I occasionally go back to visit my parents in their final resting place and take my children along as is customary in African family life.

5

The African Bank

After I had spent two years at First National Bank, a period I thought was a crowning achievement of my career, Dr Sam Motsuenyane, the Chairman of the African Bank asked me if I would be interested in taking up the position of Chief Executive at their bank. I had communicated with Dr Sam since the time I was at Citibank in New York. During his many visits to the USA Dr Motsuenyane used to say to me, 'When you finish your studying, you must come home and join us. We've started a new bank in South Africa.'

Just before my joining them, the African Bank had run into a major difficulty, which had resulted in what was then the largest foreign exchange scandal in South Africa's financial history. All but one of the senior managers had been arrested for contravening the country's exchange control regulations. That is when I was recruited from First National Bank. The request came suddenly and caught me by surprise. I felt it was a great honour to be called by Dr Motsuenyane who is an inveterate and esteemed business leader in South Africa. He had pioneered and brought the bank into being by going on a campaign to raise the requisite capital. This he did with the assistance of his colleagues and one of them was none other than my old friend, Baker Mogale. Baker had risen to the position of National Organiser for the National African Federated Chamber of Commerce (NAFCOC).

Black business people at the time were traders and conducted business under the restrictions of the apartheid laws. Under the leadership of Dr Motsuenyane, NAFCOC was the sole organised voice of black business. Baker, along with Dr Sam, had walked the length and breadth of South Africa raising money for the establishment of the African Bank in the 1970s. So the call from Chairman Motsuenyane to me was quite an esteemed privilege and I gladly accepted the position of CEO in mid-1987. This, once again, was something unheard of during those years. The sprinkling of Africans who worked in banks were, for the most part, backroom clerks and at best, tellers. My appointment as Chief Executive of the bank was highly welcomed by customers of the bank and other stakeholders in the country and placed additional leadership responsibilities on me. But this breakthrough development was also viewed by many as a foreshadowing of major new opportunities for those aspiring to improved career opportunities, particularly from the disenfranchised majority. A huge spotlight was placed on me and by this one stroke I was thrust into the public domain and carried many people's hopes.

This action, I knew then, was not only unparalleled but eroded established myths. I wondered for a moment if I was not moving too fast. My face found itself on the cover of career magazines, and invitations to address all kinds of special interest groups were difficult to cope with. I needed help and to support this career leap, Nana resigned from her job.

This was a huge sacrifice from her, because she really loved what she was doing, and she felt she was on a good path in terms of her own career development.

When I assumed the leadership position, the Bank had already been placed under curatorship by the Reserve Bank of South Africa and it was run by management seconded from Trust Bank, a large competitor bank. Inevitably, the media took some interest in my appointment and this placed me in the unenviable position of being constantly under the proverbial microscope, which quickly extended to my private life.

Given the situation at the bank I had many meetings with the Reserve Bank Governor, Dr de Kock. He promptly cautioned me that it would be important for me to ensure the turnaround of the African Bank, which had experienced trading difficulties from inception. The bank would have to increase its capital and increase its efficiency ratios so that it would be competitive and decrease its reliance on central bank interventions, I was told in no uncertain terms. Unbearable pressure was brought upon me, with the added disadvantage of operating with borrowed management from Trust Bank. In fact, all of them except for one general manager, Victor Sandamela, were white South Africans. I made a quick assessment of the management team and realised that apart from the need for recapitalisation, the bank lacked skilled staff. In effect, it was owned by the ordinary man in the street and the problem at the time was that there was not enough disposable income in the hands of Africans.

This resulted in the bank's inability to raise enough funding from the general African population – funding that was sorely needed to pep up the capital resources. Consequently, there now arose a need to create another class of shares, which would be owned by the four major banks. That, of course, made it so much more difficult for us to manage the bank, given that it was also under curatorship.

African Bank was a major challenge. We had to do a lot with a little. We neither had the capacity nor the resources to run the Bank as effectively and efficiently as the other banks I had worked for.

My first task was to improve staff morale, reduce accumulated losses emanating largely from poor quality assets and to reposition the bank as a credible institution in the marketplace. Faced with such enormous odds and meagre resources, our team embarked on an effective and sustained image versus product marketing campaign. Operating on a limited promotions and advertising budget, we targeted large corporates who were a stabilising influence in the bank's client base, and, secondly, the African community for whom the bank was created. Realising that I was to take charge personally of the bank's marketing campaign, I moved swiftly to appoint a team of our strongest managers to head up the strategic streams. By that time, we had appointed several street-wise officers such as Zuko Rwaxa, an expert in Small and Medium Enterprise business development, Joe Modibane, a Rutgers MBA with excellent finance credentials and John Bloomfield, a Canadian Cambridge educated social engineer who spent his life in the townships. I had identified some major structural flaws that, if not corrected, would lead the bank over the precipice. It was important to create key strategic units headed by competent managers who had proven experience in their respective areas. This was part of my turnaround strategy to produce positive results.

I proceeded as planned and made Zuko responsible for growing our SMME division and ensuring that he attracted quality assets into his portfolio. In addition, he was to call on professionals such as physicians in private practice, attorneys, teachers and nurses, with a view to growing our advance book. Often, one must go with one's own gut feeling and I had sensed a growing sense of identification with our efforts to rebuild the bank from our communities. In addition, we recognised the need to serve these growth markets by crafting tailor-made packages to suit their needs. Zuko excelled at this and measurable progress was made.

In addition to his key responsibilities of debt recovery, Joe Modibane was also tasked with rehabilitating the bank's asset and liability management system which was in a chaotic state. The latter was an approach for overall balance sheet management that came into common use by banks as a result of the high interest rate scenario that prevailed during the late 1970s and parts of the 1980s.

Learning from the best, my mentor Chris Ball, I had also appointed Lonnie Mamatela as my Executive Assistant and delegated most of the routine tasks in my office to him. Lonnie had to learn fast and left only the more critical decisions to me and the experienced senior management. The strategy worked well, my easy style had made me friends in the media and this meant the bank received regular and favourable coverage. The campaign allowed us, in a short period, to reposition the bank as the bank of choice for the less privileged.

Among the community projects initiated was the Mpho and Mphonyane Siamese Twins Trust Fund jointly sponsored by the bank and *The Sowetan* newspaper; the launching pad for Skotaville Publishers, which became the country's first visible publishing house; and a close association with the *Seriti sa Sechaba* Project, a high profile NGO with strong roots in the townships. I also made the bank's facilities available to the National Stokvel Association as the bank had been instrumental in its establishment. This has been graciously acknowledged by the president of the influential association, Andrew Lukhele in his book, *The Stokvel Movement in South Africa*. To want to achieve that much with so little was almost an insurmountable task. I dared not fail – the pride of a nation was at stake.

Because of this campaign, we received applications for career opportunities at the bank from young capable Africans from competitor institutions who felt that their careers were stifled. We also received several inquiries from people studying at universities abroad. That was exactly what I was looking for because I was working with borrowed management. Though we had an amiable professional relationship, I was always conscious of the fact that their loyalty lay elsewhere. As the CEO of Trust Bank had told me in a conversation, 'Gaby, surely, you don't expect me to send my best guys to your bank – I need them here.' That confirmed my worst fears. We had to make do with second best. This challenged me to train our own people.

Not too many people were pleased that there was an African Bank, never mind the way I was promoting it. In some cases I was seen as perpetuating apartheid or separateness by promoting the concept of a black-owned bank. However, when you steep yourself in your legitimate marketplace as we did, you are bound to yield positive results. Banks are by their very character known to be conservative and risk-averse. At our bank, we had created a strong and growing partnership with our clients and were under pressure to demonstrate good faith. Entrepreneurs were crying out for assistance and more importantly, loan facilities, to give meaning to their dreams. This was a national outcry and the response from Polokwane to Mthata, and indeed, throughout our branch network, was for loans and advice.

In a sense, we had raised expectations and in a small but symbolic way we helped to restore hope and confidence to a distraught community. Our business loan book assumed a new character as our systems to trace and recover bad debts slowly improved. Notable successes were entrepreneurs such as Sam Matona who personally approached me to fund his innovative portable toilet business. Sam had identified an untapped market in funerals, weddings, church revival meetings and other traditional gatherings taking place weekly in black townships. His approach to me was forthright. 'Gaby, I need R100 000 and I have no collateral to support it', he said looking me squarely in the eyes.

'How will you repay the loan?' I asked and without hesitation he talked me through his vision and opened my eyes to what I had learned years ago during my training. Sometimes you have to trust your gut feelings. I nodded in approval and the rest is history. 'I am in the shit business,' Matona would proudly announce if asked what his vocation was. His business grew rapidly and became an inspiration to others.

Another success story was that of a group of hair care experts who had earlier approached us to finance their manufacturing facilities to produce hair cosmetics. I had seen how this industry had flourished in the USA. It did not take much convincing to approve a line of credit with minimum guarantees. Manase Shole, Mos Tau and Lucky Nkosi's business produced enough products for their retail market and they became one of the first manufacturing entities in Soweto. Needless to say, the loan was repaid on time and their business thrived in a fast growing multimillion rand industry. It is these kinds of partnerships that earned us goodwill and allowed us to penetrate the market while enhancing the image of the bank which had been severely damaged by the foreign exchange scandal. Notwithstanding all these successes, we continued to grapple with our loan recovery efforts primarily due to an outdated computer tracking system. A well-known socialite once told me that he would not bother to service his debt with the bank because of our corrupted information systems. He was right and many other customers took advantage of this weakness in withholding payments. Trying to reconcile our debt book was a nightmare for our auditors. What compounded our problems of loan recovery was that some of the bank's directors were also indebted to the institution and this did not go down well with some of the customers and the general public.

Because of the profile I carried, I received numerous invitations to address various interest groups. From my understanding of business, I felt and preached that for us to succeed we needed to have our own resources, which we controlled ourselves. I saw black business potential that remained untapped, what I called 'the sleeping giant'. I felt that in spite of the tremendous odds that faced us in business, we needed to link our various forms of struggle with economic empowerment. Therefore, whenever I was asked to speak, my theme would be that the economic development for our people should not be deferred to the post apartheid era.

It became clear to me then that the envisaged political change we were fighting for would be incomplete if we disregarded the fact that national income would still remain unevenly distributed.

I was making bold and sometimes provocative statements which were widely reported in the national (and often international) media. During that time, the *Wall Street Journal* profiled me and the late Godfrey Moloi as openly defiant of business restrictions imposed by the apartheid government. Around the same time, *The London Times* ran a series of articles on what they termed the South African Revolution, where I was singled out as one of a number of black Africans agitating for an improved lifestyle for disenfranchised people. Sometimes at home my wife would caution, 'you must be careful of the things you're saying!'

My appeal for capital and skills for the African Bank had a limited response and this in turn delayed development and growth. After knocking on a number of doors, the USA Agency for International Aid office in Pretoria contacted my office for a meeting. Before that, I had a meeting with Ambassador Edward Perkins, who had intimated that there might be some technical assistance available if I made a formal request. Perkins was the first African American ambassador ever posted to South Africa.

I elaborately explained to him that our principal need was capital and human resource development.

By its very nature, a bank's growth is irrevocably linked to its capitalisation as banks are highly regulated. We also needed bankers in sizeable numbers to meet community needs. The latter request was a tall order as apartheid had ensured that there would be a scarcity of college graduates in the area of commerce and finance. South African banks had shown no interest in promoting Africans to a level beyond that of teller. In fact, I can't recall the countless occasions that I was introduced in the community as a teller at the bank, despite my position. That was to be understood; except for my predecessor, Moti Maubane, no African in South Africa had ever risen to the position of Chief Executive of a bank. These were the dark days. Even then, I was still denied membership of the Rand Club in Johannesburg. My need to join the club was to give me access to an important network in the city's top business community. After all, we had several large businesses that not only had deposited significant sums at our bank but several of them enjoyed lending facilities from us.

My negotiations with USAID resulted in what they termed 'technical assistance' and that amounted to the seconding of a seasoned US banker to work with me. Our needs, however, were monumental and I was willing to accept what I thought was a modest but symbolically important gesture.

While living in the USA, I had been personally inspired as I watched with great admiration how minority banks provided economic impetus to impoverished neighbourhoods and helped to grow minority businesses. One of the more successfully operated minority banks was the Freedom National Bank, situated on 125th Street in NYC. There were several such banks across the nation, all providing similar services.

A few weeks later, I was excited by the news that an esteemed banker named Sharnia Tab Buford would be joining me as an advisor and consultant. Tab had served as CEO of Freedom Bank in NYC and was well connected in US banking circles. Along with him and his associate Agyeman Jojo, we identified areas of weakness within the bank and they recommended remedial measures that were required to enhance operational efficiencies. Tab also engineered my meeting with the Minority Bankers Association in the United States and in 1988 I was invited to address their Annual Conference in Boston.

My campaign for our bank was not only limited to African special interests groups. I also met with several business leaders to plead the bank's cause. One of the most memorable of these encounters was at Anglo American, when I was invited by the late Mr Harry Oppenheimer, who was then Chairman of the Anglo American

Corporation. I met with him and some of his executives at their headquarters on Main Street, which was within walking distance of our offices on Marshall Street in the Johannesburg city centre. I was curious about and impressed by this invitation.

Over a sumptuous lunch preceded by cocktails, Mr Oppenheimer invited me to sit on his right and after warmly welcoming me, he requested that I state my views about the vision and objectives of the African Bank. He further mentioned that he had read about my strong views in the media, something that seemed to have intrigued him somewhat.

So I expounded my vision for the bank, as a vehicle for black economic emancipation. I thought it was a bank that would galvanise savings for African people so that they, who felt that they were sidelined by mainstream banks, could find means to finance their businesses and other ambitious initiatives.

I felt I had stated my case succinctly to the Chairman of Anglo. After listening carefully, Mr Oppenheimer responded courteously, but I was not sure if he shared our views. For a moment I was at a loss regarding how to explain our viewpoint; I had assumed it was quite obvious that the banking system in the country was not geared towards promoting emerging businesses, particularly those in black areas.

I then gently reminded Mr Oppenheimer of Volkskas Bank, a bank which was at the time blatantly Afrikaner and proudly served the needs of that ruling class. The conversation continued along those lines throughout our lunch and assumed the form of an enlightening discourse. At the end, I underscored my point by stating that an oppressed people are required to raise themselves by their boot straps.

While maintaining his courtesy as my host, I recall Mr. Oppenheimer's response as being sharply different from mine and I left the lunch in deep thought and reported my experience to my colleagues at the bank. It occurred to me that I had received attention from one of the celestial business leaders and this got me to re-assess our goals and my outspoken stance on the question of black participation in the economy and the repercussions it would have from the investor community. Our bank existed partly on the benevolence of certain powerful white interests driven by a variety of often diametrically conflicting objectives. The major banks who held all the preferred shares were publicly listed and a huge portion of their stock was institutionally owned. It did not escape my mind that some of these institutions were not necessarily sympathetic and at worst, some were hostile to the cause of black socio-economic upliftment.

I was sharply reminded of these differences when an altercation occurred between Dr Sam Motsuenyane, President of the National African Chamber of Commerce (NAFCOC) and Dr Jan du Plessis, who chaired the all-powerful Afrikaner Volksbeleggings. This fracas at NAFCOC's Annual Conference at the Good Hope Centre in Cape Town in 1988 stemmed from the main address by Dr du Plessis, who stated that African business people should stop moaning and emulate the Afrikaners who had also been oppressed by the English regimes of the past.

He reminded us how, since assuming political power in 1948, the Afrikaners had pulled themselves up by their own bootstraps to create large business undertakings such as mines and banks.

In his response, the NAFCOC President pulled no punches. In his usual calm style, and while observing the protocol of being a host, he nonetheless put his sharply differing views across. 'It is wrong to compare our brand of oppression with that of the Afrikaners; ours is complete and ruthless', he said. He then reminded Dr du Plessis that the Afrikaner did not have to be subjected to an inferior education system which placed severe limits on our understanding of sound business principles. This incident was a sharp reminder of the divergence of views on the delayed growth of black business.

A few years later, I had a similar conversation with Mr Gavin Relly, who had taken over from Harry Oppenheimer. As I recall, he too disagreed with my stance in promoting the existence of a sectoral bank but reaffirmed that the bank would continue to enjoy the technical assistance it did from First National Bank. 'It polarises the nation, Gaby, can't you see that?' he said as he pondered my bewildered face. Anglo was a major shareholder and we relied on people like Gavin to continue supporting the bank. Very recently in 2007 I asked to meet with Lazarus Zim at his executive suite still situated at 44 Main Street, Johannesburg. Lazarus had just been made the first black African Chief Executive of this giant mining house.

It was quite an experience for me to walk into this marble-walled building some twenty years later to visit with the new transformed generation of its leadership. I briefly touched on my earlier visits to Anglo and Laz and I could not help marvelling on how things had changed. 'This is the new South Africa,' he joked as he continued to crackle with laughter.

I was already on record as regularly calling for the galvanising of an African economic force for black people to stand up and create institutions that they could govern and to create a potent economic force among ourselves.

Sipho Ngcobo, who was one of the country's leading business journalists, told me once that I perplexed him by saying that Africans should devise strategies of taking equity positions in mines, financial institutions, wineries and use their collective economic muscle to create their own. In the minds of many of our people, that was the domain of the white privileged class. Consciously, I was trying to sensitise African people to strengthen the African Bank and to create their own institutions rather than rely on those who were not sensitive to the needs of the impoverished majority.

Consequently we went on a major campaign to get African people to buy shares in the bank by approaching church groups, trade unions, and sports people – encouraging them to purchase parcels of shares in our bank. There were a number of progressive corporations that came to the fore during this period.

I am particularly reminded of Kellogg's, the global cereal manufacturer. With cooperation from the management, a large number of their employees were assisted to own shares at the bank through a loan programme initiated by the company. In this regard, we worked closely with Chris Dlamini, a very able labour leader at Kellogg's.

This encouraging development motivated us to mobilise our campaign for the recapitalisation of our bank. Joe Modibane, the Bank's new treasurer, and Victor Sandamela along with Zuko Rwaxa became my Swat team. Progress was evident but painstaking. Meanwhile, the Reserve Bank had given us an ultimatum that by a certain date they would expect the bank to be fully profitable as they could no longer continue to provide support. With pressure mounting from the central bank as the due date approached, I felt as if I was slowly burning out. I was forever on the road and my family saw little of me.

The main challenge was to encourage our people to purchase parcels of shares to increase shareholding and the capital base because our capital ratio was falling far short of what was required to grow the bank into what we wanted it to be.

The media did not help. The forex case was reported daily and that undermined our campaign efforts. Ultimately, those African Bank officers who were on trial were found guilty and sentenced to long terms of imprisonment.

The task of rebuilding and re-branding the Bank became even more onerous. Meanwhile, through our chairman, Dr Sam Motsuenyane, we had initiated a channel of engagement with the ANC leadership in exile in Lusaka, Zambia. We felt that it was important that those at the forefront of the liberation struggle be kept abreast of our economic emancipation campaign.

I had developed what I thought was a strategic vision for the bank, one which would create a niche, to serve the growing under-banked markets in the informal sector. The four major banks who were minority shareholders at African Bank constantly reminded me that it was important for the bank to create its own future base and not try competing with the larger banks. 'We can't be seen to be growing a competitor,' they reminded me often enough. I quickly realised that we should resort to strategies that technology-driven banks like theirs could not compete with. That became part of an evolving strategy, which I later presented to the Bank's board. Unfortunately, they regarded it as a cardinal sin and differed vehemently with my strategy. Their view was that the Bank should not deviate from its original plan of finding a way of competing with the major banks.

Around that time, a minority group of managers had presented what they termed 'A Letter of Concern' to the board of the bank. They were opposed to my management style which was seen to be biased against some and not in the best interests of the bank.

This caused a backlash and some conflict was created particularly with the majority who promptly disassociated themselves from these views.

I thought we had workable semantic differences, but Dr Sam and I subsequently agreed that I should step down as CEO in the general interests of the bank. That came as a major blow for me and the manner in which the news about my sacking was broken was equally dramatic.

That fateful evening, hours after I had been asked to resign, I received a call from Len Kalane, night editor of *City Press*. The news had been leaked to one of his journalists and Len, who had known me from my Bekkersdal days, did not hesitate to confront me. In defending my dignity, I made an awkward attempt to explain what had happened and pointed out that I had had a rejection of my vision from the board. Len continued to question me on my personality clash with some of the managers and some unsubstantiated allegations that were made about my management style. Later that morning the radio bulletins ran the story of my sudden departure from the bank and this was followed by wild headlines in *City Press* and other major newspapers.

My critics were hard on me, with some referring to my vision of creating a vibrant economy in our neighbourhoods as a far-fetched dream. In retrospect they were right; the rise of a black middle class in South Africa remained stunted and only became reality after the advent of a new democratic order in 1994. Quietly, I lamented the delay of a dream.

If the latent black consumer purchasing power had been channelled properly it would have accelerated the dawn of access for the then disenfranchised into the economic mainstream. But mine was not a lone vision. Many supporters had openly defended me for championing the cause of economic empowerment, even at that early a stage.

In the midst of the debate, I often wondered what impact all this had on my children, Thabo and Amara. Both were in their teens and were well aware of the controversy around their father being played out in the media. I worried about the negative effects the attacks on me were having on them but was encouraged that we also received a huge amount of encouragement from a wide spectrum of South Africa's population. This was evidenced by the stream of visitors we received at our house, not to mention the deluge of positive letters and telegrams.

I found myself in a quandary. The terrible shock and disappointment just kept reverberating. That untimely step negatively affected staff members who understood the rationale behind the strategy. One of our senior managers, Joe Modibane, had written to the South African Reserve Bank to alert them to the directors' problem loans. This irritated the board and I learned from Modibane that he was asked to leave the bank after a settlement was reached with him. As treasurer, Joe knew the pressure we received from the South African Reserve Bank.

I felt the need to thank the Reserve Bank for the support they had lent us during my tenure, and I was very pleased when I received a letter from Dr Japie Jacobs, the Special Advisor of the Governor of the Reserve Bank, stating that I had done everything asked of me and exercised the required diligence to grow the African Bank. Several years later, I continued to meet with members of the board, including Dr Motsuenyane and continued to maintain a cordial relationship.

6

One for the road

In my focus on the success of African Bank, I was blind to the hidden intentions of some influential people. I didn't play the game of speaking in tongues, I was outspoken and vocalised what I really meant and did so boldly. Unintentionally and unaware, I ruffled many feathers, often those of very powerful forces. Once I was called to account by the late State President P.W. Botha. We were in Kempton Park attending a conference near the airport, where he and a few of his ministers were present. I had been asked to present a paper. Later in the evening, I was advised by one of his senior aides that the State President requested to meet with me. My wife and I had earlier sat at the head of the table with him and his wife. I didn't know what to expect, but made my way to the holding room from where I was escorted into his private suite where I found him seated.

He shook my hand politely but, with a stern face, looked me in the eye and told me he was pleased to meet me. He then told me that he had taken note of the statements that I was making and was not particularly pleased with some of my views. However, he was very courteous and mentioned that the government would not interfere with me although he felt that I was somewhat misguided. I still recall his caution that I was playing into the hands of enemies of the state.

I spent almost twenty minutes with him and his wife. The rest of our discussion was about general things and he seemed particularly careful not to offend. After a cup of tea, I was escorted out.

Incidentally, my meeting with Botha took place at the World Trade Centre, which became the venue for the Convention for a Democratic South Africa (CODESA), in 1991. CODESA was the beginning of the negotiations that began the process of transition to reach democracy in South Africa.

My leaving the African Bank and the resultant fallout could not but create a crisis for me and my family and even for part of the community. For the first time since

I was nineteen years old, I was embarrassed to be officially unemployed. I dreaded how we were going to cope both emotionally, but more especially, financially. I had just bought a new home in Bryanston and my wife was at law school. All my indebtedness was tied to the African Bank and with no alternative source of income, I was rendered helpless. Our son, Thabo was almost an adult, semi-independent and at the time studying in America. Amara was an adventurous, intelligent and opinionated growing adolescent who engaged us intellectually and emotionally. Besides all that, at the end of 1988 Nana had been to see a doctor because she was not feeling well, only to be told she was pregnant. The news came as a big yet thrilling shock to us. It was sixteen years since we'd had a child. Nana and I had tried for many years to have another baby and had come to the conclusion that it was not to be. As a result we'd stopped bothering with contraceptives. Though extremely excited, we were very cautious because Nana was then in her forties.

Meanwhile, I could not get my mind off the puzzling manner in which I had been sidelined from the bank. My fluctuating emotions followed the usual chain reaction of denial, quickly followed by indignant anger, then self-recrimination, self-pity, volatile anger and then back to denial.

I had put all the mental and physical resources I had in me into the bank with the certainty that we would succeed. And now it seemed all that effort had been flippantly dismissed. My frustration led to some unfortunate statements I made to the media, which were found to be tactless by some. Left purposeless, I felt myself sinking into an abyss of depression from which I tried to surface by looking at other avenues of escape. While I had always been abstemious, I began to overindulge in things I wasn't used to – like drinking. That mirage of distraction didn't work. Fortunately, I still had the sense to be conscious of my family responsibilities and dignity (though bruised). I didn't reach a point of total loss of control but Nana had cause for serious concern. At the same time she assured me that she fully understood that I was psychologically and mentally going through a prolonged depression and I knew I had her unconditional support.

I wanted to grieve privately and tried to be a hermit for the first time in my life by avoiding many of my friends. But none of them would let me isolate myself like that. They inundated us with phone calls and many just showed up at whatever time they could to offer their support and assistance. I remember one friend, Dr Peter Mabe, who offered me a cheque, which eventually bounced and he later explained it as a way of extending me a few weeks reprieve from my debtors.

Sadly, Peter has recently passed on and at his funeral many others shared their stories of his generosity, which was sometimes larger than his pocket. May God rest his soul!

My sudden departure from the bank was received with shock and, in some cases, anger from many people partly because of the profile that we had built at the African

Bank. Not only had my dream been shattered, but many Africans had looked at the African Bank as an iconic institution for the restitution of economic independence for African people.

The irony of 1989 was that in that uncomfortable transitory period of my career, on the 31st of July 1989, mercifully God graced us with a beautiful girl. She was bouncy, pretty, everything seemed perfect about her and I have to say even to this day, she is a wonder to us; a blessing for which we can never thank God enough. When we introduced her to Archbishop Tutu, he laughed heartily and shouted, 'This one is for the road, Gaby!'

Naledi was indeed 'one for the road', and has turned out to be our last child.

Before very long, I was recruited for a leadership position by the Foundation of African Business and Consumer Services (FABCOS). I had been watching the development of FABCOS even when I was at the bank and was impressed by their infectious enthusiasm. Tightly managed by Jabu Mabuza and his colleague, James Chapman, this coalition of several small- and medium-sized businesses was making unprecedented gains in the informal sector of South Africa's economy. One of their members was the powerful South African Black Taxi Association (SABTA). The latter had assumed a central role in the country's automotive sector. In fact, FABCOS had earlier sent a delegation to explore ways we could become their banker with certain concessions. We were just on the verge of continuing these negotiations when I left the bank.

I was invited to become Chairman of the group, which was presided over by one James Ngcoya, President of SABTA and a doyen of the taxi industry. A very vocal person within the organisation, Mr Ngcoya gave me a clear, concise and specific mandate. 'Mr Magomola,' he began, 'We know what you were trying to achieve at the African Bank. We've been watching from the sides and we would like you to come in here and create a bank for us. We'd like a bank created particularly for our Black Taxi Owner's Association, close to fifty thousand of them nationwide currently, and we're using a bank where we have no equity stake and no representation. We would want an institution where we would have a controlling shareholding and we would like to give you a mandate to start the process.'

I went home to ponder that. Another bank: problem or opportunity?

My mind raced with expanded dreams and it didn't take much time for me to appreciate the potential of that opportunity. By the time I arrived home, I had almost accepted the appointment and the invitation, particularly because Baker was secretary-general of FABCOS. I knew I could count on his aegis and I would be able to retain some peace of mind. Also, Baker, to whom I seemed to be inextricably bound since Randfontein, had come out of NAFCOC and was a champion of black business. Apart from anything else, the FABCOS team had created a coherent national business strategy and they worked in symphonic harmony. The appointment excited me greatly because I could almost see the continuum and materialisation of the dream that we had all started to see at the African Bank. It couldn't be timelier. FABCOS was a large organised business organisation. In short a platform of medium and micro businesses such as street vendors, taxi operators, and small farmers, everybody doing business on a small scale, many with scant means. Yet they had such great hopes and dreams that it made what I thought were my troubles seem like whining.

Shortly after I joined, Jabu Mabuza or Jay as I called him, reorganised the business and Jay was installed as Chief Executive. This was a calculated risk; although his previous experience was in the taxi industry, the board had recognised his managerial talent and marketing abilities. Our faith in the man paid off and helped FABCOS to leapfrog and he was always ready to take advice. I am not surprised that Mabuza has risen to become a major business leader in South Africa. Unpretentious and very funny, he and his colleagues can be credited for making the taxi industry the formidable force it is today.

Then there was the indomitable Khehla Mthembu, who was our expert in insurance matters. He brought his zeal and charisma to the organisation. Khehla had legitimacy as a former President of the Azanian People's Organisation (AZAPO), a popular liberation movement founded on the principles of Black Consciousness. I had personally identified Khehla and introduced him to FABCOS because of his leadership qualities. I had met him on my return to South Africa in the mid-eighties. Khehla had been steeped in the revolutionary politics of the 1970s and his organisation espoused Steve Biko's philosophies of self-reliance. The man had totally dedicated himself to the struggle, often at huge expense to himself and his family. Later, he was trying to get pieces together after that segment of his life had ceased and he approached me to consider selling my house to him as I was about to migrate to the northern suburbs from Soweto. The one major snag was his inability to raise a mortgage bond, primarily because of his background in the eyes of the financial institutions he approached. After a discussion with Nana, we decided to take a leap of faith and let him have the house with a deferred payment plan unsupported by any financial institution. It gives me great pleasure that Kay has become a top business leader in South Africa and our friendship and that of our children has grown.

I was very privileged to chair an organisation of that calibre with a strong national footprint and we became a major force in South Africa. We created structures and lobbied government to relax crippling legislation that impeded the growth of emerging business. We won some battles, lost others, but were able to extract significant concessions out of Government, tyre manufacturers, and spare parts and body parts manufacturers for our taxi organisation. And again, organised business could not afford to ignore the consumer power of FABCOS; our numbers were sufficient for us to exercise our options. It was during that period that the American

TV Channel, CBS Broadcasting, flew down its crew to film its award-winning magazine programme, 48 Hours. Once again, we had made world headlines and were receiving accolades and good wishes for our humble efforts.

With great confidence in our long-term strategy, we approached a number of established financial institutions to form a joint venture with us in the creation of our proposed bank. In the end we entered into negotiations with my erstwhile employers, First National Bank, and an agreement was reached for the creation of Future Bank, jointly owned by FABCOS and FNB.

My previous association with the latter was a great help; they had the infrastructure, the people and skills while FABCOS possessed a captive market. We subsequently agreed on terms and our next hurdle became the securing of a bank licence. Once again, my previous association with the South African Reserve Bank became useful in our negotiations which I had been tasked to lead.

By the beginning of 1989, a second black-owned bank was founded and I derived great joy and felt honoured to have played a role in this regard. This was considered a huge milestone for the continued growth of emerging business in South Africa. We called it Future Bank, to denote the wider vision of what we all envisaged. Our morale and spirit of camaraderie was so high that even when we did encounter obstacles, we remained confident of a positive outcome.

Future Bank was acclaimed a pioneering vehicle for black business empowerment and created a platform for accelerated growth and the graduation of several informal businesses into the mainstream economy. What was even more remarkable was that it created shareholder wealth at an unprecedented level for those at the bottom rung of the economic ladder. Jabu Mabuza became the youngest chairman of a bank in the country while Baker Mogale and I were appointed directors, representing our group's interest. The bank experienced rapid growth and we transferred some of the assets out of the FNB subsidiary WesBank and placed them into Future Bank and this beefed up our balance sheet.

Sadly, the bank soon became a candidate for a takeover and within a few years it was merged with another institution.

Without a doubt, 1990 was a different year for the country as the wheels of change started to accelerate. South Africa was clearly standing on the threshold of a new beginning that would usher in some monumental changes. This was the year when all political parties were unbanned and our leaders were released from the country's centres of repression, such as Robben Island. It was also the year when Nelson Mandela was released from prison. By that February we had moved into a larger property in Bryanston and it was there we heard the announcement by then President F.W. de Klerk that Mr Mandela was to be released. The news created unparalleled euphoria throughout the country and, indeed, in the world at large. His predecessor, P.W. Botha, had said repeatedly that Mr Mandela would not be released unless he renounced violence, something that Madiba rightfully refused to do. But

F. W. de Klerk, who could read the signs of unprecedented civil turmoil throughout the country, took a giant leap of courage and in many ways defied some of his own party members.

He showed great vision (and, by so doing, averted a crisis that would have traumatised South Africa) by taking the decision to unban all the political organisations and releasing Mr Mandela from jail.

And for displaying that foresight and vision, he received appropriate recognition and along with Mr Mandela, De Klerk became a Nobel Peace Prize laureate.

The morning of Mr Mandela's release, we gathered with friends in my home to watch the live broadcast and to celebrate the historical moment. Since our return to South Africa, Nana and I had continued to host many young men and women just as we had done in America. Our house in Bryanston had become a venue for social interaction and debate by many of our friends. But that day was especially significant. We had prepared abundant food and drinks while we waited, glued to the TV to watch Mr Mandela's release. And, indeed, we witnessed the event – saw him as he stepped out with his clenched fist, his then wife, Winnie Madikizela-Mandela, by his side. Enthralled, we watched them walk out of the gates of Victor Verster Prison. Together with those around me I knew we were witnessing history in the making. For me, the moment was particularly special. Seeing Mr Mandela leave Victor Verster Prison, where I had been detained for eighteen months just prior to my release from Robben Island, flooded me with memories too raw to hold in and brought tears to my eyes. Most people were emotional wrecks as we broke up in celebration and champagne bottles popped. Madiba's release made us extremely hopeful that real positive change was beginning for all of us in the country.

The following Saturday, Nana and I attended a private cocktail party at the Carlton Centre hosted by the Japanese Ambassador. A huge surprise awaited us; as we entered the reception room, we saw a tall slightly greying man, Mr Mandela himself and his wife, Winnie Madikizela-Mandela, and their children – all were standing on the other side of the room.

Our eyes just popped, we were in awe and hastened to meet him. I was surprised that he still remembered me. I had transformed from the child prisoner he had last seen in 1964. Madiba overpowered me with his bear hug as we met and exclaimed, 'Hey, Gaby, how have you been?'

I was totally lost for an answer, just in absolute awe. So, in a sense for me, this marked the closing of a loop that I had opened in 1964 when I first met Madiba at *Die Ou Tronk* on Robben Island. To get to see him again, some twenty-six years later, was a remarkable event that will stay with me for as long as I live. I introduced Nana to him and they shook hands. In his usual easy jocular style and hypnotic charm he said to me, 'Now I know why you're so confident; you have a beautiful young wife to support you.'

We laughed.

It was an immeasurable privilege and honour for us to be present at Mr Mandela's triumphant welcome, which was his first public occasion since his release. After the cocktail party, Nana and I went to the Market Theatre to watch a play. I can't remember what the play was called or what it was all about. But I do remember sitting in that theatre and thinking back on my life and the strange set of circumstances and the hardship and the fear and the laughter and the sheer good fortune that had brought me to that moment.

Part 3

1943–1963

7

'*Sontaha* ya *Mehlolo*': A Sunday in March 1963

'*Sontaha* ya *Mehlolo*' (Sunday of Surprises!). It all started on that Sunday of Surprises, as the day was dubbed in Bekkersdal. That is what it is still called to this day, all these many years later, for people remember how the whole small location was thrown into disarray that Sunday morning.

The usual Sunday morning business in Bekkersdal had few pressing matters besides attending services at one of the five local churches. Indeed, most residents were busy getting ready for just that that morning when all hell broke loose. All usual business was abruptly suspended, women hastily returned their costumes, high-heeled shoes and wide-brimmed hats to the wardrobes. Deacons, preachers and bishops threw their Sunday jackets and clerical robes back into the wardrobes from which they'd unearthed those only minutes before. The faithful, as well as everybody else in the location, waited for the unfamiliar dust to settle.

Word of mouth quickly spread the news from home to home and street to street. For hours, Bekkersdal watched the shiny cars – an unfamiliar sight – criss-cross the location, raising the red dust for which the township was notorious.

It was just after six in the morning.

My sister, Semakaleng, was already awake, ironing my stepmother's uniform, helping her get ready for church. Semakaleng or Smakkie, as everyone called her, recalls hearing car doors banging outside – another rarity. Who owned cars in our township? Curious, although she knew I was not in any trouble right then, she nevertheless thought to check. Even as she did that, she was quite sure whoever had stopped in front of our gate had made a mistake – they had stopped at the wrong gate. Well, she would just direct them to the right place then.

Smakkie peeked through the lace curtain that covered the long narrow kitchen window. And got the shock of her life.

White men.

Striding up the path of white bricks that led from the small low meshed steel gate – the pedestrian gate – they came.

One of four cars blocked the wider car gate.

Paralysed, my sister saw them stomp onto the highly polished black *stoep* that ran the length of the house. Then two went around to the back of the house.

The doors closed, they had to knock. And knock, they did. Knocked loudly, back and front doors.

And that is when I heard them.

At the same time, I heard something else.

Until then, I'd been fast asleep, I reigned on my two-week old special single bachelor bed that I had just bought for myself on HP (higher purchase – with interest which was two times the cost).

It looked just like my friend Monty's bed. I had placed it in the best room of the house, the dining room, which also housed overnight family guests. No protests from *Ntate;* I was a working man of nineteen. I was very proud of my modern purchase; it was light in weight, had an Edblo mattress and was made of blond wood that contrasted with my parents' thick dark wood of the table with matching chairs and a sideboard-display cabinet. This was my statement of emancipation.

Loud voices. Outside. Speaking to my sister, who was fifteen then.

Semakaleng tells us they said they were looking for Thabo, Gabriel Magomola. She recovered enough to quickly think of a way to warn me to escape. She went to *Ntate*'s bedroom and, in a loud voice, told him that there were policemen. '*Whites*,' she stressed, '*all over the house.*'

Some were at the back door, she said. And that is what had roused me from sleep.

At first, I thought Smakkie was being melodramatic. She was excitable at that stage. But I think this was wishful thinking on my part (or the working of a sleep-fogged brain). I say that because, even then, even as that thought crossed my mind, I could hear unfamiliar noises out in the yard. Some of the police, I later heard, were already poking the ground outside with long steel spikes, searching for weapons caches.

Suddenly, I was wide awake but stayed put, feigning sleep. That didn't stop my stomach dropping and tying itself in taut knots.

In stiff competition, my heart raced a marathon and beat so irregularly, I had to open my mouth to catch my breath.

Inside, I heard striding, firm footsteps accompanied by *Ntate's* sleepy shuffle. From the sound of it, they were leaving the house, going outside. However, they were soon re-entering the house.

It was all very dignified – eerily dignified.

There were no raised voices, or kicking – the expected police etiquette during a raid. In our location, that rowdiness was a well-known fact, especially when the raid was lead by Sergeant Schoeman. That man absolutely terrorised Bekkersdal with his yard raids. Armed with a long metal spike, he would poke the yard, searching for buried illicit brew sold by the mothers of Bekkersdal.

Abruptly, my reverie was brought to a halt. Someone pulled off my blankets. '*Areye!*' (Let's go!) a white male voice said in SeSotho.

Like a jack-in-the-box, I sat bolt upright. And found myself surrounded by four big white men. They were in plain clothes, but their police authority was beyond any doubt.

Anger burned from their eyes and I feared they would *klap* me. But despite those enormous, rough hands that looked more than ready to fix me up well and good, I tried to remain calm. Tried to look that when, in fact, I felt very small – small and exceedingly vulnerable in my semi-nakedness.

One of the officers politely asked my sister to bring a glass of water while he gave me pills to swallow.

Without any protestation, I obliged. Was the state of shock I felt that clear then, despite my attempts at appearing calm?

That is a question I did not ask. What I did was take the water and tablets and just swallow – gulp down the lot.

That is how numbed I was. I never even stopped to question what those tablets were. Neither did *Ntate* ask. Semakeleng was too young to consider the horrendous possibilities.

The raid was so unexpected, I didn't even think of running or slipping through the window, which I always did to evade *Ntate*.

'Are you Gabriel Magomola?' One of the plain-clothes policemen asked in a calm tone. If I had not known any better, I could have mistaken him for a friend.

I nodded. Nodded, for I'd lost my voice.

They then looked through the papers they carried and when they came to my name, ticked it off from what appeared to be a very long list.

'Is your name Thabo Mosebetsi?' another asked in that same conversational tone.

Frowning, I shook my head. Denial and disbelief flooded me as a deep, cold realisation hit my solar plexus.

Thabo Mosebetsi was my underground code name.

How could they have known? Even my very inquisitive sister, who tried to know everything I did, had no idea.

I knew then, I was in serious trouble.

'Where are the minutes?'

I nearly bolted – got up and dashed out, when another soft voice asked that one. I caught the speaker and one of his colleagues exchange looks. I was sure then they knew. Knew the answer to each and every question they asked me.

I hoped I appeared calm. Frowning slightly to register mild bewilderment, I shook my head.

I did not trust my voice to speak.

A trickle of sweat slid down my back, I could almost hear its drip. The enormity of what was at stake weighed on me. But how could our plans have gone asunder? Done so to the extent that the Security Police knew that we minuted our meetings?

I was not the only one thoroughly thrown.

Ntate was sure the police were making a huge mistake. Shaking his head, he kept saying, 'Not my son. Not *my* son.'

Nonchalantly, the police went about their business. They pried into my books and a few fell without too much force, just by what appeared to be accidental swipes.

I was grateful when I realised that Smakkie had hidden some of my banned books among her own schoolbooks. Their search did yield a jazz album by the famous American jazz drummer, Max Roach. I had just bought 'Freedom Now Suite'. One of the tracks, 'A Tear for Sharpeville' was dedicated to the scores of people who had been brutally shot by the apartheid police during a protest march in Sharpeville, in 1960. Now, the police seized the album and ordered me to get dressed.

Out of respect for *Ntate*, I obeyed the instruction without making a fuss. But in my head, I noted that as one more transgression I had to avenge. Still numb from shock, I grabbed my *boggarts* and t-shirt from the back of the chair near my bed and slipped on my shoes without bothering about socks.

When I'd finished putting my clothes on, for a brief moment I closed my eyes with the hope that it was all a nightmare. But when I opened them, it was to meet *Ntate*'s quizzical face, his eyes wide with disbelief.

My heart bled for my poor father for I could see, plain as day, he still thought – believed – this was all a terrible mistake. That if he could only convey to the Special Branch that they were making a mistake, and convince them of the fact, that would be evident to them too. And all would be right again.

In his customary low but firm voice, *Ntate* asked the men where they were taking me.

The police were courteous to him and they reassured him he had nothing to worry about. They said they were just taking me in for questioning and I would soon be back.

My father trusted me. He would never accept that I could do anything to disgrace or harm our family. After all, I was his first-born son and he and *Mme* had brought me up in the church and the tradition of our people. If this was hard on me, it was killing my father.

The police walked me out as old friends. They led me to the waiting cars.

Outside, a small crowd had gathered and I heard some from among it shout, spreading the warning, '*kuyabheda*' (it's bad!)

As though to reaffirm the terrible news, seated at the back of one of the cars was a comrade, his head cast down.

I tried to read his eyes. Considering the gravity of our situation, I desperately needed reassurance. But the comrade's eyes mirrored the horror in my own heart.

Who else had been arrested?

I feared especially for my best friends, Leopard (Lepe – Lips) Mosito and Monty Seremane. Those two and I were inseparable and our friendship meant the world to me.

Lepe and Monty were older than me; each by four years. They were also tall, athletic, and boxed and played soccer for the Western Division. Of average height, I was small of build, and only liked reading and music. Fortunately, my friends also liked music; we shared a great love of music, especially jazz.

We lived in close proximity, went to the same school, played together, and shared dreams. To this day, all my memories of life before Robben Island involve one or both of them, in one way or another.

And because we grew up together that way, our parents offering distant supervision to all three of us, our identity and kinship was as strong as blood.

Despite some competition among the three of us, we shared a deep trust and loyalty; and knew, without doubt or hesitation, that we'd always have one another.

Leopard lived at the back house opposite our house. There was not even a fence that separated our homes. Our doors were never locked, and if they were, the keys would be left with other neighbours. What he ate, I ate. I often escaped the crowds and cockroaches in my own home to catch restful sleep in his dining room. He only lived with his mother and sister, *Ousie* Maria and Mamorero. His father worked somewhere far away on contract and we saw him rarely. Monty's father, whom we fondly called 'Mjerry', came from Zimbabwe. His mother, whom we called, Momjerry was a close relative of my mother's and used to prepare a great curried mutton stew, way back then.

'Ziyabeda!' the crowd shouted as I was quickly bundled into one of the cars. Then the four cars proceeded along the main road of Bekkersdal that ran about four blocks from what we called 'uptown' to 'downtown'.

My heart thudding, as the cars made their way to God only knew where, I looked at the familiar sights without seeing much. One thing was clear though, despite what the police had said to *Ntate*, we were not going to the police station.

Where were they taking me? All too soon, my unasked question was cruelly answered. We had stopped outside Monty's home.

My fears were compounded when I overhead neighbours gathered around there saying his younger brother, George, had already been picked up. The police cars were certainly busy that Sunday morning in Bekkersdal. Later, I would hear that when Monty got home and heard the news of his brother's arrest, he went bananas. That is just the kind of man he was; protective of those who were weaker. Monty went straight to the police station to hand himself over.

But outside Monty's house, while the police put their heads together, the crowd, hungry for details, screeched, '*Areng, Maburu*'? (What are the Boers saying?)

I looked down on my hands, seeking my own answers. Who had told them about the minutes we took? How could they possibly know my code name? Know my home address?

Later, I was told that, that morning of surprises, six cars – each chock-a-block full of white policemen – had driven up and down the length and breadth of Bekkersdal location. The police went into our houses, hunted down men they wanted and, one by one, ticked off the names of their targets from the long list they had so painstakingly put together.

By Monday morning, on the buses and trains heading for schools, firms and farms, the residents of Bekkersdal still didn't know what, exactly, had happened. We, the apprehended, were not that sure either. To tell the truth, I was not overly concerned because I was convinced I would soon be home. Then I would certainly catch up on my sleep – so rudely interrupted – in my own comfortable bed in 686 Tshepe Street, Bekkersdal.

Home, Sweet Home!

8

Bekkersdal

That home was in Tshepe Street, Bekkersdal; a house identical to all the others in the township, distinguishable only by the freshly painted white outside walls. A compact three-roomed house – one bedroom, for my parents; a dining room; and a big kitchen with an adjoining narrow room, we called the laundry. The laundry had a concrete sink and a separate bath area with a concrete bath in which, for some odd reason I no longer recall, we used to store fresh water; and used portable plastic basins for washing ourselves.

Although I claim Bekkersdal as my home, I wasn't born there but it is where my family relocated when I was about six years old. Before that, my parents, my younger sister and I lived a simple life in the married quarters of the Venterspost mining compound, where I was born on the 9th of September 1943.

It is therefore on Venterspost Mine that I grew up, living with *Ntate* – my father Malebelle Magomola, also named Israel; *Mme,* my mother Sophie *Matlakala* (Out of the ashes) – ten years younger than *Ntate*; and my younger sister, *Semakaleng,* (Don't be surprised), who was born three years after me. From what *Ntate* shared with me as a child, I got the sense that the whole world was consumed by World War II around the time of my birth and during my early childhood.

The family's first-born son and they named me Thono, in Sepedi, the last sediment of liquor in a calabash, the most concentrated, delicious, precious drop. Gabriel, my middle name, comes from my paternal grandfather.

From these names, I gather my parents were more than glad to have me. From their actions, ever since I can remember, I knew I was cherished.

Ntate was a store clerk. *Mme* worked as a casual in nearby Westonaria. I don't remember experiencing hunger, there was always enough to eat. Every month *Ntate* supplemented his mine rations with a sack of mealie meal, a sack of sugar, tea, a box of tins of condensed milk so that we had something to fall back on when there was no milk at the store (which often happened). We never felt deprived.

My ancestors had migrated from Botswana to the village of Gopane, near the town of Zeerust, in what is now called the Northwest Province. *Mme*'s family, the Modisanes, were from Groot Marico, also in the Zeerust area. My grandparents needed money to pay land taxes on what limited land they owned. Thus, their generation, and the generation before them, were migrants. My parents also immigrated south to Johannesburg, and then westward, seeking opportunities in the mines of the West Rand, as thousands before them had done since the discovery of the world's single richest gold deposit, the Witwatersrand Basin in 1886.

Ntate worked on the compound as a privileged clerical employee or *umabhalane*. Having completed Standard 6 (Grade 8), he was considered to have a high standard of literacy. He was very proud of his Royal Readers' English, which he spoke most of the time. His meticulous appearance attested to his elevated status and integrity.

The memory of my father, ingrained in my mind, is that of a very serious, placid man, clean shaven, dressed in a starched white shirt, the sleeves suspended by sleeve cuffs, a thin black tie, a heavy tweed jacket, black pants (the legs also suspended by cuffs, for he rode a bicycle), and a pair of highly polished black shoes. *Ntate*'s trim hair, which remained the same length and texture year after year, was always parted on the side. Thick black-rimmed spectacles framed his eyes. The outfit was completed by a tilted Stetson hat without which *Ntate* never stepped out of the house. He always had the same type of hat – the same shape, grey in colour, same size. Before the hat became worn out, he would get himself a replacement. Rarely did *Ntate* show any emotion on his stern face. Growing up, I thought he was strict and harsh. His thick shiny belt doubled as an instrument of punishment whenever we strayed. Later in life, I came to understand that *Ntate* had experienced the harsh hard life of the mines, which most probably carved the hard streak in him that I found almost cruel.

Later in my youth, I learned from adult whispers that *Ntate* was meant to have married another woman with whom he had two children, until he was knocked off his feet by my mother's quiet beauty. Officially, we never met our half-siblings. But I once went to peek at them out of curiosity, and found myself staring at faces resembling mine.

The compound was headed by the mine manager, who was also in charge of the underground section. In adherence to the strict hierarchy observed at all mines in South Africa, this man was always white and called *Baas*. Usually, *Baas* could converse in the vernacular languages. If he could not, he improvised and used *fanakalo*.

When I opened my eyes and began to understand life, I must have been five. However, I was still blissfully unaware of apartheid. But while I ran around, chasing the wheel of a bicycle in play, the apartheid system was becoming more and more deeply entrenched after Dr D.F. Malan's election as Prime Minister in

1948. But for me, life was a smooth progression, with no threatening or jolting experiences.

I went to school, which I enjoyed tremendously. I had good friends. I was told and I believed that I was extremely intelligent and basked under the praises of the adults. I worked hard. I was a precocious reader and, with *Ntate's* coaching at home, was rewarded with praise and encouraged with sweets and small coins by uncles and our neighbours and smiles from the teachers at school. But then, we left Venterspost in 1949.

From the compound, we relocated to Bekkersdal Township. *Ntate* had secured employment away from the mines. At Bekkersdal, there were no basic town amenities and the streets were untarred except for *Kgomo ya Hlaba* (the cow pierces), the main street which cut through the township. There was no electricity, no flushing toilets – we used the bucket system.

Samponkaans (night soil bucket collectors), would enter the location in their trucks promptly at 6 pm to collect the buckets of soil from the toilets and replace them with empty (and supposedly clean) ones. This arrangement was far from pleasant for both residents and collectors. Long after the *samponkaans* had left – amid clanging of metal bucket and the men's shrill whistles, a foul stench lingered in the Bekkersdal air. Of course, the task was also unsanitary as well as demeaning to all concerned.

My parents were not unhappy with our home in Bekkersdal. 'You just needed furniture,' they agreed with our new neighbours. They compared Bekkersdal to other locations and found it far better; 'resplendent,' they said. They said that because here the houses had cemented floors, plastered walls, and indoor running water, and a toilet outside with an adjoining plastered and cemented coal shed. The adults always joked that Bekkersdal was built before the government became wise and decided to build black townships with just bare walls. What was most special about Bekkersdal was that each house came fitted with a black steel Welcome Dover coal stove – a freebie from the municipality.

That stove was the centre of life and provided all-year-round nourishment and warmth. To support its importance, my parents had promptly installed a spacious steel lemon-yellow cabinet scheme with a silver trim, in the kitchen.

It is here in Bekkersdal that Malefetsane, my younger brother whom we called Fetsa, was born. From my aunts' whispers, I gathered that *Mme* had also borne – with strength and virtue – the loss of two children who had died in their infancy. These aunts also lived with us. They were *bommangwane* (aunts), *(Mme's* younger sisters).

My parents erected a church just outside our house; they were both ecclesiastical. *Mme* was a preacher and *Ntate* an elder of our branch of the St John's Faith Mission church. Spiritually, *Mme* was the more dominant of the two. She had incredible healing, clairvoyance, and prophetic powers; all totally in line with the St John's

Church strong matriarchal oracles. The Church of St John's was founded by a woman, *Mme* Manku, and her husband, in Evaton in 1940.

Bekkersdal was a lively, hospitable, peaceful, and friendly community where everyone was treated with respect and consideration – a large, extended family, you may say. Our parents didn't dwell on the injustices of the time but bore the harsh life with fortitude and righteousness. They worked long, hard hours for little remuneration. Despite the hardship that was their life, they ensured that we were fed, cleaned, schooled and stayed of sound and virtuous moral footing.

How, then did I end up arrested, the police coming for me at the crack of dawn, hunting and hounding me as though I were a hardened criminal?

I do believe good people like Archbishop Tutu had something to do with that – in ways they may never have planned or even considered.

C1: My parents' wedding day, 1946

C2: My father, Mr Israel Magomola, in a 1960 pensive mood pose

C3: Taken about three months before being arrested and sent to Robben Island, a photo of a young tender-looking 18-year-old Gaby

C4: A young Gaby at home in the family front yard age 16, in 1960 Bekkersdal

C5(a): My sister, Semakaleng

C5(b): My brother, Malefetsa, on the right with a friend

9

Growing pains

My parents had enrolled me at the local high school in Krugersdorp, some 40 kms away from my home. That was the nearest high school for Africans. I travelled by bus to Randfontein, then took a train to Krugersdorp, then took yet another bus to get there. The two-hour commute, each way, was a sore trial. Not that the trip was ever lonely; to the contrary, my great friends, Leopard, Monty, and the garrulous Moss Mokotong, and I shared hilarious times during those daily trips to and from school. Looking back, I do believe it is around this time that I began to notice that things in our country were beyond just unjust.

At Munsieville, we met older boys. These were boys to whom I looked up for they were, in my youthful opinion, almost grown. I learned from their courage and wisdom. They were from a big town; older, wiser in the ways of the bigger locations.

It is also at Munsieville that I first met Archbishop Desmond Tutu in what was reportedly his first teaching post. He taught us English and Music. I remember one of his favourite songs:

Tlong Tlong Thaka Tseso Re Sa Bina Pina (Come, Come Friends, Let's sing this song)

E Tla makatsa bohle batla e utlwang (This will surprise all who hear it)

I remember him as an eloquent, thin, frail-looking and well-dressed young man with a tapering chin and short hair. His home was adjacent to the school and his father an ordained minister.

Later in life I would be re-acquainted with the Archbishop in his different role of a fiery opponent of apartheid dogma. That school teacher and his colleague, Stan Motjuwadi, as well as the principal, G.G. Mamabolo, were real masters – role models – and the years spent at that school were, for me, years of enlightenment. It is here that my political awakening took place. Other influences were also at play, however. I was in the big city, and I had to grow very fast.

Munsieville, called the Wild West, was notorious for its colourful gangsters and pick-pockets – such as the infamous Lefty and Jeffrey. But the most feared gangster was Buller. That man was reputedly capable of single-handedly causing a riot. Very adept with his knife, Buller was known to have vanquished many an enemy silly or stupid enough to challenge him. Rumour had it that even the police were scared of him.

Then, in 1958, I passed the Junior Certificate with honours and proceeded to Madibane High in Western Native Township, near Sophiatown. That is where I met my friend Gigi Mbere and his late brother, Aggrey, and forged a rewarding friendship that has lasted a lifetime.

These were times during which apartheid – the idea of separate races and the self-proclaimed superiority of whites – was heavily enforced.

Crimes against African people were inconsequential. My constant confrontation with antagonistic white men with heavy moustaches tested newly-politically-aware me to no end. The contemptuous dismissal with which these men always treated us made me feel I was an annoyance by my very existence. My resolve to fight for my rights not only grew but found expression.

At the end of 1959, aged sixteen, I (with others) was expelled from school for truancy and holding political meetings. We had incurred the wrath of the principal, Mr Madibane, whom we called the Shark, and the school didn't even give us our year-end results.

'Don't you ever come back to this school!' That was all we were told.

Ntate, totally in the dark about my clandestine political activities, was extremely upset at what he perceived as an injustice, especially since, with no explanation given for my expulsion, he couldn't even question the action.

Therefore, in 1960, for the first time in my life, without purpose or clear future plans, I enjoyed a period of indolence. Later, I decided I was mature enough to work. I wanted to dress and feed myself. I found a job at Delmas Milling Company, a food producer and milling plant in Randfontein.

As a manual labourer, I worked with much older men, patching mealie-meal bags, earning a weekly wage of one pound, eleven shillings.

With my meagre wages and lunch money savings, my wardrobe improved and I also bought myself a bed, which I installed in the dining room.

10

My political awakening

While outwardly we emulated the lives of rebellious youngsters everywhere in the world, there was a more serious side, a hidden, secret side to some of us.

Since my days in Munsieville, I had woken up to the deprivation of my race. But since early in 1960, on the 21st of March to be exact, more and more, I simmered in indignation and resentment against the government. More than that, I knew I had come to understand and accept that I couldn't just sit and watch while black people were being wantonly mowed down.

That day, at Sharpeville, a township outside the town of Vereeniging, what started as a peaceful protest march against pass laws, the mandatory carrying of what was called *dompas*, saw sixty-nine men, women and children killed and up to three hundred and eighty wounded. The march had been organised by the Pan Africanist Congress (PAC) and an unarmed crowd of about seven thousand people gathered at Sharpeville police station to hand over their passes and offer themselves for arrest. Their slogan 'No bail, no defence, no fine!' That says it all. The protest was peaceful. The outcome sought? Jamming the jails.

But, without warning instructing the crowd to disperse, the police started shooting – using live ammunition. Fleeing, people were shot in the back.

On the same day in Langa Township outside of Cape Town, thirty thousand people had gathered to hand in their passes. Violence was again unleashed by the police on the protesters and resulted in the deaths of two people and the injury of fifty.

Swiftly, black people reacted in an uproar. There were mass demonstrations, protest marches, strikes and riots throughout the country. At the end of March, the government declared a five-month state of emergency, detaining thousands of people. Robert Mangaliso Sobukwe, the Pan Africanist Congress (PAC), leader was among those arrested. He was later sentenced to three years in jail for burning his pass. The African National Congress (ANC) and PAC were banned on the 8th of April that year and membership of those organisations became illegal. From then on, the stage was set for the political drama that would play itself out in South Africa, over the next thirty years, as positions on each side (government and liberation movements) hardened.

By then, I was already a member of the ANC Youth League, thanks to the mentorship of an intellectual from Bekkersdal, Motsamai Mpho, who later returned to Botswana. Thus, the banning of these organisations had a direct impact even on me. We were all forced underground.

Until March 1960, the PAC's policy, as expressed by Robert Sobukwe, was that while 'We are ready to die for our cause; we are not ready to kill'. However, the Sharpeville massacre changed the direction the PAC would subsequently follow.

Like the African National Congress from which it had broken away in 1959, the PAC pursued an aggressive but non-violent campaign. Not realising the deep-seated anger among African people, the government continued and even hardened its brutality.

On March 30 1960, thousands of protesters marched through the city of Cape Town demanding a cessation of pass laws and the release of political leaders.

For once, the protest marches were brought into the cities of South Africa and this instilled fear and mayhem. The government reacted by unleashing its security apparatus and introducing even harsher measures. All this helped to drive the struggle underground and transformed the PAC into a militant organisation thus leading into the formation of Poqo and subsequently the Azanian People's Liberation Army (APLA).

When I joined the PAC in 1962, I was driven by years and years of accumulated outrage; the pressure within me was ready to explode. I had found an outlet for my youthful zeal. My attraction to the PAC was not founded so much on their much vaunted policy of African nationalism, as I was too young to understand the complex arguments contained in political philosophies.

The literature is awash with reasons why the Pan Africanist Congress which had been founded in April 1959 in Orlando, Soweto, had split from the African National Congress. The birth of the PAC came about out of the rejection of the multi-racialism that had been expounded by its parent body, the ANC. Nelson Mandela states in *Long Walk to Freedom* that the formation of this new organisation was based on similar grounds as the founding of the Youth League in the forties. 'Like those of us who formed the ANC Youth League fifteen years before, the founders of the new organisation thought the ANC was insufficiently militant, out of touch with the masses and dominated by non-Africans.'

The PAC had devised a strategy to overthrow white rule by force, through a rather ill-founded Grand Plan prematurely announced by its inept leader, Potlako Leballo who was based in nearby Lesotho. Such militancy found immediate resonance with me and many who were later jailed and ended up on Robben Island. One of these was Mxolisi 'Ace' Mgxashe who was aged sixteen and in the first year of high school in Langa township just outside of Cape Town. 'I was an inquisitive youth and had been gathering tit-bits of information about the PAC and was impressed by the outspokenness of its spokespersons. Its emergence excited interest even in apolitical families like mine,' he remarks in his work *Are You with Us?* As part of our mandate, I also recruited others to join the armed struggle, to challenge the system of violence with violence. With the pervading anger, we had no difficulty finding candidates; all those I personally approached came on board without much exhortation. 'Enough is enough,' they all said, as they signed up.

As I mentioned earlier, we knew little about the basic philosophy of the PAC which was in itself a recently formed organisation with an evolving philosophy based on Pan Africanism. This philosophy was widely advocated by emerging African leaders such as Kwame Nkrumah, Prime Minister of Ghana, and several other eminent leaders in the African diaspora who supported the call for a united Africa to overcome colonialism. Nkrumah's eloquence and that of leaders such as Patrice Lumumba of the Congo, Sékou Touré, President of Guinea and the fiery Jomo Kenyatta of Kenya helped to fuel the burning spirit of African nationalism that was consuming parts of the continent. It was around that time, 1963 to be exact, that the Organisation for African Unity was founded, just shortly before my arrest. Robert Sobukwe, the founding president of the Pan Africanist Congress, held up the beacon for this continental movement and he was arguably the most inspirational of his peers in South Africa in articulating these refreshing ideals.

As new adherents, we were tasked with the objectives of expanding the membership, learning the basic objectives of the movement and amassing assorted weapons to prepare for the onslaught at a date to be announced.

Our first task was to bring about an end to white domination in South Africa by overthrowing the apartheid government and thereafter, the leadership of the PAC had promised that the year 1963 was decisive; that was the year for the liberation of the African in South Africa. Meeting after meeting was held at clandestine venues in the veld, churches, football stadiums and a variety of venues. Often times we met at the local cemetery to avoid detection and to maintain absolute confidence about our activities.

At these meetings, we were schooled on the history of the struggle for self-determination from the days of the founding of the African National Congress in 1912 and later, the expulsion of the Africanists in 1959. We were taught of the heroes of the struggle such as Chief Albert Luthuli, Oliver Tambo, A. P. Mda, Anton Lembede, Nelson Mandela and Robert Sobukwe, to name a few. Selfless service to the nation was deemed as paramount and over and over again we were told of the importance of laying down our lives for the cause of our liberation.

We had all the ingredients of success – devotion, gallantry, bravery, unlimited zeal. Well, mix all that with the unpredictability of youth, lethal determination, some (perhaps overrated) intelligence, and a perception of injustice we would crush – and, you're talking tenacious followers! We believed we were the wronged, for far too long. Surely, we told ourselves, we were morally entitled to retrieve what was ours. We had leg-shaking impatience. Therefore, when we heard the call of war, we offered to be in the forefront and die first because we didn't have responsibilities of children and wives.

I, definitely, had had enough. I was no longer willing to endure the miserable existence we called life in our townships. I didn't want to be a man casting my eyes down at another man, a foreigner in my own land.

Izwe Lethu! (Our Land!) resonated in my head and my soul. I had heard how my ancestors were dispossessed. Landing in the unfamiliar territory of industrialisation, squashed in three-roomed hovels, pretending to be happy while at the mercy of their conquerors. We saw the glimmer rise, and then quickly fade, in our uncles' and fathers' eyes when they told of the old life. We heard their sighs when they remembered the villages of plenty – when a man could have his own homestead, farm whatever he wanted on his own land, have his own wives, with a herd of his own cattle and have unlimited heirs without any fear of hunger.

To my impatient, boiling, youth blood, the idea of spontaneous and bloody popular uprising had decided appeal. I clasped the promise of the pamphlets and impassioned speeches that declared:

'The white people shall suffer! The black people will rule. Freedom comes after bloodshed. Be a real man, join the struggle for liberation!'

I was the man they called; I had found my calling.

Intoxicated by the ideal, I saw the promised liberation of all black people – in 1963; the year the PAC declared as the year of liberation.

We embellished the heroic exploits of Poqo in the Eastern Cape, which had been formed in 1961. I never wanted to become one of those men who held their hats in their hands while a young white boy gave them orders.

And, above all, I was never going to call any white man *Baas,* I vowed.

Well then, the crunch had now come.

11

The initiation

After the Security Branch swoops, we were locked up at the Randfontein police cells, just ten kilometres away from Bekkersdal. I was processed in the charge office – fingerprinted and my personal details noted. Then the officials frisked me, not that they bothered telling me what they were looking for. I was incensed, my jaws tight with suppressed rage when I was put through a mouth inspection. But I held on to my confidence – I wouldn't let that slip just then.

Although we were not prisoners officially, we were kept away from each other – isolated – and fed the usual fare given to people in police cells. I kept thinking about how the others were, how they were holding up wherever they were held.

Finally, late into the night, the interrogation stopped and I was allowed to sleep. Still in isolation, kept thus so we could not exchange information. The police of course hoped the isolation would raise the feeling of uncertainty and anxiety in us; weakening each one of us, breaking us down and rendering us more pliable.

For a week we were continually interrogated by the three white members of the Criminal Investigation Department (CID) – Terreblanche, Van Wyngaard and Botha with the African detective sergeant Mhlongo and one Indian man whose name we never got to know. They wanted to know what our plans were and who the leaders were. Then they produced gory photographs they said were of atrocities committed by Poqo initiates in the Eastern Cape.

I was startled by my own shock and pity for the dead people I didn't know. They had lists of Poqo attacks in Langa and Paarl where suspected informers had been executed. More pictures were produced; these were of a raid by Poqo members in Paarl. Five members of a family were killed in that raid and two teenagers were hacked to death.

The police then asked me, 'Is this what you boys intended to do? Is this what you really wanted to do?'

At this stage, they showed me photographs of five white adults who were killed in caravans on the roadside at Mbashe (Bashee) Bridge near Umtata, in the Transkei.

The interrogation by the police was thorough. Their combination of courtesy and calm together with our vulnerability was a disarming mix. They played on our emotions, testing and feeling us to elicit information. Initially, I was amazed by their apparent self-control – with all that tension (palpable) between us – but the thought did cross my mind that nothing prevented them from shooting and killing us right then and there. Later, however, their tactics changed and they jeered, 'We have a truck full of witnesses,' said Wyngaard. 'C'mon,' he cajoled, 'We know everything.'

Then turning sympathetic, they told us they knew we were just misguided souls and that the PAC leader in Lesotho, Potlako Leballo, had boasted about the impending uprising. The police, we were informed, had raided the PAC offices in Maseru and seized all the lists of those involved and that was how they had our names. We just didn't know what to believe. But it was crystal clear that our captors were prepared to obtain every ounce of truth out of us.

Every gesture they made seemed to have a sinister underlying meaning. I soon realised that they were playing us against one another. All their moves seemed to be deliberately calculated. At that point, I decided not to believe anything they said.

'Eh, Seremane says you were planning this attack on innocent people,' one said and further insinuated, 'He's in the other cell, telling us everything.'

Looking at me, he slowly raised his brows, letting the point sink. I looked back, trying hard to not be rattled. The man went on, 'You're the only who's going to prison. Everybody is confessing.' Then, he added, 'C'mon, Magomola!'

'Bring him in,' I shot back.

At that, their disguised hostility flared into outright vicious assaults.

By the time we left the Randfontein cells, most of us had a broken rib or nose or something else.

Personally, I was suspended, by rope, from a hook in the ceiling. My handcuffs cushioned so that I wouldn't have bruises. *Very clever.* My interrogators placed bricks on the floor on which I was forced to stand. With my wrists secured, they kicked the bricks away from under my feet so that I dangled from the ceiling like a carcass at the butchery.

Totally incapacitated, I swung back and forth.

'Praat die waarheid!' (Speak the truth!) they shouted.

But I refused to say anything.

Next, they flogged, punched, kicked and struck me anywhere they pleased. I felt the blows of batons and fists and objects I couldn't identify.

This pattern of assault – we would get to know later as we compared notes among ourselves as prisoners – was quite common and resulted in the death, from internal bleeding, of many activists. Those who lost consciousness during these assaults were revived with a splash of cold water.

Of course, the police had other methods of forcing 'confessions' from those in their custody. There were those who had a wet sack tied around their heads. The sack was then twisted to choke them. To others still, electric charges were applied to wires attached to their fingers. Those deemed too stubborn for these 'reasonable' methods, were suspended upside down by sacks tied over their bodies and struck to the ground and pulled up by the hair. We were told only confession would bring salvation. I knew from the anguished screams and the scraping chairs followed by moans emanating from the other interrogations rooms that I wasn't the only one who refused to divulge information that would incriminate others.

We cried out purely as a natural reaction to physical pain, torture; we never pleaded for mercy. I understood we were at war.

Several of our comrades were broken by the coercion. Unable to read through the trickery, they wondered, wavered and conceded. 'If my leader has talked, then there's something wrong here ...' They then co-operated with the Security Branch.

By their actions, they betrayed us.

Some of those comrades were released on condition they gave evidence as state witnesses. That couldn't happen to me. I couldn't be that. Anything but that, dear God, I prayed, remembering that, after all, I was the eldest son of the respected *Ntate* and my dear late *Mme*.

It had been just five years since *Mme* had passed on after a long struggle with pulmonary tuberculosis. I was once again reminded that my mother had left us all too soon.

By the end of that first week, the sieving had resulted not only in the identification of the culprits but also the identification of the ringleaders.

However, the informers, or the forces of darkness as we called them – people who had allied themselves with the government by deceiving, spying and lying – they too, had been identified. They were known.

Twenty-nine captives remained in the police cells – twenty from Randfontein and nine from Bekkersdal. Around the country the Special Branch had circled pockets of known PAC intellectuals and activists, who were quickly arrested and neutralised.

We were not perturbed; our strategy was to have leaders for each group, like platoons. If something happened to an individual, like death, there was a succession plan of leadership in place. This was to safeguard the revolution so that it would continue and survive even without our presence.

On that belief rested our faith in the righteousness of our struggle.

On the 23rd of April 1963, that belief was sorely tested when the Security police told us, with glee:

'We've got you now. We will charge you!'

We didn't know who had spilled what secrets.

Shortly thereafter, we were transferred to Krugersdorp Prison under warrant of commitment for further examination.

Strange to say, my reaction to the arrest was a deep hollow disappointment that festered unceasingly in my heart.

I had been convinced liberation was within reach. To be caught just before we even began our mission to embark on a final onslaught and liberate our people was intolerable – totally insupportable.

Called *Kothabeng*, the prison was an imposing red brick building surrounded by thick iron bars that I can still visualise. It was visible from miles away. The town of Krugersdorp, named after Paul Kruger, President of the early South African Republic, was built on a summit near the end of the western ridge of the Witwatersrand. It lies on an exquisite, rugged countryside criss-crossed by several streams. The town itself is on the gold reef, where mining was still carried out in some parts. Apart from gold it was reported to hold other precious metals that were also mined. Krugersdorp also lies in the heart of the old Transvaal Republic where massive protests were staged by the Boers against annexation of the province by the British after the Anglo-Boer War.

Because of the close geographical area from which we came and friendships that went back to school days and, later, work, the Randfontein-Bekkersdal-Krugersdorp groups identified as one unit. Our bond was further strengthened by the fact that we were all captured within days of one other.

From Bekkersdal there was Hubert Boyce; Matthews Letlhake; Abraham (Shakes) Matsile; Moses (Moss) Mokotong; Eret Radebe; Joe Seletesha; Joseph (Monty) Seremane; Samuel (Sam) Thabapelo and myself. In the chaos, at one home, instead of picking up Shakes Matsile, his confused co-worker was taken instead because they didn't have his real name; they only had his code name 'Action'. Later Shakes went to the police station to hand himself over for his co-worker to be released.

We were accommodated in one dormitory cell. Each was given a sisal mat to sleep on and two grey, scratchy, filthy, lice-infested blankets.

From the first day those insects bit us with no mercy; every warm crevice of the body with hair itched incessantly. Day and night we scratched the scathing, stinging bites from the fat lice that seemed to multiply overnight. In the mornings, our white underwear would be covered by a sea of lice. At the courtyard showers, where we were allowed half an hour, mornings and afternoons, we undressed in the sun, picked the lice and crushed them between our thumbnails. The blood from each would cover the whole fingernail of a thumb.

We were forced to stay inside the cell. So, to keep our minds and bodies occupied, we organised singing groups and dancing, we made *morabaraba* boards and with our rations of soap we played ludo. We picked the sun-softened tar from the courtyard to make dice, pieces of toilet paper made the dots for the numbers, and, for tokens, we used pieces of sunlight soap. We sat there for hours playing the ludo and snakes and ladder games. These group activities were not permitted, and so, whenever we were caught, we were punished.

Not punishment, but apartheid stratification, applied when it came to food and who got what in prison. To our consternation, we discovered even though we regarded one another as colleagues and comrades, even friends, even though we were charged under the same laws, served at the same institutions, when it came to the menu, we were treated differently.

Africans received the ghastly breakfast of acrid *motoho* served in old rusty metal dishes, and a small cup of black coffee and *phuzamandla*. Lunch was *kaboe* mealies, usually dry or with a sprinkling of beans. Supper was soft porridge with barely-there boiled vegetables and, on top of that, there floated a few pieces of fatty meat.

Abomnomzana, as we teased coloureds and Indians, were given slices of bread with a smear of holsum (instead of porridge). Our friend, Archie Jacobs, classified coloured and therefore entitled to bread, generously shared his.

While we were awaiting trial, we had to go to appear at Court once a week for a formal remand. One particular day, feeling rather bold and reckless, I smuggled out one of the prison's rusty dishes to show the magistrate what we had to eat out of. His response was cold and uncaring – formulaic:

'Your case is still under investigation. You're remanded,' he howled back at me.

On another day, again in court, it was Derrick Bila who had something up his sleeve – literally. He had a big fat louse crawling on his back. He complained to the magistrate who didn't seem to believe him.

'Would you like to see?' Derrick asked, reaching over his shoulder.

'No,' said the magistrate, almost jumping away.

Then, on the 17th of July 1963, we were transferred from Krugersdorp Prison to the Fort Prison, nicknamed Number Four by the people of the townships of Johannesburg. We were to remain there for the duration of our trial at the Johannesburg Magistrates Court.

But not all of us were going there. Four inmates from Krugersdorp had been charged with the murder of a Special Branch policeman.

We knew all of them very well. Peter was a trombone player for a group called the Newport Jazz 8; Thami attended the same school I did at Munsieville; Champ Molahledi was a well-known boxing trainer on the West Rand; and Joe Motsumi, the oldest of the group, was a community elder and the disciplinarian. He's the one who took us through our morning exercises to instil discipline among us. Each of these four men was isolated for interrogation. Not one of them ever returned. Through visits, we heard they had been sent to Number Four for a speedy trial in which they were expeditiously found guilty and sent to *intambo* (the rope), as the gallows at the Pretoria Central Prison was called. Sent there, to be executed by hanging.

It was quite shocking – frightening – to lose them so quickly. They were just like us. They *were* us! We had shared the awaiting-trial experiences with those four men.

The knowledge that these men had been sentenced to death on a trumped-up charge was both extremely horrifying and revealed our vulnerability.

Information reached us that their folks were told to collect their bodies from Pretoria Central Prison for burial.

That is something that will stay on my mind for as long as I live because even as I write now, I can see their faces clearly. Therefore, as we left for Number Four, we felt extremely vulnerable.

12

The betrayal: Number Four Prison

July 1963

The Old Fort Prison complex – commonly known as Number Four – is one of the oldest remaining buildings in Johannesburg. Virtually every important political leader in South African history from Mahatma Gandhi to Nelson Mandela and Robert Sobukwe, as well as scores of other South Africans caught in the web of colonial and apartheid repression, have been imprisoned in these jail cells. The old stone walls tell a century's worth of stories of an iniquitous political system, a brutal penal institution, and the resilience of generations of prisoners. Without warning or any preparation, my turn had arrived to experience the harsh reality of Number Four.

There was nothing glamorous about the harsh violent inhabitants of Number Four. We encountered debased souls who had surrendered to the life of crime, a reflection of the damaged society we lived in. What I saw there challenged everything I believed about humanity. The experience of that first night felt way beyond my realm of any perceptions or experience of life.

New to this harsh and violent reality, we tried to maintain our dignity.

Askance, we watched the food area, where prisoners shoved one another for a chance to grab the runny porridge and a mixture of *kaboe* mealies from trolleys before they moved off to eat, grunting like animals.

In the poorly ventilated dormitory cells, the blankets were also grabbed in a rush by the common-law prisoners, some of whom boasted to have been born in jail. The overcrowded stinking cells with bloody floors had no adornments of any kind. They were cold, dark, filthy, barren concrete cells filled with masses of unwashed bodies boasting hostile stares from the scarred and brutal men. We were definitely out of our depth.

For the first time, we experienced eastern toilets; the prisoners called them 'long drops', holes just dug in the ground with no partitions so that we had to relieve ourselves in full view and hearing of other men. Mind you, these latrines were right across from the concrete floor platform from where we squatted as we gulped our morning porridge and what passed for dinner. The floors covered with human waste from the overflowing latrines were almost impassable. In our homes, we were taught that an immaculate home was a reflection of the household's essence. The only familiar sight at Number Four was the lice infestation on the filthy sleeping mats and blankets.

However, it was a relief to finally know our predicament, although we had no expectations of acquittal. We had come to Number Four to stand trial, finally. We had been in the prison system for three months and awaiting trial for two months. All of us knew Number Four by reputation. As young boys, we were told to behave ourselves or we would end up in Number Four with habitual criminals such as rapists, murderers, big-time robbers we read about in *The Bantu World.*

That whole week, my first week in Number Four, my experience revolved around the clatter, screams and howling voices; the disquieting, fear-filled silence; groans at night; the bloody but inconsequential fights of the inmates among themselves or with the vicious bloodthirsty warders. However, *ubuntu* is a sturdy, stubborn plant and its seed will often prevail to flower in the most barren of soils. Some of the African prisoners showed us the way to survive in that place, survive from one day to another. And we often relied on these good Samaritans to offer advice to avoid confrontation with these fearsome people.

For nourishment, we only had *motoho* in the mornings. On the way to court, we just gulped black coffee in small cups and that slippery congealed mealie paste with floating rust – and remember, it had been dished hours before we even woke up! Fortunately, we were always in a rush with no time for anything else anyway.

Court days were vicious days, hard days for we returned evenings, too late for any food – not even leftovers. So, we just crawled onto the floor with or without bedding – and slept.

Everyday we went to court by *kwela-kwela.* We were exceedingly lucky that the High Courts were busy. That is why our case was brought before the Johannesburg Magistrates Court in Fox Street, which saved us from a harsher sentence.

Our case began on the 22nd of July 1963. It lasted for all of four days: Monday to Thursday. For those four days, the routine was the same for the nine of us from Bekkersdal. From the courtyard, we were ushered into heavily locked dark grey concrete basement cells where we waited to be called for the commencement of the proceedings. The first day in that dungeon I felt the same paralysing dread I had felt when I was a little boy and *Mme* told me a story about the day they went to visit the Sterkfontein caves. This was when she already had me. She said first they had to crawl inside the narrow entrance. It was dark and she remembered being told that they had to follow the guide very closely otherwise they could get lost and if that happened, they would never be found. That had put the fear of God in me, then. Then she said towards the end of the ten to fifteen mile walk, there was the miracle of a subterranean lake whose entrancing sight was worth all that discomfort.

But right then and there, waiting to appear before a hostile magistrate, I could not think what could ever be worth the fear, discomfort and dehumanisation I was suffering. No two ways about it, the court appearances were a harrowing experience, with no relief in sight.

On the very first of the four days, a warder barked each of our names and directed us up narrow, dark, cold, black concrete stairs into the courtroom. As we surged up those stairs, we sang protest songs to enter the courtroom in defiance.

We sang bravely and in that confined space our voices echoed throughout the courtroom.

We sat on benches in the enclosed dock in the small, poorly ventilated courtroom with low ceilings. Our attorney, Dan Bregman, sat to our right.

We wore the clean shirts and trousers and polished shoes our families had brought. When Magistrate Vos entered, we were told to rise.

The first day was chaotic. The cases had to be sped up to accommodate the expected rush of cases of those charged by the recently amended Suppression of Communism Act 44/50.

I was charged on two counts under that Act. First, for being a member of a banned organisation and, secondly, for participating in the activities of a banned organisation.

Our trial took place just a week after the Rivonia Raids had started on the 11th of July 1963.

Thus time had saved us from being charged under the General Law Amendment Act (2nd May 1963), one of many to amend the Suppression of Communism Act of 1950 and its predecessor, the Communism Act of 1944.

This new security legislation was deemed necessary to fight the recurring acts of sabotage. By upgrading existing legislature, the State sought to counter the surge of nationalism gripping the African continent – a surge that had reached South Africa.

The government enacted further laws to counter the influence of political organisations which had been banned by law, notably the African National Congress (ANC), the Pan Africanist Congress (PAC) and the South African Communist Party (SACP). Added to that was the Indemnity Act of 1961, which granted indemnity to police officers for acts committed in good faith. The act was made retrospective to the 21st of March 1960 (the date of the Sharpeville and Langa massacres). Thus began a process of placing the police above and beyond public reproach and, more seriously, effectively above the law.

These webs of laws created and entrenched an environment of surveillance and repression in which the police were beyond public scrutiny, criticism or challenge from the opposition in Parliament and/or the judiciary.

After the Magistrate had recited our charge to us, he asked, 'What do you plead?' We pleaded not guilty.

We felt we were innocent for seeking restitution; there was never a question that we were guilty. The sin, or the crime, was that we were being prosecuted for demanding back what was legitimately ours and defending ourselves from injustice. We were going to do what should have been done a long time ago, we believed.

The state called its witnesses.

We sat absolutely entranced while our brothers testified against us. Each day had its own star witness. Witness A was Sasa (not his real name), who was referred to as 'Mr X' by the court to mask his identity. Sasa was the one comrade who sat at the back of the car when I was arrested. I found out later that his role that day was to point out our homes to the Security Branch. It was ordered that his name not be revealed though he sat there in the witness box in front of us with no disguise.

He described one of our meetings in the graveyard – described how that meeting was opened by the greeting: 'Sons and daughters of the soil.'

In excruciating detail, Sasa elaborated how we assembled in secrecy in the graveyard at dusk, how we started rotating the venues, away from the homes with ears that could betray our plans for a countrywide insurrection. We shook our heads in utter horror. This man was not only one of us in Bekkersdal, he was our treasurer and he had toured the country on our behalf.

He knew everything. Everything he knew, he told. He told the court how Monedi, from Munsieville, opened our first cell in Bekkersdal. That I convened the first meeting with Harrison Mbambo, Denis Molete, Peter Nchauke at 149 Johnson Street in Bekkersdal. That it was at that meeting that I was elected chairman of our cell. Sasa told of our subsequent meetings and named the delegates at those meetings. He revealed how he, Monty and I had gone to Lesotho to receive instructions from Potlako Leballo. He told of our plans to bomb Libanon power station, at shaft Number One. We had already made contact with mine workers to supply us with explosives, which we were going to use to disable the power station and darken the whole area around Randfontein and Westonaria before attacking the residents. Sasa was head of the Task Force. The Intelligence unit had gone on a reconnaissance mission to study the installation of the mine and reported what should be done when handing over to the Task Force for execution.

I was floored. Flabbergasted. I sat there open-mouthed and I wondered if the man singing like a harp was the same Sasa I knew – he, who was a *chommie,* who lived right across the street from Leopard's home.

Was this the Sasa with whom I had attended the same higher primary school in Randfontein? For high school, he had gone to a boarding school in Basutoland. At his home, they couldn't manage to buy him books, so during holidays I used to give him my own books to take, and beg *Ntate* for new books.

With detached equanimity, this stranger parading as Sasa looked at each one of us with barely-concealed hostility. The sting of his betrayal, however, was far worse than his hostile stare. His arm, the arm of an obviously well-nourished gentleman, stretched out and pointed across the courtroom. That was Sasa as he identified us – each, in turn – with cold precision. It was in seeing that firm, plump and rounded flesh on his arm that I realised how emaciated we had become.

After Sasa's testimony, we knew we were doomed.

As if to confirm my worst suspicion, the next day, one of the *Rand Daily Mail*'s headlines read, 'Attack planned in graveyard, court told'.

But God is merciful. He works in mysterious ways. Just when I thought all was lost – that I was lost – my faith in my comrades was miraculously restored.

The next witness – after Sasa's damning betrayal – was also supposed to be anonymous. This was Dadu (not his real name), whom I had known in my early childhood at Venterspost Mine. He knew the workers in the mines and the building structure of the power station and had facilitated getting the dynamite to build the bombs. He also gave the inside workings of the mines to the intelligence team who went to conduct the reconnaissance mission to ascertain where to strike for maximum effect. Dadu was big-framed and stood over six foot. He had played fullback sweeper for our football team at Madibane High.

No striker from our regular competitors – Orlando High, Kilnerton, or Wilberforce Institute – could easily go past Dadu.

An eloquent speaker, he was on the school debating team and was renowned for his rhetorical prose. He was also proficient in many languages, with a brilliant infectious smile. A good-looking man, he was poised and confident.

However, that day, I saw another Dadu. In Court, Dadu played illiterate and stammered in isiZulu throughout his testimony.

When the prosecutor asked him, 'What did these people say? And where did they go?'

Dadu replied, '*Azange bakhulume lutho. Bathe nje baya eHQ.*' (They didn't tell us anything. They just said they are going to the HQ.)

The prosecutor coaxed for more detail. Dadu shook his head, '*Bakhulume nje amazwi amabili bathi, HQ.*' (They just mentioned two words, they said HQ). He demonstrated with two fingers.

The frustrated prosecutor kept prodding, 'What does HQ mean?'

'*Angazi, Nkosi,* (I don't know, My Lord) responded this educated man we all knew was fluent in English. '*Bakhulume amagama ayi 2 nje.*' (They spoke just two words.)

'What else was said?'

'I don't know, I just remember, the words HQ'

With defeat on his face, the prosecutor gave up. Dadu had contrived a brilliant plan; to give as little damning evidence as possible. He was brilliant.

The last witness called contradicted himself in many ways and yet he was found to be a 'reliable' witness.

On the 24th of July the state closed its case. We consulted with our attorney and conceded to his advice that we change our plea to one of guilty; the evidence against us was simply overwhelming. He was of the opinion that the court might be lenient to us for not wasting its time by going through a protracted trial. Everything had to move swiftly, numerous trials were pending.

We had been caught in the jaws of the numerous laws.

On the 25th of July, after the four-day rush of a trial, Magistrate Vos pronounced our sentences.

'You have been found guilty of being a member of a banned organisation and of taking part in its activities. For that, you are sentenced to three years on each count and, in all, you will serve six years!'

That sentence was directed to us, labeled ringleaders: Seremane and me from Bekkersdal; Boxy, Archie, Harrison and Martin from Randfontein. Dazed, I heard the rest of the sentences as from a great distance, 'five years, two years … four years …'

Behind us, members of our families gasped and wailed while we, as though we had rehearsed it, angrily shouted, '*Dis vokol*' (That's nothing!)

Then, after the initial blunt shock, we laughed heartily at the absurdity of the sentences. 'What's six years?' we scoffed. 'Six years is like six months, we'll be back!'

The magistrate tried to remain composed, his beet red face and stinging words betrayed his contemptuous anger.

'You are lucky that you're appearing in the Magistrate's Court. You are saved in that I am limited by the powers under the jurisdiction of this court. If I was wearing a gown as a judge of the Supreme Court, I would be sentencing you to ten years on each count.' With that he collected his papers and huffed out of the courtroom.

I glanced at my family then. I noticed *Ntate*'s grave raging helplessness. In the four-odd months since I was arrested, *Ntate* had aged ten years. His normally strong face was loose and softer than I remembered.

Eyes gleaming with unshed tears, *Ntate* fastened his eyes on my face. I could see he was still trying to grope with this new reality that his son, the apple of his eye, could commit an offence against the law. *Any law*. I was not only his son but, in his eyes, an intellectual, a gentleman. The fact that I was going to prison was simply beyond his contemplation. Right before my eyes, I saw Ntate's faith and hope for my bright future crumble and collapse – complete devastation.

At last, sadly, *Ntate* shook his head and a voice I didn't recognise croaked:

'Ngoanaka? (My child?) Thono?'

I had no answer, no comfort to offer my father.

But like a man, I tightened my jaw to suppress the surge of helpless rage inside me. My heart a bleeding lump, I raised my right hand and saluted *Ntate*, then quickly turned away. We went down the stairs with fists raised, singing, 'Afrika! *Izwe Lethu*!'

I felt all gutted inside. Not by the terrible sentence and what awaited me, but by the sight of my beloved father, all shook up and shriveled right before my eyes. Devastated, by what I had done. *O, Ntate*!

After the sentencing, we went back to the Fort to wait for the sentencing of the Randfontein group. As expected, they had also changed their plea from not guilty to guilty the day we were sentenced. They were sentenced the following day, the 26th of July.

So on Saturday, the 27th of July, we were all called to the courtyard and told to strip naked, starting with the shoes, and dress into the bandit attire of cream white tent canvas shorts and matching small short-sleeved triple buttoned jackets. Those uniforms shrivelled our maleness into small boys in the eyes of the authorities.

They stripped us of our individuality and diminished our humanity – not only in the eyes of those who wielded authority over us but even in our own eyes.

'*Haak*!' the warders instructed us to go into the waiting *kwela-kwelas*. Hopping with our soft feet on the cold, sticky, painfully sharp gravel of the courtyard, we entered the cold steel vans.

On the way, the Randfontein group told us that Sasa had testified because he had been threatened by the Special Branch and, also, his girlfriend was expecting a baby. They'd heard all this the previous day while in court for their final day of appearance. They said Sasa's reward was swift; he already had a job as *umabalane* at the Municipality offices in Bekkersdal. Semakeleng would later tell me that from the court, the Special Branch would follow them home then escort Sasa to a hiding room somewhere in Bekkersdal, where he was little known – or, better still, not known at all.

'*Haak!*' But we needed no such bidding as we left the Fort Prison. We didn't look behind us, we were just glad we didn't have the misfortune of being permanently commuted to Number Four.

13

Welcome to my farm.
Welcome to the party

27 July 1963

Leeuwkop Maximum Security Prison – that was our next port of call. And did we get a warm welcome!

This prison is situated just north of Johannesburg. We got there in the late afternoon. Lumped into the back of police vans with jokes for windows and round ventilation holes not much wider than a child's mouth, we saw little during the drive from our point of departure, Number Four, but our relief at what we had left behind carried us forward.

A hush fell as we entered Leeuwkop; disbelief on every face. This was the last thing we were prepared for – Leeuwkop! One of South Africa's top maximum-security prisons, made to hold particularly hardened criminals. Leeuwkop Prison is where Ezekiel Dlamini, otherwise known as King Kong, the notorious serial murderer of the fifties, had chosen to throw himself into a lake, take his own life, rather than stick it out in that place. The authorities at Leeuwkop boasted they could soften the most hardened of criminals. Talk about shock! Just when we thought we'd escaped from the horrors of Number Four!

To welcome us, there was a pair of warders, one black and the other white. The two officers were in identical dark brown khaki uniforms. This pair would be our main caretakers for the duration of our stay at Leeuwkop.

Taking over from those who had brought us there, the pair inspected us, coldly looking us up and down as they counted us to make sure there was the number they expected and that we were all in good health. I suppose they didn't want 'damaged goods'.

The Head Warder, Sergeant Liebenberg, nicknamed Magalies, had been a farmer before he joined the Prison Service. I guessed he originated from the Magaliesberg Mountains, North West of Johannesburg. Beetroot red, he was an imposing six foot four, thick-necked and broad of shoulder. His ice-blue eyes reminded us always that he hated us – and couldn't be bothered to hide that fact. Even his fluency in Setswana only emphasised that deep-seated contempt in which he held us. Looking down at us, Sergeant Liebenberg said, 'You are the twenty-nine from Randfontein,' paused before, in measured tone, he continued, 'Welcome to my farm!'

He stalked us in a slow broad walk; his body seemed to fill the whole corridor. In contrast to our silent bare feet, his strides thundered in his highly polished shiny boots in tawny red – almost military blood red with striking sharp, pointed shiny brown leather tips and black soles.

His colleague, Sergeant Major Khumalo, a pompous Zulu man with a jovial exterior, was extremely cruel. He was short and stocky, had the biggest, ugliest nose I have ever seen. The thing spread over his whole face. This man had, as an extension of himself and the authority he wielded, a hand-made baton sheathed in leather with a club at one end.

The weapon reminded me of a dormant snake that could be brought to life at the instruction of its master. And, indeed, when Khumalo instructed us on what to do, invariably, he gestured with his stick of authority – as we found out, that very first day at Leeuwkop Prison.

'Strip!' Khumalo told us to take off our bandit uniforms. Stark naked, we shivered in the cold, all twenty-nine of us.

'*Haak! Teen die muur!*' (C'mon! Against the wall!) shouted Magalies.

We turned slowly, shrugging, shaking our heads, *what now?*

Thick and fast, the orders came, each more bizarre than the one before it.

'*Kyk vorentoe!*' (Face the wall!)

'Don't look down! Or up! Or sideways!'

'Put your hands against the wall!' Khumalo barked, hitting the baton-*sjambok* against the palm of his hand in a fast tempo. And to make his point, he hit anybody who moved with a stinging knock (with the baton) on the back of the knees.

Striving hard to appear obedient and courteous, we complied; lined up against walls of the two-metre high hall, our palms against the wall.

From the beginning of the row, '*Phahlalatsa maoto*' (Spread your legs!) Magalies shouted. He stood, arms folded against his chest, his legs spread wide apart. Several African common-law prisoners stood next to him, adjusting surgical gloves.

We heard the hissing and snapping of rubber and wondered what it was and what it meant for us, but we dared not look.

Next, I heard a piercing cry, a horrified and horrifying cry, quickly followed by grunts and moans of pain. Or, was it pleasure? Pleasure from other voices – different voices from those that cried out in desperate anguish?

Khumalo and Magalies answered my silent questions:

'Bombs! You have bombs, in there!'

'We're looking for megaton bombs!'

They kept shouting. The shouting would be followed by screams. And that, in turn, would be followed by the sound of feet, of someone running out. Finally, that would be followed by Khumalo's excited shout:

'*Sheshisa! Sheshisa*!' (Hurry!)

Perplexed, I waited. Whatever was happening was coming closer and closer to me – to where I stood, waiting, legs wide apart, hands plastered to the wall.

I smelled him. A primitive, unwashed smell. As of a wild boar. A memory from visits to the farms in my youth, suddenly dredged by now's terror.

The small hairs at the nape of my neck rose, bristling; a reaction to the creature's heavy breath hitting that spot.

Without warning, two fingers thrust up my rectum, shoved in deeper and wiggled inside – to reach even further.

A gush of blood pounded in my head. Searing pain tore through me like a fire consuming dry grass. Then – darkness. I must have died temporarily.

I couldn't see him. I didn't want to see him. I had never thought that excruciating pain possible.

I don't remember what I did.

The man (creature, as I thought of him at the time) didn't say a word, throughout the whole ordeal. When he was done, he moved to the person next to me. And another took over from him, coming to inspect a different part of my anatomy.

This one told me to click. Say, '*Qa, qa, qa,*' he said, prying my lips open, a finger tapping my teeth to open wider. Then he began prodding inside my mouth – still searching for bombs. By now, I had completely dissociated from any feeling. Next, they poked and prodded my ears, my armpits, dripping with sweat although it was July, the middle of winter, and the concrete floor was icy cold.

They were still searching for bombs.

After that, I followed the procession, itself following the order that was shouted at us:

'*Sop, sop!*' (Soap, soap!) to be smeared with a brown gooey soap gel.

Another row of common-law prisoners stood at the ready: Pa-ah! Pa-ah! They slapped the gluey stuff on my forehead, in my armpits, and on my groin.

Khumalo then shoved me into the shower room. I had noticed how those ahead of me had to run because if they did not, Khumalo was ready to knock their knees with his baton-*sjambok*.

The freezing cold shower pressure from the big nozzle swept me back out with a forceful blast; Sergeant Khumalo, ready with his baton, threw me right back. I had to be thoroughly cleansed. I slid, slipped and fell. There was neither rail nor wall to hold on to for balance. Our warders told us the cleansing was to de-lice us as we had come from Krugersdorp Prison known to be infested.

His face bathed in glee, 'Welcome to the party,' Magalies smirked at the door.

We shuffled out and into an enormous reception hall, where we were processed. Here, we were immediately stripped of what identities we still clung to. Instead of names, we were assigned and called by numbers. Gabriel Magomola, prisoner number 1/1236, and my vital physical details were duly recorded on the prison register forms. It was duly noted that I was a single, Roman Catholic (which I had told them), 20-year-old Bantu Pedi, well built male, weighing 148 pounds, born in Randfontein and possessed matric (which I didn't). I was recorded to have a square face, high forehead, brown complexion, deep set eyes, a prominent nose, a medium mouth, good teeth and large ears with short hair and a short beard. I was declared to have a normal heart, lungs and all other organs. A note was made that I had distinguished vaccination marks and other abnormalities, which were also noted; anything else that could be used for identification in the event I escaped was all noted. That description would be circulated for my capture. We were then photographed and fingerprinted. Our heads, beards and moustaches were shaved by the common-law prisoners. My mental state was declared normal and my physical state good.

From the intake statistics, I was in tip-top shape. It came as no surprise, therefore, that hard labour was recommended.

We were then issued with identification four-sided cards like the *dompas* that contained our names, crime for incarceration, the nature of the sentence, educational level, occupation, religious affiliation, and the date of incarceration. Strict instructions were given that we carry the cards at all times. So, what was new? Africans carried passes all the time. Now, in jail, we had to carry jail passes. That's life, for you.

We were bundled into what would be our accommodation for the next five months; separated from the common-law criminals, as we were labelled of higher risk – a threat to the State. Our quarters were a double volume dormitory cell. It boasted a toilet right there in the cell and had no partitioning at all. Privacy, for such as we were, was not a matter to be entertained. We were given one roll of toilet paper – ONE – for the whole entire group of us – TWENTY-NINE grown men. Sometimes, when the roll ran out, we were forced to use pieces of the blankets. Out of sheer frustration and anger, I usually just tore pieces of my shirts. The result was that often, by Saturday, I'd have half a shirt.

The mesh-reinforced windows were high above and offered just a glimpse of light from the sky, the colour of which we had almost forgotten. At the very top, there was a vertical strip of plank that formed a catwalk, where the warders strolled and peeked at random, to observe what we were up to. We didn't have to see them to feel their presence, though. We knew we were under constant surveillance and so took turns watching out for them while we talked – which was forbidden.

Each of us was given a three feet sisal mat, two inches thick, and three grey, coarse, low quality blankets. In silence we made our long bed, as we had done in Krugersdorp Prison, joining the mats together, using some of the blankets as under sheets and the rest for cover.

But, that awful night, we slept without our usual animated and defiant singing. Famished, weary, lost, forlorn, and subdued, like wounded animals, we lay ourselves down, each to lick his bruised and bleeding soul. We were so down, we couldn't even acknowledge the inmates from Pretoria, whom we found already there.

Before that late afternoon, we had thought we were hard; we had believed we were ready to face anything – even our own deaths. For the first time since I had signed up, I was assailed by serious doubts about my own commitment. I wondered if the life of my dreams was worth all that pain.

I was not alone in such soul searching. Later, nobody could describe the ordeal, even as we sat and wondered among ourselves.

All everybody remembered was that the instruments of our violation were Africans, just like us; the rest is a blank. None among us could remember, never mind describe, those men's faces or other physical attributes. Blank.

But I can still smell the damp, mouldy, sweaty, vile stench of them.

Intuitively, I felt that our fresh experience at Leeuwkop was just the beginning of real hell. My mouth was still filled with bitter bile when I finally dozed amid the anguished groans and moans of my mates. I didn't know or wish to know if they were awake or in painful dreams. My own private personal agony was too deep to share even with them with whom I had avowed solidarity. I pretended I was home asleep on my new bed. Bedtime here was 8 pm every night with blaring lights; for the six years of my incarceration this was bed time – 8 pm.

The first morning at Leeuwkop, Magalies and Khumalo supervised our mandatory thirty-minute sprinting around the courtyard. For exercise, we had to run at full speed, while we were tripped and lashed by Magalies's cane. '*Hardloop!*' (Run!) and Khumalo's stick with the head hitting us behind the knees; '*Nges'dumo mfana.*' This, while some of the common-law prisoners jeered. Finally, short of breath and with our knees shaking, we went for breakfast.

That, too, was served with enthusiastic encouragement from Khumalo: '*Hamba nges'dumo mfana.*' (Go with haste, boy!)

'*Nges'dum'o!*' (With haste!) He sang and screeched; and we had to run to grab from the table to get our ration of food. As a prisoner grabbed a rusty metal bowl of porridge, Khumalo shouted again and again:

'*Nges'dumo! Shesisa!*' We scampered, grabbed and scuttled off and away to his beat. A prisoner grabbed a cup of *phuzamandla* and hastened off. There were no utensils. If one ran past a plate, missing it, too bad; that spelt a missed meal for that prisoner. It was against regulations to go back in the queue; and, eagle-eyed Khumalo watched, ready to strike accurately with his baton, accurately, *behind* the knees. When that happened, we would hear his ominous hiss-laced laughter.

When we'd run the obstacle race and got what passed for food, we ran back to the cell to eat in a corner.

In the mornings, we were woken up at six by the clanging of keys as the heavy grey steel doors were opened. This was accompanied by the lethal brass bell. Just to wake up, we had to follow a precise routine: fold the blankets in a specific and uniform rectangular shape; then roll up the sisal mat and lean it against the wall and, lastly, place the blankets in front of the mat to create a seat. (Nelson Mandela describes this routine eloquently in his book, *Long Walk to Freedom*.

After that, came the rush to the outside concrete basins, to wash hands and face, in preparation for the pre-breakfast count.

For that, we stood in front of our blankets and waited to be counted. This was to ascertain that no one had escaped or died in the course of the night.

The showers were in a separate building that was kept locked and only opened at the discretion of the warders – a rare occurrence; twice a week was considered more than adequate.

'This is not a hotel!' Was the curt answer, when one of us was rash enough to ask that the showers be opened. Again, these showers, as the toilets, had no partition of any kind. In fact, none of the facilities had dividing walls or partitions for privacy.

Saturday mornings, we were provided shavers, to remove all visible hair, and fresh uniforms, which were laundered by the common-law prisoners. There was no system of distribution, the warders just barked, '*Hoe veel is julle?*' (How many are you?)

One or another prisoner would shout, 'Thirty!'

And exactly thirty of the articles we were being allocated would be thrown at us. There would be a mad scramble and one grabbed what one could grab, irrespective of size. Shorts or shirts, in various sizes, would later be exchanged for better fit.

Sometimes, for any of a variety of reasons (or, indeed, at whim) the warders would take the clothes from us and we then roamed around naked, for hours, even going to meals in that disgraceful, dehumanising state. For the entire length of my incarceration, all of six years, we were not supplied with any underwear.

Routinely, Sunday morning was the inspection, followed by the *klaagtes en versoeke* session (complaints and requests) conducted by the Commanding Officer of the prison.

To demonstrate that he was on duty, he carried a baton under his left arm. It was absolutely crucial to be flawless for his inspection – a clean uniform; the three buttons of the top neatly fastened, faces and heads cleanly shaven with no visible hair anywhere. For his arrival, we stood up straight in a guard of honour, our identification cards prominently held in front of our chests. The Commanding

Officer would stroll between us, looking each one of us up and down for any faults – before moving on.

At question time on our first Sunday, I surmounted the courage to ask, '*Ek vra asseblief, kry ons nie koffie, Meneer?*' (I ask please, can we get some coffee, Sir?)

The corpulent Commanding Officer and his warder entourage derided, '*Kyk net vir hom.*' (Just look at him.) '*Hy soek sy elf-uur koffie!*' (He wants his eleven o'clock coffee!)

S'dumo, the nickname we had given Khumalo, was almost hiccupping with laughter; his arrogance concealed from the Commanding Officer, he screamed:

'Open your eyes and ears … *Eh he he*. Oh, these people!' and shook his head pityingly at our ignorance. He turned to the Commanding Officer, 'When they get the food here,' he said, pointing at the kitchen counter, and continued, 'they run away. I don't know why. They speed past the coffee. *Eeh- he!*'

Later, my friends marvelled at the daringness of my request. Puzzled, they scratched their heads and cautioned: '*Ei, Eh, Monna, Otlorebolaisa kamaburu?*' (Hey man, you'll get us killed by the Boers. Why are you even thinking about coffee?)

However, the next day we had our very first small cups of black coffee.

The ins and outs of prison provided ample opportunity of abuse or fun, depending on which side of the fence you were on. I remember another meal routine, this one belonging to Sunday mornings, and what havoc it played on us before we knew better.

Just before one reached the kitchen, there stood a big oil drum containing this Epsom salts concoction. Little did we know that it was an optional extra. That first time, innocent of such knowledge, we were very happy to see it as that meant we would get a chance to cleanse ourselves – inside. After gulping the Epsom salts mixture, we moved towards the kitchen to get food.

But the warders stopped us, '*Nee, Nee! Het jy Epsom salt gedrink?*' (No, No! Did you drink Epsom salts?)

Confused, we nodded. I began to fear we had been poisoned.

'*Nee, jong. Jy het klaar gedrink; jy kan nie drink en eet nie.*'

Loosely translated: You cannot have your breakfast if you elected to have Epsom salts.

There would be no meals for that day. Our runny stomachs growled the whole day and throughout the night.

By the end of the first week, our will would remain only in our minds. We had quickly learned to adhere to the stringent routine of drills and that we couldn't act on impulse – the fear of punishment was real, ever-present, and palpable. We had to wait to be instructed by unnaturally loud voices on what to do, when and how. This was a whole new ball game – a harsh environment, hard to comprehend at that stage of young, inexperienced me.

Because the situation was that dreadful, we desperately needed hope – something to hold on to. Thus, we waited for salvation in our night-time dreams, in the moments of our waking up and before the horrors of the day made their inescapable claims on us, in our muted conversations, and in our choral singing of defiant struggle songs. Our internal energy was conserved for that period of reckoning, when we would be vindicated. *Ntate* Paul Masha strengthened us.

He was trained in the judo martial arts and his soporific demeanour encouraged us to seek guidance from him and we looked to him for courage when things were really tough. In many ways, this man reminded me of my father for he was almost his age and was greying at the temples as dad was. At my age, I was young enough to be his son. We could always count on *Ntate* Masha to stand up for us, restoring and replenishing what remained of our diminished humanness.

Ntate Masha's nurturing us did not come without cost to him. For some reason I would never know, the older prisoners seemed to provoke Magalies' most sadistic outbursts. Stalking us, he would call out to the married men, scolding them for the bad influence they were on us, the younger ones. That is not to say Magalies was enamoured of the younger prisoners – oh, no!

For the youngsters, Magalies' and Khumalo's tricks were inexhaustible. Those two could be trusted to always find new ways of punishing us.

One day, the duo showed us an old crack in the wall and accused us of drilling through the thick concrete, attempting to escape. They then told us we would be charged with attempted escape from the maximum-security Leeuwkop Prison.

Next thing we knew, without warning, we were marched to the isolation cells and committed there while an investigation was conducted.

We were scattered about the cells so that we couldn't communicate with one another during the interrogation period. But how could we possibly tunnel through the thick cement wall with no tools except our bare hands?

Suddenly, I found myself in a dark single cell – a hell-hole. The cells were carefully designed to psychologically torture, taunt and haunt, create despair and instil utmost fear. That first time in there, I was overcome by an unreasonable but real fear that the walls would suction my brain and swallow it – together with the rest of me – my whole self – into their deep dark depths. That feeling was so painful I often think what I suffered there, that time was worse than any physical torture I had experienced up to then. Deprived of all socio-physical and natural stimuli – visual, aural, tactile, auditory – the abyss felt deeper than hell. Throughout my struggle in that twilight isolation, I wondered how my colleagues were coping. I became disoriented, all my senses hyper-heightened and, with no outlet to vent my feelings, I began to hallucinate. I heard echoes; I smelled damp rot and felt something or someone touch me on my legs. At one and the same time, even as I experienced all this, a part of me (or another, different me) knew and understood that this could not be – it was not possible that I was experiencing these things I was experiencing.

For twenty-three hours, over a fortnight, we were each on our own – total isolation.

In those crammed, confining, cells – dark and badly ventilated, the only light, a trickling flicker from the ventilation hole, fifteen feet up – the only sign of life, the warder voyeurs who peeked in through a peep-hole on the steel door.

Then, twice a day, for 30 minutes, mornings and afternoons, we were let out for exercise. It was physically excruciating to run on hungry stomachs at twice the normal speed. They really wanted to kill us – were bent on killing us. We were told, '*Hardloop!*' (Run!) as S'dumo chased us around the courtyard.

Hubert Boyce, who was the first to experience the isolation cells for frequent insubordination, had become a regular in isolation and familiar with the warders. Now the warders found him something to do: he was made to hand us our food. Before that, our food was just left outside the door, and we'd wonder, '*Hoe gaan ek die kos kry?*' (How will I get the food?)

Then, without any explanation, one day we were returned to the main cellblock. We didn't ask for reasons for that action; although we did wonder. Wonder as we had wondered at the onset of our isolation.

Four months after our trial and sentencing we were still languishing at Leeuwkop when on the 24th of November President John F. Kennedy was assassinated in the United States. We mourned and sorrowed.

His death extinguished a beam of hope for our own salvation. Kennedy's solidarity with the Civil Rights Movement encouraged us in our own struggle for freedom. We believed he was assassinated by conservative forces not sympathetic to our plight. Our hope for foreign intervention to aid us was not totally extinguished, though. The world had reverberated with moral outrage after the horror of the Sharpeville massacre. Surely the world would not abandon us, it would look out for us, we were convinced. The Organisation of African Unity (OAU) had just been established in Addis Ababa, while we were awaiting trial at Krugersdorp Prison.

One day, a random search by the warders resulted in the discovery of a newspaper, smuggled in by one of the common-law prisoners sympathetic to our cause. Maximum security prison regulations forbade us any and all newspapers. The warders raised hell. It was unheard of, for a smuggled newspaper to be found in a cell at Leeuwkop. Cigarettes were common. Within minutes, our two tormentors, Khumalo and Magalies, blocked the entrance of our cell.

'Whose paper is this?' Magalies asked, his voice cold and quivering with rage.

No-one owned up.

He immediately ordered the dreaded strip and anal search. 'Face the wall and take your clothes off!' he barked. I felt like spitting in his contemptible face.

Automatically, we complied, dissociating ourselves from the act. Then it was '*Sop, sop!*'

We had nicknamed this procedure the sign of the cross, for performing it resembled the same sequence of actions – the smear of gooey gel soap on the forehead, under both armpits and genitals. Unlike that holy ritual, however, ours was, invariably, followed by the blast of a cold shower.

Still unsatisfied, Khumalo whipped out his *knobkerrie* and chased us around the courtyard.

'Nges'dumo!' (With haste!) I felt light-headed, my legs ached and buckled. Wheezing and breathless, I swallowed. But my throat was bone dry.

Huffing and clutching my burning chest, I fell.

Seeing that, the others refused to run altogether.

All of this drama ended up earning us a ses *maaltye* penalty or six days in isolation cells. For the first three days, we didn't get any food. Day four and day five, we had rice water.

Finally, came what we'd all been waiting for – manna from Heaven. From then on, we had half-cooked *kaboe* mealies. And how was this meal served? What about thrown in under the door, as though we were rabid dogs?

During all this time, underfed and hungry all the time, do not think, for a minute, we were exempt from the compulsory exercise: thirty minutes, morning and afternoon. Supervised by a warder, we had to run around the courtyard. Once, I just refused to run. Out of sheer exhaustion. And got away with it.

We held on steadfastly to our dreams of rescue before serving our six-year sentences, dreams that were further fuelled by the build-up created by African statesmen such as President Ahmed Ben Bella of Algeria who made a statement that he would soon be parading through the streets of Johannesburg with his military forces to overrun this country. Prime Minister Kwame Nkrumah of Ghana, a towering force within the movement of Pan Africanism, advocated the quest for the unification of the African continent.

In the afternoon of Sunday the 9th of December 1963, some time after visiting hours, when the animated voices of visitors had long subsided, we suddenly heard unusual noise. Moments later, a phalanx of coloured warders in private clothes swarmed and opened the cells.

'Two-two! *Umthetho wasejele!*' (The law of the jail), Khumalo ordered.

I was momentarily puzzled by the warders' air of jubilation, if restrained. Not sure whether we were being taken to a place of even worse torture or, like cattle, being taken for dipping against disease or, indeed, to be given diseases.

The warders guarded their secret, but there was electricity in the air; anticipation was undeniably there, tangible as the very air we breathed.

We fell into line and on we marched like disciplined soldiers. We went through the maze of the prison corridors – to the courtyard. There we were made to sit in rows. And wait.

Patiently, we sat and waited; wondering and on tenterhooks. But it was beginning to be obvious what the big secret was. The moment had arrived.

Knowing something of prison by now, we had always suspected that our departure from Leeuwkop would come unannounced, yet the element of intrigue was nevertheless still too much for us. We sat waiting for confirmation. But we had not been informed because the prison authorities did not want the prisoners to tell their visitors of what we used to call the 'draft'.

How I wished I had known I was leaving so I could've told Leopard who would go to my family and let them know.

The visiting warders strutted about with barely-concealed smirks of superiority. They were accompanied by a number of common-law prisoners, whom they used for whatever purpose. The common-law prisoners seemed to share a camaraderie from which we, the security prisoners, were excluded; not that we minded the honour. It fell on the criminals to hand each one of us a cream white canvas shirt and matching short pants – both made of a very hard fabric.

We were instructed to remove our clothes, right there in the courtyard. It was so undignified and disrespectful, especially taking the age difference among us into account. In the African tradition, there is deep inter-generational respect: a son (any young man) is not supposed to ever set eyes on the body of a father (an elder). I remember that when we were children, we were often told that it was important for a child never to witness the nakedness of an adult and if they did, they would go blind. Filled with shame, we avoided one another's eyes, kept our eyes cast down in an attempt to give one another the distance and shield our captors denied us, for we remembered we were human.

Remember now, not one of us had underwear. And there we were, a hundred naked men, changing into these brand new stiff clothes that were extremely uncomfortable. We did exactly what we were told – did so with dignified courtesy.

In no time at all, we were again made to stand in twos.

'Choose your mate! Next to you! *Ha! Ha! E, he!* You are embarking on a journey which will require you to be close to your best mate all the time …' Magalies was in his element; he was enjoying himself.

I chose to shackle myself to my childhood friend, Monty. I drew courage and inspiration from that man; he and Leopard were my surrogate brothers. We were soul mates.

'Clang, clang,' the keys in the heavy bags rattled. Soon, there was even more clashing and clanging: in pairs, handcuffed at wrist and shackled in leg irons at the ankle, we made an unwieldy troop, doing the obstacle three-legged walk.

We were all used to handcuffs – had used them ourselves. But the leg devices were a new aberration – a totally new form of degradation – something we had only seen in Western movies, where violent homicidal maniacs were portrayed, chained on the legs and the wrists. It was incomprehensible to me that these would be used on us. After all, we were helpless, defenceless, unarmed captives of the apartheid regime. The brutality to which we were now subjected was unfitting and inexplicable. The only reason for using them, the only reason I could think of, was they were used in order to humiliate us and break our souls.

We slept like that.

We had planned a concert that evening. Needless to say, that concert didn't take place as the musical group, 'The Limelighters' totally forgot all about it.

Tugging and pulling to find comfortable positions that could accommodate (if not encourage) sleep proved futile. There was nothing for it but to wait for the morning. We waited for the morning. Perversely, that whole night, I thought about my magnificent bed at home (something I did every night). But, this night was different. This night, I just couldn't let go of the thought of my new single bed at home. I believe this is what is called 'obsession'.

14

Journeying to Robben Island

December 3, 1963

From that awkward torturous sleep, we were woken up at 4 am by the commotion the warders made. The familiar cling and clang of keys against the bars somehow seemed magnified that morning. '*Umthetho wasejele!*'

In pairs, we formed a neat row and sleepily followed the direction the warders indicated. Outside, it was a warm summer morning, the sun already casting a silvery gleam that was busy chasing away the last of the dark of night. But, up there the pre-dawn sky still sported the moon and the stars – things I had almost forgotten existed.

Like a desert traveller, I inhaled deeply, my heart soaring with undiluted pleasure. Surprised, I smiled, thrilled I could still experience the joy of simple nature. Beyond the prison walls, birds chirped and chirruped, busy communicating among themselves from the trees. Dawn, beautiful dawn! The sweet smell of the just-watered grass and soil of the prison's immaculately manicured grounds added to the sense of wholesomeness. Suddenly, I thought of my first sweetheart, Mamodipane or Papai. I was apprehended just when I had finally reached the end of my confusing puberty and was experimenting with the mysteries and pleasures of adult life. As I thought of her that morning, I didn't realise, didn't know, that I would never see her again.

My thoughts were broken by the serving of breakfast. Even on that special day, there was nothing special about our food. We got the same old *motoho*. The only difference was that, this time, the *motoho* was still warm. But so we would not be carried away, it was still served in the same small rusty metallic bowls and still made slightly palatable by that frugal spoonful of brown sugar sprinkled on top.

We gulped it down. But my stomach growled for more food. *Fat chance of that!*

Soon after our introduction to Leeuwkop Prison, I had resolved to banish fear for I understood that unless I did that I would never survive those damp dark walls.

Within an hour, like cattle, we were herded into the police vans. To send us off the Commanding Officer of the prison addressed us. He told us that we were leaving his presence and heading for Robben Island. Then he warned us that if we thought we had been subjected to pain at Leeuwkop Prison, we had 'seen nothing yet'. We were leaving with no illusions this time around.

Limping, squirming, pulling and yielding, in a clanging, clashing cacophony of the shackled and barely awake, we stepped up and into the five vans – twenty of us in each van. Our surrogate parents, Magalies and Khumalo, along with a Colonel from Leeuwkop, were part of a group of warders' escort taking us all the way to the end of the universe.

We still could not escape the company of those two bullies – truly rotten souls.

We drove out of the high steel gates of Leeuwkop Prison in the partial dark of pre-dawn. The five vans carrying us were escorted by two cream coloured Security Branch cars with four big armed men in each – two in the front and two at the back. Those cars were followed by two vans full of coloured warders, also fully armed. Quite impressive when you consider that not one of the hundred prisoners had so much as a nail file!

Hunger for the outside world gave us extraordinary skilfulness. For a glimpse of the familiar, somewhat awkwardly, we scrambled to the small steel-reinforced windows and ventilation holes. Greatly discomforted by the chains binding us hand and foot, we turned, twisted, pulled and adjusted till we were crouched on the low benches of the van, for that is all we could manage – there was no other possibility as we were bundled and tightly packed just like a bunch of pumpkins thrown into a bag. As you can imagine, finding those positions, barely endurable as they were under the circumstances, caused absolute chaos.

Our journey from Leeuwkop Prison just outside of Johannesburg to Cape Town would be 1 200km. We sang our freedom songs loudly to banish any fear.

Senzeni Na? (What have we done?)

Senzeni Na?

That song (and others like it) spoke of our deep feelings and our pain – things too intimate to articulate in plain, everyday words.

Though I desperately hoped the vans would take the road that went past Bekkersdal, Westonaria, and other townships on the West Rand instead of the faster route through Johannesburg, I tried not to think about home.

And, wouldn't you know, as if in answer to my wishes, I saw the rocky reddish yellow valleys and hills changing into the flat topography of the West Rand. The only crests among the tall veld grasses were the gold domes, those monstrous aliens erected by the mining industry. For a while, we were silent, each deep in thought.

I can tell you what was going through my mind: *Will I ever come back? Is this the end? Will I ever see my family again?*

My hopes rose higher as we passed the main street of Randfontein town. Spontaneously, we broke out into joyous howls and screams – the other ten Randfontein guys in the van and I – as we passed through the industrialised, lively street. We had not seen our home towns for about the same amount of time.

If the warders wondered what kind of hell had broken loose in the back of the van, they didn't bother to stop the van and come and look.

We passed the Mill site, a patch of veld where Tunkie, a friend and former schoolmate, was knifed by *amabhaca* on his way back from his nightshift at a progressive company that employed African matriculants. His death was a hard time for us and created resentment for the outsiders from the Transkei who worked in the mines. That was the very first time I experienced the violent death of a close friend; and I couldn't comprehend that senseless violence.

Then I saw the house where I worked as a garden boy, weekends, for pocket money. I was introduced to this 'Afrikaner family' by Ganantios, another one of my friends. Ganantios worked for this family's neighbour, at that time.

But now, the vans were going past the Bantu Affairs Commissioner's Offices in Randfontein, where I – together with the coloured woman I had bribed with one pound per week instalments for five weeks to claim she was my mother – had appeared for a hearing. I had taken that drastic step to get myself reclassified 'coloured'. This was not because I hated my race – far from it. But as a coloured, I would get a better paying job in Krugersdorp. Upward mobility is something I have always valued. Mind you, while I (and other Africans light-complexioned enough to make the attempt) was doing that, there were some coloureds who declared themselves white.

There again, the incentive (usually) was the chance for a better life. The outcome of all this was that while that 'better life' was perceived to have been achieved, families were torn apart. Unforeseen reactions from 'loved ones' brought emotional pain that had not been expected (or suspected) as when some of the new whites didn't want their old dark skinned cousins and boyfriends claiming them as kin. But, hey! I was young and somewhat ambitious.

And so, the debonair, (hopefully) sophisticated, partly emancipated Slideman Montgomery took over the life of Gabriel Thono Magomola. I was 17, armed with my new green coloured identity card, and had a job as a part assembler at Rubber and Wheel Industries in Krugersdorp. The English surname of Montgomery I had borrowed from Ntate's war hero, famed British general, Bernard Montgomery, Field Marshall of the Allied Forces during World War Two. The arm of the law is long, indeed; it reaches even the hidden recesses of the heart. During the entire period of my incarceration (and some years later) I was haunted by that fraud. At any time,

I expected to be hauled back to court and charged for that same act, and then get another sentence – additional years behind bars.

Delmas Milling Company came next. This is where I had my first job, at sixteen. However, the drive through Randfontein town was inconsequential – outside it was all quiet, the stores closed, not one soul stirred. But that didn't stop us making a commotion – just for those sights of remembered places.

Then we were upon the grassy vacant buffer zone that separated black and white Randfontein, so that whites in town would be able to see Africans approaching from the township. Under that grass, away from the nuns' and teachers' eyes is where we had our fair fights to settle scores. That was where the Bantu No. 95 Greyhound bus turned away from the town centre. Malome George, the driver, was an obliging *ntate*, who always wore a white straw hat to conceal his balding head. He had a huge wide scar right across his neck.

And here was Mathlare – trees bus stop, where people who lived on the semi-urban plots alighted. When we were growing up, we used to tease those people, calling them *moegoes* for we believed they were not as smart as we who lived in the townships. The bus stop was surrounded by a lethal thicket where it was reported that no-one could pass between 8 pm and morning and still have their life with them; that infested it was with *malaitas* from the mine hostel, who knifed pedestrians. At least, that's how the legend went. But now, Mathlare signalled we were approaching Bekkersdal!

The singing stopped as, with baited breath, we waited.

After a few kilometres, we passed the dam always covered by a rising film of mist. When we were children, it was called Bekkersdal Dam. The dam was later renamed Donaldson Dam. Nobody knew what good this settler who had lived in the area had ever done to have a dam named after him. But most residents called the sunlit lake 'Blue Sky', for it always reflected the clear blue sky of the West Rand.

When I was a child, we used the area for our pranks; stealing liquor and escaping to the dam with girls. My business-inclined mind, even then, envisioned Blue Sky as a well developed resort with amenities for boating, fishing and all sorts of water-themed activities for the whole family. With the enforcement of the Reservation of Separate Amenities Act, the dam was, indeed, converted to a leisure spot – but, for the enjoyment of the white community only.

That dam was steeped in mythical mystery. As children, we used to stand on the edge of the water and witness an imaginary rhythmic movement right in the middle of the dam where, according to legend, there was a huge snake, which consumed people who tried to swim in it. Many boys drowned because (we believed) they were 'swallowed' by that snake, called *Noga yako damong.* I had great respect for Blue Sky.

Girls never ventured anywhere near Blue Sky but swam in the smaller, dirty, muddy dam, called, *kolobe* (pig dam) not far from Blue Sky. They would skip school, and spend the day there, armed with a bottle of vaseline, so they wouldn't return ashy-skinned, a dead give away to the parents.

One day, Abel, a boy we were swimming with, disappeared. One moment we were all laughing and splashing, and when we came out, Abel was gone. First we thought he was playing a prank, hiding under the water with his nose pinched. As dusk approached, we knew there was big trouble. We ran back to the location to report that Abel had been pulled by water, he wasn't coming up.

The police came and searched for a long time before they found him on the other bank, dead. Then, not long after, another boy from nearby Carletonville drowned.

I stopped going to the dam after that – altogether – except when there was a *mokete* – a ceremony at our Church home branch. Then we would go to the dam for baptism and blessing; which is when we would be dipped in the water.

Now memories flooded me; and they were faster than the speed of the roaring vans. Now, as we drove past Blue Sky, with maturity and the wisdom that comes with that, I wondered how we could have ever thought the dam ominous. We had believed its depth was beyond measure. Yet now, looking at it with my grown-up eyes, the dam looked quite quaint. Quaint – and not the least bit dangerous.

Mme! The vans had gone beyond the dam. Here we were, going past the graveyard where *Mme*, my beloved mother, *Nkhono,* Grandmother Christina, and others lay. Sombre and grieving anew, I said a silent prayer, asked *Mme* to continue to preserve me. From the distance, I could see the tree under which her grave lay, marked by a zinc cross with a number on it. As a family, we had feared that someone, sometime, would move the cross or desecrated the grave; so we had all memorised the number. That way, the office clerks could check and tell us where the grave was.

From my youth, ever since I lost my mother, she has come to me in many visions; and I believe that she has been beside me and has ensured my well being and what success has been mine through all my life. So now, I had the usual silent moment of prayer for salvation and for safety as we journeyed to Robben Island. I thanked *Mme*, and remembered her generous spirit. How she dispensed her incredible powers that God had given her.

Up to this day, people still talk about my mother; they remember her healing powers – how she could cure many ailments and possessed the gift of accurate precognitive future prophesies.

I still grieve for *Mme*; we didn't have enough of her. She was only in her mid-thirties when she passed on. We didn't learn enough of what we could have from her because we took our time with her for granted. I still can't forget her, she remains in my heart.

Finally, we saw the thirty or so rows of houses that formed part of Bekkersdal. It was just after six in the morning; smoke rose from the chimneys; announcing preparation of the morning meal; bread, tea and porridge. We knew that in all the homes, people were starting fires in the coal stoves.

Suddenly deflated, in resigned silence, we watched the smoke hover over the location – a black cloud that could be seen for miles and miles.

That morning, looking at our homes from the back of a police van, crammed and bound in chains, we looked at the rising sun, and its brilliance was no different to that of other days – days we remembered – days when we used to be free.

A deep, painful, cankering nostalgia struck me. We were going past my own home. I was leaving, abandoning my younger siblings there. Who would look after them? With *Ntate* ageing and caring for his new family, I was designated to be their caretaker, chosen by nature – being the eldest and male. And, I didn't expect to find my father alive, even were I to be released after only two years, because I had heard that his health was deteriorating and he was just disintegrating – the impact of my arrest, I knew.

Semakeleng entering puberty: and I wouldn't be there to make sure no boys took advantage of her and made her pregnant. All these thoughts jammed my mind; they pained me more than the chains on my wrist and ankles. I had let my family down. Everybody … including *Mme.*

15

The reception

Around midday we had not yet been given an opportunity to relieve ourselves – in the 12 hours we'd been on the road. It was in the middle of summer; inside the van it was sweltering hot, our faces and bodies were dripping with sweat. With no facilities for relieving ourselves, those who couldn't hold the water any more just knelt at the door, waited for the van to ascend so that the urine would go down, and the wind swept it all away as the vans sped along.

By now Bekkersdal was miles behind us. My last sight of the place was *Komojuteng*, a store opposite the beer hall. Opposite the store was the Municipal Offices building where we paid rent and, across from it, the clinic. And some way from these, towered the high pointed cross of the AME Church.

The van roared towards Potchefstroom; past the Western Reef, Carltonville; past all the western conservative towns, through the maize territory of the Free State just across the Vaal River. Then, somewhere along the way, we turned at a road sign that said Bloemfontein; Kroonstad. Throughout that drive since we'd passed Bekkersdal, between naps and conversation, random thoughts flitted through my mind. Uppermost in these were thoughts of family, home. And my mind stubbornly refused to venture so far away from home – and my special bed in the dining room.

When our stomachs reminded us, we snacked on a bag of *katkops* of brown bread and water we'd been given by the authorities. The convoy drove through the Free State Province – a first for most of us. There was some excitement when we crossed the Vaal River and finally arrived at the first stop: Kroonstad Prison.

Apparently, the whole town was expecting us; spectators lined the main streets, craning their heads for a better view as the vans approached. And when we got there, we could see that the prison authorities were also expecting us. As the vans approached, there was a sudden burst, a flurry of activity; and then a number of warders poured out from all corners of the establishment. You should have seen the metalwork: guns ablaze, rifles and artillery. That was our welcome to Kroonstad Prison.

'*Senzeni Na? Senzeni Na?*'

From the depths of our hearts, our song of defiance roared.

'Shut up! Or else, *ons gaan daai kos uitvat.*' (we'll take the food out.)

What difference would it make? We simply shrugged and continued singing.

At the prison yard, the vans stopped, and we were told to alight, 'Two-two!'

The big man in charge of the prison came forward booming with laughter to welcome us, '*Waar's daai sang groep?*' (Where is that singing group?)

His subordinates accompanied his jeer. With the crashing and clanging chains around our ankles, we shuffled without balance. Our stiff, swollen and discoloured wrists were frozen into fists, the bones having suffered the most uncomfortable position.

With speed, we were commandeered towards the toilets, the use of which was no mean feat in our condition (we were still bound in pairs). Then we walked, still barefooted, to the hall where we were told to sit in rows for lunch.

Prisons around the country were served a uniform type of meal: lunch was *kaboe* mealies – loose maize kernels boiled with salt added. Then we had the liquid with solids, a thickish brew, *phuzamandla*, to which every prisoner was entitled – for sustenance.

After the meal, we were made to wait in another hall while the warders rested. No consideration whatsoever was given to us, no relief, other than that we were unchained and allowed a thirty-minute walk around the prison yard for exercise before the next phase of our journey.

When the warders felt rested, we were bundled back into the vans. Now, we started to feel that we were really getting into the unknown. Our songs continued, but with less vigour, less volume; most of us were exhausted by chains, the discomfort of being bound to another body, lack of sleep, and, of course, the drive itself – under the crammed, far from hygienic conditions.

Note how, unlike the warders, we had not rested at all during the break. They had most probably stretched out flat on their backs or sides, closed their eyes in a darkened room in which all was quiet and peaceful. We had had no such privilege.

We conversed, snoozed on shoulders and slowly fell asleep to the drone of the van as we penetrated the dry Karoo desert. Then, by a terrible stroke of bad luck, one of the vans broke down. In that sweltering heat, the prisoners from this van were spread into the remaining four vans; which cramped us even further.

A couple of hours later, just past Colesberg, we entered the sleepy town of Richmond. The sun was setting now. We had not known that, but this was where we were going to spend the night.

We were received in a similar fashion to Kroonstad. And duly served the same supper we had come to expect at Leeuwkop Prison: the semi-hardened *motoho* with two pieces of meat, and for the fortunate, a small piece of vegetable. We also had *rooibos* tea.

It was obvious that the local warders were in a hurry to be gone. Normally, prisoners were locked up around four, four thirty. It was already way past that 'knock-off' time and the hurried treatment meted to us reminded us of that fact. It served as an indication of their annoyance.

But, by then, we were somewhat inured and were indifferent even to the surroundings.

We didn't even wonder what was out there; it could have been anywhere for all we cared. The fact that is was already dark, also didn't help. Moreover, we were all totally unfamiliar with the place and, to us, it felt like hostile territory. The language, the speed with which the locals walked, spoke; their sarcastic laughter – all these things – rankled us.

In a way, therefore, the local warders' impatience to leave us as soon as possible was to our advantage too. We were quickly whisked into four cells, fifty of us in a cell with common ablution facilities. Though encumbered by the chains, we didn't complain; experience had taught us that no amount of pleading or complaining would earn us relief. So we resigned ourselves to the fact – the reality – that we would, again, spend the night in chains – bound hand and foot.

Clearly, this harsh, inhuman treatment dished out, particularly to security prisoners, was meant to demoralise us.

But, as the saying goes: You can't keep a good man down. I have fond memories of the late Norman Nkosi, who hailed from Rustenberg. Norman, who had a great command of English, a boisterous disposition, and a keen sense of humour, was a teacher when he was arrested. He was a good-looking fellow, and wore dark horn-rimmed spectacles that made him look more like a pastor in training than his status of the time – a prisoner in shorts, chained, barefoot, his wrists and ankles looking like rising dough.

Now, if Norman was anything, he was a pragmatist. Many a time, his loud laughter, that shook his whole body, gave us a brief respite from our predicament.

On this occasion, which I remember very well, his infectious laugh was laced with cynicism as, looking at the pair next to him near the urinal basin, obviously anguished, Norman, with a false gaiety, cracked:

'How do you guys feel about the prospects of spending Christmas on an island?'

The couple just gave him lethal stares that said he was out of his mind. But we all doubled up, laughing, momentarily forgetting our position of extreme discomfiture – pain – and embarrassment. That was Norman, for you.

Now, after emptying our bladders we found our way back to the sleeping quarters and tried our best to make ourselves comfortable (as far as that was feasible). Monty and I had practised the night before, so it was a little easier to get around with the chains.

Unfortunately, some of us were afflicted with stomach disorders probably due to the slight adjustment in the diet. To add to the inconvenience and embarrassment of the afflicted co-chained who had to drag his partner to and fro, there was no toilet paper provided. Also, his partner didn't only suffer inconvenience but his reluctance (understandable as it was) embarrassed him. That went on all through the night, until morning. The men who had to use the soil buckets endured an ordeal.

As always, the warders were indifferent to our discomfort. Any words or gestures to get their attention would be futile, we knew. We didn't even try.

I couldn't sleep. I couldn't stop thinking about what lay beyond Colesberg. What was I to expect? And I felt the others' fears, betrayed by their thrashing as they dreamed.

Then, at dawn, just as I tried to grasp some sleep, we were rudely awakened by a loud knock on the cell window, alerting us it was time to begin the final leg of our journey to Robben Island.

Still manacled in pairs, we managed to walk to the makeshift bathroom and, each man using one hand – his free hand – poured water over our faces to obliterate the indecencies of the night. Hey, we were all brought up to be gentlemen. So, without any toiletries, we had to make do with our fingers to brush our teeth and to wipe our faces.

Breakfast, as usual, was the scant lukewarm porridge, with sugar sprinkled on top. On bruised and swollen feet, we shuffled back onto the vans just as soon as we'd had our breakfast. We had *padkos,* our provisions of *katkops* smeared with holsum.

No matter how hard I tried to separate my thoughts from my feelings, the nearer our destination came, the more fierce the anxiety that attacked me. There was a tremendous build-up as the vans approached Paarl. What a scenic area! The strange-looking mountains covered in dark green vegetation loomed over stretches of perfect vineyards.

This scene, to me, looked more like pictures of Europe than Africa. I was certainly in a different world.

I know how the condemned man feels the last night before execution. I had been incarcerated for months by now. But, suddenly, the finality of it all bore down on me – heavily. The questions that had assailed me when we passed Bekkersdal returned, only, they had bred and multiplied a thousand fold.

Would I ever see my family again?

We knew just then that there was no way back. The vans bounced at lunatic speeds on a long and winding road. That turned out to be a trip I never wished to repeat, a wish I have managed to keep. That was the only time I've ever driven to

Cape Town in my life. Even after all these years after my release, I have never again motored to Cape Town.

We had a brief break at De Doorns. It was the first time that most of us saw flyovers (highways). I remember the breathless drive along cliffs, as we sped on our way towards Du Toit's Kloof. There was a pass through the tunnel. Just before the tunnel, the road, right on the very edge of the mountain, wound up steep cliffs. At every vibration of the van, we couldn't help but imagine what would happen if it were to just tip over those sharp precipices. A very grave and real possibility, I felt, given the reckless driving we were experiencing. But, then again, this may have been my errant anxiety talking.

What is true, though, is that of the four vans, the leading one was easily six kilometres away, and speeding away. We could spot it here and there – way ahead – as the road twisted and turned, winding around the mountain.

And, then – CAPE TOWN!

'Now we're in Cape Town, Cape Town!' we mumbled, excited and awed by it all. If we were wearing suits, we would have straightened our ties, coughed, and clasped our hands. For that was the dramatic finish of an incredibly long, painful journey – a journey that we would remember for a lifetime.

We were not oblivious to the beauty of the bright, cloudless, splendid afternoon as we approached Cape Town. We drove through the pristine, visibly white populated city, until we arrived at the docks. We didn't see much of Table Mountain because the day was a bit on the cloudy side by then and the mountain was enveloped in a mystical mist. I remember the rays of the sun stabbing the ocean as we alighted from the vans that had faithfully transported us over the 1 200km journey from Leeuwkop. The hairs on the nape of my neck stood to attention.

Briefly, my mind flew back to Bekkersdal. To that Sunday, light years away, it seemed now, when white plain-clothed police had burst into our home, in the early hours, before sunrise: *Sontaha ya Mehlolo*. Unbelievable. But that I was here, like this, was evidence of that Sunday of Surprises.

We tumbled off the vans; sweaty, lethargic, our limbs numb from poor blood circulation. We tried to stretch our cramped legs, and stifled yawns of exhaustion.

Soon, however, sounded the familiar shout from one of the warders:

'Haak! Come on! Four-four! Four-four!'

That meant that we had to stand in the customary rows of four, we knew. We complied. That was the beginning of what was to become a conventional occurrence on Robben Island.

Still manacled and under the watchful chaperon of our faithful guards, Magalies, Khumalo as well as the whole entourage of warders, we embarked onto the ferryboat, the Dias, on our way to Robben Island. Most (if not all) of us had never seen the ocean before, let alone been a passenger on a boat. Climbing on to that rocking boat was quite an affair, I assure you. It was the kind of thing one sees in movies depicting the equivalent of a 'Jim Comes to Jo'burg' character – but in a more sophisticated way, a way involving such luxurious lives as would have anything to do with boats and oceans. We, on the other hand, had never even contemplated doing anything like this – even as a remote possibility. We grew up in the townships; our dreams were made of different stuff. Looking at that boat, climbing onto it, frankly, I wasn't sure we would reach the island alive. That ferryboat looked too narrow, too ancient, to accommodate all of us. Yes, it had been freshened with blue paint and trimmed in white. The deck was made of wooden strips that looked as though they might be knotty pine and there were ropes lying all around.

While some of us were told to remain on the top deck, others were herded down a wooden staircase to the lower deck. We stumbled weakly on the unstable surface unable to balance, dependent on our partners to synchronise our uncoordinated movements.

The boat chugged off slowly from the docks into the green blue sea.

My memories of that virgin voyage are blurred, fragmented, unreal images. I must have been physically and mentally delirious. Of course, all the way from Leeuwkop Prison to Cape Town, all of us had talked about this voyage – the boat ride to the island. Now, here it was, at last.

With the sun setting on the horizon, the reality of our fate began to sink in. This was the beginning; we were about to start a horrible, long journey of captivity – in the middle of the ocean – on an unassailable island. There was no possibility of a Papillon-like escape here at all.

For the first time, as the island drew nearer and nearer, the possibility of never returning struck me. Till that moment, I hadn't lost the quixotic optimism we all cherished, had cherished, from way back in Leeuwkop; that the rescue by the mighty OAU forces was still probable. However, the reality that it had been almost six months since the formation of the OAU and we had not seen any action yet from that body was enough to begin to get the truth to dwell on me that, perhaps, just perhaps, I might serve longer than I had anticipated. I had just turned twenty and although naïve, I also had some understanding of what lay ahead of me. My thoughts ran rapidly back home – to my family.

I couldn't help but reflect upon the fate of my younger siblings. I knew life had changed for all of us – irrevocably. Only the future would tell what would become of me.

The power of the cold Benguela current from the icy Atlantic Sea was quite evident, especially to those of us on the upper deck. The strong gale winds propelled the Dias, which reminded me of a slave ship.

It also reminded me of me – buffeted by the might of the apartheid government; I was just as powerless as those slaves of yesteryear. And, like them, I was journeying into the unknown. This line of thinking came to me unexpectedly, helped, perhaps, by the lulling rhythms of the sea. Now, as the small ferryboat soared and dipped with the crests, dips, and swirls of the deep dark unfathomable sea, so did my anxiety soar. This same sea with its secrets of the goings on on the island since the 15th century – secrets it buried in the vastness of its oceanic bosom – that sea of Table Bay, the only witness to the screams and last breaths of Makana, who risked and lost his life attempting to escape the soul-killing confines of Robben Island – what would it be to me?

Would I return or, Makana-like, perish on the island or in trying to escape it? The gales swept stinging salty sprays from which we couldn't even shield our eyes due to our manacled hands; they threatened to whisk us off into the ocean. Now, not only could I see Table Mountain but it seemed to grow larger and darker as we got to mid-ocean – more pronounced and brooding.

Perversely, as though to taunt me with its unreachability, the city remained much evident by means of its twinkling, winking lights. To rouse myself from my gloomy thoughts, helped along by the eerie trip itself, I turned my thoughts to our heroes, the most valiant African fighters. Leading the roll, of course, was Robert Sobukwe, the then President of the PAC, languishing on the very island I was headed for. Nelson Mandela and others had also served time on Robben Island in 1962. Now, my thoughts and feelings more sober, in the essence of my soul, I felt honoured to be touching the soil on which some of these great men had set foot albeit, like me, that had not been a voluntary act.

I felt an irrational sense of pride, as though I had achieved a great feat. Somehow, in those magical moments, the thick layer of anxiety and fear that had blanketed me subsided.

Dreamlike, I watched the big city almost completely disappear, dwarfed by the immense size of the ocean and even Table Mountain receded into the mist that blended with the clouds. The whole atmosphere was surreal. My mind was in turbulence; too much was happening all at the same time.

We could feel the water deepening and feared we would be thrown overboard and plunged into the depths to be devoured by the gigantic sea creatures that kept splashing about the boat (we later found out they were whales and seals), sending my heart into my throat.

The motion made my poor stomach unstable. I felt it wobble and, without warning, I gagged, then vomited. My empty stomach cramped painfully as Monty propped me over the rail.

Later, I learned that Warder Khumalo had also suffered from seasickness. How I wished I had seen that myself. To watch Khumalo suffer helplessly against the forces of nature is something I'm sure I would have relished.

As we neared the island shore, we saw large colonies of penguins, birds I had only ever seen in textbooks and 'The National Geographic' magazine.

We landed.

To receive us, there was a contingent of warders. They were all White and led by the island's Commanding Officer, resplendent in impeccable khaki uniform and matching military caps with a green band, with sparkling brass badges that read: '*Suid-Afrikaanse Gevangenis Diens* – South African Prisons Service'.

The officers stood in upright rigid military positions in their shiny brown army boots. Others reined in their disciplined fearsome Alsatian dogs.

That's how Robben Island would always be: White warders presiding over black prisoners – on the whole.

In the background of that ostentatious officialdom was a large number of common-law prisoners who kept disciplined faces and gracefully accepted the orders given to them to move this and that out of the boat, anchor the boat, and to basically ensure that there was order. The process was something to behold, it took about 30 to 40 minutes to unload the supplies bought in bulk from Cape Town; a necessity, as there were no production facilities on the island.

For a moment, I thought those workers were some of the political prisoners who had arrived there before us, but the majority seemed to be coloured and were too docile and compliant. They didn't even acknowledge our presence as we alighted from the ferryboat.

That initial chilly reception said, to me, we were being introduced into an environment of near hopelessness, where there would be absolutely no support system.

Once this became clear to me, it also became quite evident that I had to rely heavily on my own inner being and inner strength.

It was on December the 10th 1963 that bewildered, we stood on the docks of Robben Island's Murray Harbour under a signboard that read, 'Welcome to Robben Island. *Ons dien met trots* – We serve with pride.' A crudely drawn justice scale illustrated the signboard.

Promptly, an instruction was barked out by one warder:

'*Val in!*' (Fall in! Four-four!)

So, what was new? *Umthetho*. We had heard it over and over again. All it meant was that we should form rows of four; the queues had to be disciplined – made even, with the assistance of the warders' batons anywhere they could land on our bodies and their barking dogs nicking our heels.

Disinterested, we complied; and then patiently waited for the handover by the Leeuwkop Prison Colonel – by which we'd cease being his responsibility.

Addressing his Robben Island counterpart, Colonel Liebenberg announced:

'*Kolonel ek het jou honderd hardegatte gebring.*' (Colonel, I've brought you a hundred intransigent hard arses. From now on they're your responsibility.)

We could tell he meant we were irredeemable – which we regarded as a compliment. We also understood his heartfelt relief at being free of us. The feeling was mutual.

Politely, in a soft voice, a gentleman's tone of voice, the receiving Colonel replied saying, '*Nee Meneer hulle sal regkom. Dis die eiland, ons sal hulle reg kry.*' (No Sir, they'll be fine. This is the island, we'll get them right.)

Part 4

1963–1967

16

Robben Island, Prisoner Number 837/63

Early evening – the sun still up – but we had no watches and, on this foreign island, didn't know how to read the sky to estimate the time.

The officers exchanged a few formalities, and the *bandittis* handover was done – over. Armed warders herded us and, like sheep to market, loaded us on open-backed lorries. We then made our way to the prison reception, about a kilometre from the harbour.

The day seemed to stretch and stretch, endless – like my life seemed about to stretch in this place. The only difference was that the day was God ordained; my life, apartheid-government condemned.

The reality of abandonment – of being all alone – cut off from the rest of the world – seeped deeper and deeper as my eye took in that desolate arid patch of rock in the middle of the ocean. Nature had devised the perfect prison. No bars were needed here: the chances of escape were nonexistent. Most of us just paddled in water, how could we even attempt to swim across an ocean? Like nothing had shown me before, this place told me loud and clear we were truly consigned to damnation.

Robben Island is a small island, some 2km wide and perhaps 4km long, comprised largely of hard rock and sand. It lies anything between 12 to 15km from the Cape Town coast and is separated from the mainland by icy cold and choppy waves. Its name is said to be derived from '*robbe*', the Dutch word for seals. Available evidence indicates that the island was established as a source of food for sailors and explorers during the early colonial times, when Bartholomew Dias and his ilk accidentally happened upon the shores of South Africa and decided it would be a convenient outpost. The island was also reported to be the last resting-place of sailors drowned at sea due to some unfortunate mishap or shipwreck. Later, it was lunatics, lepers and others suffering from incurable diseases that were banished to languish and die in isolation.

Later, the apartheid government declared the impregnable island a maximum-security prison – for non-white males only. No ships were allowed within a mile of the island's rocky shores because the prisoners there were considered the biggest threat to the State. Right now, the group thus perceived included me. I, Gabriel Thono Magomola, eldest son of Malebelle Israel Magomola and Sophie Matlakala Magomola, both respected leaders of the Church of St John's – I was on Robben Island – a prisoner. And there was no likelihood of escape for me, or any one else, for that matter.

Not even the great commander of the Xhosa Army, Makana, also known as Nxele, who had been banished by the colonialist marauders, could escape the wrath of the cold Atlantic Ocean.

In 1820, Makana and scores of others escaped from the island. It is reported that all but eleven perished in the high seas separating Robben Island from the mainland.

Our destiny was sealed.

From the lorries, on our bare, bleeding, and swollen feet, we shifted our weight to gain some balance as we walked on the rocky luminous white sand. Only then did the warders realise it was after office hours, and the reception would already be closed.

Still bound hand and foot, we made our way to the cells – about a hundred and fifty metres away. In neat rows of fours, we trotted behind the leading warder. Suddenly, a huge flock of large birds resembling white pigeons flew over us. With deafening squawks, like vultures coming to a feast, they swarmed and hovered over us in a dark flapping cloud. In their scary welcome, these escorts stayed with us until we reached the prison yard. Later, we found out that they were seagulls.

We squatted outside on the massive courtyard to slurp *motoho* in big dishes, that we nicknamed, *izikebhe*. Making light of the anxiety we all felt, we joked that we could use the seagulls to escape.

After the quick meal, it was: '*Val in*!' again, in pairs – fifty in all.

Thankfully, our handcuffs were finally unlocked! But the sudden rush of blood that came at the release initially brought more pain to our clotted wrists and ankles. But there was more relief than pain. For this, we were grateful indeed.

Our group of a hundred men was divided into two groups of fifties, and housed in two of the most unimaginatively constructed cells of the H-shaped prison block in Section A. Section C had just been completed, but was less secure. So, the common-law prisoners in Section A had been moved to another section to make room for us, the political prisoners, by that fact considered more dangerous than mere criminals.

Each cell was one large hall of approximately two hundred to three hundred square metres. The walls were made of solid thick concrete bricks, covered with slabs of slate on the outside. The window sills were so wide that we could lie on them and, indeed, did on occasion sleep on them, quite comfortably. For maximum security and to prevent smuggling, the windows were covered with mesh wire on the outside and further reinforced with four- or five-inch thick iron bars made of a hollow metal pipe, inside of which there was a rotating iron rod that couldn't be sawed off. The windows ran all around the entire cell so that, from all sides, the warders outside could see what was going on inside.

Now and then we would hear a threatening shrill, '*Bly stil!*' (Keep quiet!) through the windows.

For further reinforcement, there was barbed wire around the perimeter of the prison. The building was surrounded by guard posts manned, at all times, by heavily armed guards.

A cell usually accommodated sixty men. We each got a dirty, stinking sisal mat and three scratchy grey blankets that were neatly folded by the previous owners.

To the annoyance of the rest of us, when he was given two half blankets, John Mohapi protested, 'I want a full *kombers.*' It seemed trivial to cause such an uproar over a prison blanket.

But, from experience, he knew blankets were checked thoroughly and if any part was found missing, he would be severely punished. All the blankets were threadbare with the ends torn off by the common-law prisoners, who used the strips to strangle each other during their all too frequent fights.

Right next to the entrance to the cell was a walled bathroom area with two uncovered metal bucket-toilets, we called *balies*. For washing, there were three deep concrete slab basins and showers with only cold water.

The first morning, we woke up to the customary loud ringing of the brass bell – at 5 am – followed by the stringent command:

'*Word wakker! Staan op!*' (Wake up! Get up!)

We didn't need to be instructed to fall in line for the bathroom. Overnight, the buckets had been overused and with no toilet paper, it was not a pretty sight to see first thing in the morning – or at any time of day, for that matter.

In the early years, this aspect of prison life was pretty rough on us. Later, we did receive rations of eight squares of toilet paper, per day, and a bar of soap for the week, for each man. We brushed our teeth with our fingers or used pieces of cloth we'd rubbed soap on.

From the lessons of Leeuwkop Prison, we folded our sisal mats and blankets to rest against the wall. By 6 am, we were ready in line to be counted before the opening of the cell doors for us to be let out.

Here, *we* were the *samponkaans*.

*W*e took turns to carry out that unpleasant task of emptying the buckets every morning, and ensuring that they were thoroughly cleansed to avoid a lingering stink.

Then we proceeded to breakfast. This banal routine did not change one bit over the long years of my incarceration on Robben Island.

My hope that being in the Cape, so far away from home, would bring change to the routine and prison food – improvement from the situation at Leeuwkop – was quickly dashed. Warders opened the cells, directed us to the kitchen, some a 150m away from the cell block, and encouraged discipline and speed with batons. '*Val in!*' Regularly came that call for the usual queuing, but here we didn't have to do that running. However, here too, if one deviated from the straight-line queue or talked, a rapid strike from a hand or baton would remind whoever had forgotten that we were forbidden to talk or even whisper to one another.

That first morning, we each grabbed the dish of cold congealed *motoho,* which had been dished three hours earlier and stacked. Each dish had a little bit of sugar, just half a teaspoon or so, placed right at the corner. The only way of getting more sugar, double if you were lucky, depended on how close the bottom of your dish had come to the food in the one beneath it. As the dishes were not covered, the dish on top of another would often get its bottom caked with the sugar from the one below it. The giddy prize winner then quickly scraped that crust onto his dish! A mug of warm coffee from an enormous urn accompanied the *motoho*. After that, we proceeded to a huge courtyard where we squatted in long rows to quietly eat the unpalatable breakfast. Usually, we poured the coffee, (which we later learned was just roasted, blackened ground maize that was brewed) over the *motoho* to soften it.

On Robben Island, the *motoho* was always undercooked. But worse still, it was made from decayed mealie meal infested with live maggots.

As we poured the coffee over the *motoho*, the fat thick white wriggling worms would surface and swim in the *motoho*-coffee sludge; a revolting sight to which I never became accustomed.

In fact, when we first got there, for days I refused food; starving to death was an option I was willing to accept rather than eat maggoty food. I rapidly lost whatever was left of my weight.

My elder brothers urged me to accept the conditions in which fate had put me and not kill myself as that was the intention of the authorities. Under that sober context, I learned, especially at breakfast, to just close my eyes, pour the coffee over the *motoho* and stir, then gulp the whole mess down – get it over with in the fastest possible time.

All through that first morning on Robben Island the strangeness of the place struck me: a hot, chunk of rock on which grew reluctant shrubs and weird grasses. It sits in the middle of the ocean, surrounded by high gleaming fences of razor sharp wire, its hostility alive and throbbing. All around and everywhere, warders milled and meandered by the score, their eyes alert and frankly hostile. There were some among them who never, but never, walked without their sinister Alsatian dogs at their side. And those dogs seemed trained to silently watch our every movement, everywhere we went. I felt, 'one wrong move and that dog will be at your throat'. I prayed the dogs were trained well enough to distinguish between a random move and whatever move was a 'wrong' one. And more warders looked down at us from the lofty heights of brown steel and wire watchtowers.

Processing was the same monotonous, tedious routine of being commanded to file into twos and fours to facilitate the endless repetitive counting process of our often naked bodies. Files were opened for each of us.

We were numbered, stripped of any identity: I remained nothing more than a number, nothing more than a quantitative object, to be constantly watched, counted, deprived and punished. My prison number, 837/63, meant that I was the 837th prisoner in 1963. Then we were each tagged with a pink identity card marked '*Maksimum*' (Maximum). We had to carry those cards at all times. The card displayed the prisoner's number, surname, first names, aliases, prison section and cell, religion, age, sentence, scale of gratuity, date of sentence, date of discharge, with/without remission and number of previous offences.

On the scale of gratuity, all of us were labelled and graded D, the lowest wrung on the A, B, C, D spectrum; it carried the least privileges and very few rights. Annual appraisals were conducted to determine whether a prisoner deserved an upgrade, this according him an improvement of privileges. The upgrade was from D to C, and so on, until one became an A-group prisoner.

After processing, we were handed supplies; and found apartheid alive and well at the island prison. Africans were given mismatched, any-size-should-fit-all uniforms of hard cotton cream white shirts (with a small front pocket to fit the prisoner identity card) and short pants while Indians and coloureds received socks and long pants. We also received any-size-fits-all dirty brown coloured sandals made of old hard leather – the mismatched pairs of size nine and size six or whatever had us bewildered and shaking our heads.

Needless to say, by the next morning, the sandals had been swapped around; people just helped themselves to whatever would fit. Remember now, regulations stipulated that we line the sandals in the corridor outside the cells at bedtime. By the end of that very first week, most of us had given up on the slipping sandals; we just trudged about barefoot. Sooner than expected, our feet adapted, thickening and hardening till shoes to them became but a dim memory.

Later we were introduced to Major G. C. Visser, one of the highest ranked officers on the island. Visser then introduced us to the man two levels below him who was responsible for the day-to-day running of the prison, Chief Warder Theron. A clean-shaven short stocky man, who turned out to be a thorn in the flesh just about all the time of our stay on Robben Island, it wasn't long before we experienced his bitter hatred of black people.

Theron was extremely neat, his pants always pressed and, his tawny-red boots always shined. He was one to strut, showing he knew he was superior. A quietly assured, patient man who carried the knowledge of absolute power that was his as a badge and who wielded it without mercy, Theron conducted his own kangaroo court, and there presided as a magistrate. He dispensed cruel punishment.

The prison was run with a strict military code guided by rigid prison regulations, as we were constantly reminded. Most of the warders came from poor families, didn't start off as intellectuals and had received little education.

They faced bleak futures on dying farms or the mines unless they were sprung out. Most of this kind entered the service for the opportunity it offered them to better their lives; and not with malicious intent to make the lives of prisoners a hell on earth.

But there were those, like the Kleynhans brothers, who were following a family tradition going back generations – a tradition nurtured through brainwashing. People like those took their role seriously and played it with religious zeal. That role, they reckoned, was: to ensure that the *kaffir* would never rule the country. They entered the service with that belief firmly rooted in their minds. Generally, the warders were ignorant, crude bullies who used foul language and brute force to assert their dominance over the prisoners. Only their individual unimaginative styles of punishment enabled us to distinguish between them.

Chief Warder Theron, with prominent webbed blue veins on his nose, in his ceremonial welcome address had reminded us very quickly that, '*Jong, julle's nou in Robben Eiland*' (Boys, you're now in Robben Island.) 'And here, there's no room for *hardegatte*.'

What this gentleman failed to understand was that we were resolved to revolt against their trenchant political domination; resolved to the point of death. We had vowed that we would not compromise our dignity in any manner. It was all that we had left.

After processing, a warder barked, '*Val in*! Four-four!'

We filed in fours, and proceeded in disciplined silence on the gravel dirt path. I was among the first rows of that snaking queue of a hundred men, as we were marched from the old prison to Section A through the prison yard. Section C, still under construction, was a hive of activity. Scores of men, comprised mainly of common-law prisoners, formed the *bouspan*.

The scene resembled a primitive slave camp and reminded me of the movie epic, 'Ben Hur'. There was the frantic running to and fro; pushing old, unstable, overloaded wheelbarrows, ferrying stones from here to there; and constant shouting.

Some of the men were pulverising the medium stones to a finer grade to be used as concrete for the building foundations, others were breaking larger stones to medium size, while others still chiselled those to fit into the building structures. Ben Hur!

Though it was around eleven in the morning, the sun was already scorching as a couple of warders, some on the sides and others behind us – led our procession.

Suddenly, I was struck by something, the odd behaviour of a small group of common-law prisoners (three or four), who kept running and crossing the road a little ahead of us. We would walk for ten or so metres, and there they were again. From the furtive glance they cast our way, they seemed to be sizing us up.

But why? Then, as I looked closer, their strange behaviour leaving me no other option, one of the figures struck me as quite familiar; he had the same physique (especially the facial structure) as most of the males on my maternal side of the family. The prisoners came closer. Then the man who reminded me of people I knew stopped and gave me a long stare – a searching look. After that, after a few seconds of staring at me like that, he turned about and ran away. Except for that impression, the vague familiarity of his build, reminding me of my maternal uncles, I didn't recognise him at all. Outside of prison, people all look different. However, there was a total lack of variation, singular sameness in the way we looked inside. Shaven clean, with no beards or moustaches, wearing the same uniforms – nothing distinguished one prisoner from the next.

The man was back with his mates again. I saw him point at us – at our group. Then a strange thing happened. He came back. Came right back to us.

That act was in defiance of the warders who grunted half-hearted warnings. But the man did not heed those warnings but came right up to me.

My blood relative!

Uncle Ishmael Modisane had long been imprisoned and the family had no idea what prison he was currently in. Uncle Ishmael looked like a man possessed, obviously dumbfounded at seeing his young nephew at that condemned piece of rock called Robben Island.

When he'd last seen me, I was at school (with such a bright future, everybody said). He kept shaking his head in sheer disbelief.

Finally, Uncle Ishmael touched me, laid his hard as rock hand on my shoulder and said, 'Thono! Thono! *Oetsang mo? Obatlang mo?* – Thono! Thono!' (What are you doing here? What do you want here?) His voice was sadder than that of one announcing a death.

Because he was a common-law prisoner, the warders mistook Uncle Ishmael's act of defiance for an act of the taunting of one prisoner by another. Totally misreading the scene, the warders not only ignored Uncle Ishmael and what he was doing, but their loud guffaws proclaimed their total approval.

My uncle went back to his group and I clearly saw him wipe away a tear from his cheek. I could well imagine the thoughts that were going through his mind.

That meeting left me very sad, for my uncle was not the man I had known, back home, all those years ago; he was but a shadow of himself; emaciated, he had lost some teeth, and his eyes were bloodshot and glazed. Clean-shaven like all of us, he had peculiar marks on his face and head.

Nevertheless, despite that drastic change, the terrible erosion, I could see clearly that this was my uncle, taken away from us some ten years before.

Later, Uncle Ishmael told me he came to Robben Island five years before our arrival.

But he had no idea why he was sent there, usually only incorrigible prisoners were shipped to the island – as a last resort toward redemption.

One day, when I had been on the island for a while, I asked Uncle Ishmael why he had cried that first day we met. His answer was that he'd thought I wouldn't be able to make it there.

Thereafter, conditions permitting, my uncle supplied us with newspapers, smuggled, of course. Newspapers were a precious commodity to us, our refuge and beacon for the future. The common-law prisoners would pretend to clean up after the warders. Then, surreptitiously, they would straighten up the crumpled papers. Some, like Uncle Ishmael, worked as domestics in the warders' married quarters and took it upon themselves to salvage any newspapers. Most were in Afrikaans. The most surprising source of information was *Die Stem* (The Voice), an Afrikaans publication.

This provided us with information we shared. A network of smuggling newspapers developed. From newspaper cuttings, torn pages, medical journals, in whatever language, we devoured everything, just to glimpse what was happening on the outside. It didn't matter that some of the smuggled news was outdated – that huge was our hunger for news. Sometimes, though, we received misinformation on what was going on.

Soon after our arrival, we had occasion to again strip naked – for medical inspection.

This was so we could be assessed for *spans* – the stronger men were assigned to the quarry *span* while a few of us who were visibly weak and fragile were given tasks that were less strenuous. This was not done out of benevolence or altruism but practical considerations – necessity.

The prison had to be built in a rush. The countrywide arrests had resulted in numerous mass trials and convictions thus raising a pressing need to accelerate the building process at the Robben Island facility.

The first few weeks, because of ill health and youth, I was assigned with others to perform light mundane duties. There was a sense that we might not be ready to be integrated into the briskly moving hard labour at the quarry. However, just a few weeks later, the need for labour overrode any humane considerations and now we were suddenly considered mature enough to work the quarry. That first day on the quarry *span* was a day I will never forget.

Later that day, the warders asked in hesitant heavily Afrikaans-accented English, 'Who of you can drive? All the licensed drivers raise your hands.'

We paused, unsure we'd heard right. But the request was repeated.

From some of our ranks, a few hands rose with much hesitation. At once, those who had raised their hands were separated from the rest of us.

Although I could drive, I decided against raising my hand, adopting a 'wait and see' attitude.

'Now that you have been driving and you have experience,' the warder jeered at the volunteers. 'let me take you to where you'll be working.' He then took those men around the corner and showed them a stack of old battered wheelbarrows.

'There are your vehicles, now get on with it!' he shouted at the top of his voice. Was I glad I'd held my horses! The rest of us, I and the other non-drivers, were assigned to be *malaisha*s.

Sound was much a feature of our lives as the warders on the island. Within a few hours of our arrival there, we were puzzled and not a little unsettled by an eerie, pounding noise that seemed to come from the direction of the ocean. But we soon realised that it was the sound of water crashing upon the rocks down by the shore. And above all that noise was the booming sound of the foghorn, with its sickening repetitiveness. Day and night made no difference; what variation there was in its haunting call depended on weather conditions. When visibility was low, which was not uncommon on Robben Island, that foghorn would sound at more frequent intervals, warning approaching ships off and away from this rocky island that had claimed many other ships as victims.

17

Unzima lomthwalo
(This burden is heavy)

Institutions run on ritual or, if you prefer, procedure. And what soon became a ritual here was that after the third count of the day – post breakfast – as day follows night that count would be followed by Head Warder Delport's command, 'Quarry *toe!*' (To the quarry!)

Delport was a tall, heavily-built ogre with a permanently red face. Your stereotypical slave master, the man was possessed of inexhaustible energy. And an equal measure of cruelty. His reputation preceded him. Long before we set foot on the island, we had received warning of him. We had also been warned about his weapon of choice – a hosepipe. The man wielded that hosepipe at whim, on any part of a prisoner's body, at any time he felt like doing so, for any reason he deemed fit. But apparently, he was an expert on quarries. So, after the third count of the day, in his heavily-accented English, he'd shout to us: 'Quarry *toe!*'

And, '*Val in! Val in*!' – his warder subordinates chanted.

At that, all of us, hundreds of prisoners, formed rows of fours and, in what couldn't be but long and unwieldy queues, walked towards the quarry. On all sides, we were surrounded by warders. Herds of sheep have sheepdogs, prisoners have warders – it is just a fact of prison life.

Apart from guarding us and making sure we did not escape, the warders' function appeared to be constantly urging us on '*Kyk voor jou, agter is donker.*' (Look ahead, behind is dark.) And they had help from their Alsatian dogs which constantly nipped at our heels; thus helping their masters to speed up the procession.

The infamous four brothers Kleynhans usually led that escort task, something they seemed to relish. These men had a special propensity for violence, unavoidable perhaps, considering that they came from a long line of warders. And, as though that were not enough of a burdensome inheritance, the brothers now had Head Warder Delport to nurture them. It was under that gentleman's mentorship that the Kleynhans sons served their apprenticeship before they were released to do their dirty work.

As a mark of the esteem in which we held the Kleynhans four, we even had a code: *'Die Blok is warm!'* (The block is hot!) When a prisoner heard that, he knew that the Kleynhans boys were on the war path. More times than I care to remember, have I heard those four hurling insults at inmates or, in their kinder moments, shouting with glee, *'Laat waai ... Laat waai!'* (Move it!)

They beat and assaulted; and often threatened to '... break every little bone in your stupid body!'

Such outbursts were not infrequent. The countless times I found myself at the mercy of the Kleynhans four, I struggled to remain me – remain human.

Tears were rare; I only felt them under the eyelids, but never released them. I wouldn't give them that much satisfaction – not if it killed me.

Another outstanding warder torturer was Sergeant Zille. A tall man of six foot two, he strutted in a military rhythm with his rather prominent protruding stomach. He had a sun-induced dark red complexion and dark brown hair.

Usually, he wore thick horn-rimmed opaque sunglasses and we couldn't see his eyes. Zille's conduct reminded me of the Nazi stories I had read. He went the extra mile when it came to giving punishment. His idea, when it fell on him to mete punishment, was not just to punish the culprit but also – and perhaps this was the more important goal to him – to provide entertainment for his colleagues and/or appease his superiors. The exercise, of course, was at our expense. Frequently and without warning he would kick us. Almost everyone I have spoken to about this remembers being kicked by Zille. Of course, we reported him to the authorities. Of course, nothing came of that; Zille went scot free. Chief Warder Theron (to whom we reported Zille's abuse), a known Broederbond sympathiser, would shout his reprimand in a sharp shrill voice, laced with parent-like indulgence, *'Zille! Ek het nie volstruise hierso nie.'* (I don't have ostriches here.)

In barely-suppressed glee, Zille would reply, *'Oooo, Meneer, ek het hom net getik'* (Oh, no Sir, I just touched him) to the great amusement of the other warders. They all chuckled, enjoying the sport, secure in their immunity. Zille knew, understood, believed he had unquestioned immunity. He was right, of course.

On the way to the quarry, we always passed the leper graveyard, just before we came to Robert Sobukwe's cottage. At the time, Robert Sobukwe, the founding president of the PAC, had been on Robben Island for four years. He had completed his initial three-year sentence, but because of the restriction of the 'Sobukwe Clause', remained caged, lonely in that small cottage, guarded by an armed warder.

He was the first victim of the 'Sobukwe Clause' of the General Laws Amendment Act of 1963 which enabled the police to perpetuate the detention of individuals after the expiration of their sentences. From an initial sentence of three years, his incarceration was extended indefinitely. To my knowledge, Sobukwe is the only person, in the history of South Africa, to have been subjected to that law, concocted and named after him.

The conditions of his banishment forbade him to talk to us. In fact, we were not allowed to talk to anyone – not allowed to talk even among ourselves. However, as we marched past the cottage, about a hundred metres away from him, Sobukwe would acknowledge us with his brilliant smile and the open hand salute, held just below his waist.

Then he cheered us on, in his own way, by picking up sand and slowly pouring the sand back, from near his shoulder. This was reinforcement of an idea. He was telling us, reminding us, that the land belonged to us and our struggle was, therefore, a legitimate one.

As can be imagined, we derived great joy from this encounter. And, of course, in return the PAC cadres (we fondly called one another Mo-Africa, Son of the Soil), would all raise open palms at him while the ANC cadres raised their clenched fists to show their solidarity. That is something I miss sorely these days, that solidarity, demonstrated in the very early years, irrespective of organisational allegiance. On Robben Island, I can safely say, Robert Sobukwe was revered by all of us because of the man he was and what he stood for. The Kleynhans brothers, our perpetual tormentors, would shout in their customary screeching voices, '*Kyk voor! Moenie na daai man kyk nie!*' (Look in front of you. Don't look at that man!)

We ignored them, most of the time.

Besides the prison barracks, there were civilian buildings: a school for the warders' children, family homes, two churches, a general dealer store, and a bright red and white lighthouse up on the hill. To us prisoners, it seemed perverse to have this cosy family life in such close proximity to the brutality of the prison.

The walk to the rock quarry was approximately thirty minutes.

On arrival, we would once again be counted before we took our places on the piles of stones to be crushed. All around us, strategically positioned at elevated posts, armed warders stood watch, their firearms at the ready, their trained dogs alert.

Under the soaring Cape summer sun, with little rain and no shade for relief, we held onto our small prison khaki sunhats to protect our bare and shorn scalps. Prison regulations demanded that, to show respect, we take the sunhats off whenever the warders addressed us. And if we forgot to salute in that way, the hats were knocked off our heads for the impertinence. In the end, to avoid unnecessary clashes and clubbings by the warders whom we had thus offended, we just kept the silly sunhats off, choosing to brave the sun and the fine powder from the rocks rather than face the unreasonable, unpredictable ire of our keepers.

One day, as we were allocated positions at the start of our daily routine, Delport warned that it was important that we filled our quotas. Authoritatively, he added, '*Luister, julle moet daardie klip vyner kap. Verstaan julle, my bandiete?*' (Listen, you must crush this stone to fine pieces. Do you understand, my prisoners?)

We nodded, even though we didn't really understand how we could pulverise rocks.

I was just transfixed, studying this man who had such visceral hatred of anything that was not white.

He didn't discriminate among African, coloured or Indian prisoners – none of us escaped his stinging racist insults.

I've never known any man who could reach that blinding level of pathological hatred. Coming from me, that is something, let me tell you; for I had thought I'd experienced racism from the ultra conservative West Rand where I grew up but I had never seen a man who actually enjoyed and revelled at seeing other people suffer – Delport did. Everyday, he would make sure that several prisoners were charged for insubordination; did that by inventing one excuse or another. That much did he enjoy seeing us deprived of meals. Delport reminded me of Magalies – a little. Both stand out as people born for their jobs; but Delport is the superior of the two.

The warders ganged up against us, and used a group of common-law prisoners, nicknamed the warders' *handlangers,* as allies. Those prisoners didn't work, their focus was to taunt and torture the political prisoners. In between the jeers and the kicks to please the warders, they performed extra duties for them, ingratiating themselves to their masters. They could be seen, eager as beavers, rushing about, carrying the warders' jackets and *skaftins* or, brushing the warders' uniform buttons and buffing their already shiny boots. All that sucking up – done for just day-to-day survival, and earning the rewards of a few trifling pleasures: a cigarette (tobacco was a precious commodity), bread crust (which was the thickest slice), or, perhaps, an extra plate of food from leftovers, or the satisfaction and sense of relative security, in serving and gaining the approval of the masters.

We were each given lots of medium-sized stones to pound and pulverise with the heavy four-pound hammers with which we'd been equipped. These stones were to be used in the erection of new prison cell blocks. I (and, certainly, most of us) was not that adept at wielding a hammer, not used as I was to manual labour.

And it was very awkward to squat on the sand listening to the warders' instructions for the day; which often went like this:

'*Hierdie plek is Robben Eiland. Hier gaan jy leer om 'n groot klip klein te maak en 'n klein klip fyner*'. (This place is Robben Island. Here you will learn to make a big stone small and a small stone finer.)

Digging of the old bluestone quarry seemed to have been taking place for many, many years, judging from the scars and obviously man-made dongas on the rock face, yet there were still large amounts of bluestone residue, approximately 250m in diameter, dug down to about 100m. Some common-law prisoners drilled to loosen the rock while others pounded away at the huge, steel-hard boulders with fourteen-pound and eight-pound hammers and various other tools. We fried under the sun as we laboured.

At the beginning, understandably, I had no idea just how much energy it took to fill the designated quota for the day – 15 to 20 lorries – for our group, the 'One hundred intransigents'. If you're like most people out there, mercifully, you have no idea how tedious and bone wearying that task was or how slow it went. Imagine how many minutes it would take to fill a lorry with sand? How many shovelfuls it would take to do that? Now, none of us were, as I've already indicated, master rockbusters; moreover, we were not in what can be remotely considered peak form.

The whole long day, under the scorching sun, heavy hammers weighing down weak and wearied arms, we broke stones; bludgeoning our hands and feet and lacerating our fingers in the process while the dust and flying stone fragments and other debris plastered and coated our exposed limbs and faces and some of that even strayed into our unprotected eyes.

All that physical suffering, to say nothing of the hazard to our health – for what? Simply put, non-productive work that could have been much more efficiently done using machines. The only reason I could think of that that was not done (and, instead we were abused in that manner) was that that provided our captors with yet another means of crushing our spirits.

Determined not to succumb, we coped with the drills the best we knew how. We formulated our own linguistic code to enable us to communicate, share and converse without detection.

With subtle gestures, facial expressions, jerks, twitches, sighs, exclamations, utterances and singing, we spread our messages without the warders being any the wiser. To relieve the pain, we sang melodies which softened the brunt of that unbearable hard labour, making it less so. Also, the songs and harmonies gave us a chance to breathe, thus helping us conserve some energy. We sang:

Unzima lo mthwalo (This burden is heavy)
Woyisa amadoda (Heavy even for men like us)
Andikhathali noba kunjani (I don't care what it is like)
Sizimisele inkululeko (We're determined for our freedom)

Unfortunately for the prison officials, the human body has needs which would be folly to ignore. Much as it must have pained them, they had to give us some sustenance. And this they did – if grudgingly.

For the morning's brief break, we each received two hundred and fifty millilitres of brackish water from a rusty metal oil drum. Pleas for more water were just totally ignored. I suppose we should have been grateful that was all the reaction we got for our trouble; there are worse things in life than being ignored. Let us take the case of Johnson Mlambo.

Legend has it that before we arrived on the island, Johnson Mlambo, who was serving 20 years, once insisted on his right to more water when he was in the *landbouspan*. In response, he was buried, up to his neck, face up, in the sand. But that was not the worst of it. No.

While he was thus totally disabled and helpless – incapacitated, really – the warders took turns urinating into his mouth.

Yes, we can count ourselves very lucky that when we made our request for more water, we were simply ignored.

Lunch, delivered to the *spans*, was served at midday, after the head count. As mentioned before, diet in prison then, was differentiated according to race classification. For us Africans, lunch meant the customary plain *kaboe* mealies with weak *phuzamandla*. The D-diet, for coloureds and Asiatics, was of mealie rice (coarsely chopped maize) or samp with soupy beans or vegetables. (See now why I had wanted to play coloured? Even in prison, I would have fared better!) Soon after our arrival on Robben Island, we accepted (had no choice, really) that we had to share our food with the seagulls. Those skilled hunters came for meals with such accurate precision, one would be excused in thinking that somewhere in their bodies, there is a built-in clock. And don't think they have no manners.

Grateful we had shared food with them, they thanked us by leaving us calling cards – those unmistakable large droppings. A deafening silence followed their departure; and marked our return to the *spans* – after a head count. Of course!

Courage has many faces, colours, shapes, and smells. On our first day at the *spans*, my friend, Baker Mogale, asked Delport if he could go to the makeshift toilet.

As all prisoners did, respectfully, Baker stood at attention opposite Delport, looked him squarely in the eye, his dark face a blank mask, and asked, 'Excuse me, sir, I would like to use the toilet please.'

'Wat het jy gesê?' (What did you say?) Delport hissed.

Baker repeated his request.

'Wie is jou sir? Sir is a *kaffir predikant.* (Who's your sir? Sir is a kaffir preacher.)

'What do you expect me to say?' Baker remained obstinate. Curious, I went nearer the two; I wanted to hear what was being said.

'Sê baas. Ek is jou baas, hierso ...!'

'I will never call you baas,' interrupted Baker. 'Sir is sufficient.'

By then he was urgently pressed, but the altercation continued. 'Listen, *kaffir*, every prisoner calls me baas here and you are no exception ... It's that or no toilet, finished and klaar!' barked Delport so incensed he was red with rage.

'I'd sooner shit into my pants than address you as my boss,' snapped Baker, and, then and there, let loose – defecated in his pants while casually walking back to his workstation.

We watched all this in absolute awe.

But the warders burst out laughing, '*Die kaffir het vir homself gekak!*' (The *kaffir* has shit on himself!)

For me, however, that was a feat of sheer courage. I shared Baker's moment of triumph.

But that was something the authorities couldn't understand – just could not understand that a prisoner could have that kind of courage. On principle, this man had vowed he would never say *baas* to a white man. Baker's valiant stand, his magnificent, sweet-smelling defiance earned him the respect of the prisoners of conscience. He had set an example for all of us. And I certainly took notes, preparing myself for when my turn came.

The following Sunday at the *klagtes en versoeke* (complaints and requests session), Baker raised the matter with the Commanding Officer who seemed to empathise. Thereafter, we were informed that we need not address warders as 'Baas' – Meneer (Sir) was enough – to Delport's annoyance, I am sure.

This is the stuff of legend; and it would remain just that on Robben Island, for years to come. Even when Nelson Mandela and the Rivonia Trialists arrived, in June 1964, (their second time around on Robben Island), they said they had heard about these *hardegatte* who refused to say *baas*. This uncompromising stand was later adopted by all who followed and ended up on Robben Island. Within the PAC, the ethos was 'No collaboration with the enemy!'

At the end of that first day, after all that shit and the rest of it, the warders signalled us by shrill whistles. We downed tools only to be told we had failed to fulfil our quotas. The punishment was 'no Sunday meals'. Talk about adding insult to injury.

Unaccustomed as we were to such hard labour, on that first day on the *spans*, we also got raw red blisters on our hands – things I had only seen before this – seen on the hands of others. That is what we'd got from the hammering.

We had no idea how to heal the stinging water-filled lesions on our palms; only the slow creep of time would, eventually, harden the skin.

Everyday, upon our return from the quarry we, as all the others, had to '*Val in!*' into long queues, strip naked, and put our clothes to the side and wait for the warders to search the clothes. Then we were to *tausa,* that is, turn around and face away with hands held up high and legs spread wide apart – then bend down for the anal search – by the warders. To our utter amazement, some of the common-law prisoners seemed to relish that moment, as we had witnessed at Number Four and Leeuwkop Prison. With energetic agility and masterly coordination, they would clap their hands above their heads while spinning around and, at the same time spread their legs to land already bent forward for the anal inspection. Not at all out of breath from what, certainly to uninitiated us, seemed exhausting, they would then exclaim, '*Nkosi yam!*' (My king!)

Not since Leeuwkop Prison had I ever experienced anything that dehumanising.

The last step of the search was to open our mouths, while the warders clicked, 'qa, qa, qa, qa' conducting the oral search.

After that routine, we were again counted before going to the kitchen for supper – at four o'clock; as though what had just happened was just part of normal everyday life – which, in retrospect, I suppose it was; for that time, for that place, for that reality. Normal.

For the F-diet, supper consisted of stiffened *motoho* (again), in bigger dishes with a piece of fatty meat, which officially should have been fifty grams of real meat, on alternate days, but never was. What passed for food was just barely nutritious, to keep us alive so we could go on toiling; paying for our perceived sins.

Coloureds and Indians on the D-diet had *katkops* (the cat's head) – a quarter of a loaf of bread and a tiny spread of fat, some soup with floating vegetables, a few more nutrients (than we received) to strengthen them, and 250g of meat. Two hundred and fifty … I hope you noticed that. See why I tried to play coloured?

Occasionally, there would be a shortage of food supplies caused by the common-law prisoners who worked in the kitchen and exploited the weaknesses in the controls. They never stopped stealing food, a practice called '*smokkel*' or smuggling. Those prisoners stole just about everything: bread, cigarettes, money, drugs, weapons, and other items … all these were smuggled by the common-law prisoners into their cells and later sold, bartered or given to their friends.

We, the political prisoners, who were not allowed to work in the kitchen, would be the ultimate victims of this misdemeanour as we would be made to suffer at the hands of our captors while the common-law prisoners went unscathed.

During meals, there was a warder who would quietly stand immobile in a corner, Parker pen in hand, and watch out for offences – anything that chagrined him or which he thought might possibly chagrin the authorities not there present. Whatever it was: stepping out of the queue (possibly cut off by somebody else), a shirt not tucked into the pants properly, talking (even saying sorry for stepping on someone's toe) … anything

That, and anything else too petty to remember or mention here, irritated Van Tonder terribly. He would say, 'No *pararara* (talking), *een maaltyd*!' (you miss one meal). Oh, how power does make some drunk!

After supper, before going back to the cells, *again,* we were counted. That happened every single day – without fail.

I suppose that was to make sure that any prisoners who had (don't ask me how) managed to somehow make an escape did not get that much of a head start before that was discovered. Definitely, with all that infernal counting, there was hardly a period of little more than three to four hours in between. Now, with the final count of the day over, frazzled, we would rush to the bathrooms, shower the dust and grime off, prepare our beds and thankfully rest our worn bodies.

Finally, for a few hours, we were free to do as we pleased though still under the watchful eyes of the warders. Grouped according to our levels of maturity and ideological or political leanings, we would then assemble into discussion groups and get educated, on life skills, by the elders and teachers. It is in those discussions where seeds of tolerance and the true meaning of liberation were instilled in us. It is true that where there is a will, there is a way because, even under the stringent surveillance of that prison, we managed now and then to swap prisoners from one cell to another without detection; this was good for the rich discussions and the sharing of information – that is, among the various cells.

Alternatively, to bring some distraction and variety to the stultifying evenings, we played draughts, checkers and other board games – without the boards, of course, but improvising. We sang and, in time, we did that to the accompaniment of musical instruments. Here is a sample of some of the songs we used to sing:

Eh! Madala, ujikelezi umzi wenyindoda (You stalk another man's house)

*Owakho uwushiya nabani (*Who did you leave yours with?)

Occasionally, some of the sympathetic common-law prisoners, such as Uncle Ishmael and his friends, would smuggle food into our cells in the evenings.

They would mix all the scraps they collected during the day and bake them into bricks we called *'indalafu'*, which they hid under their uniforms.

This support – illegal as it was – was most welcome as it came just at the right time. By then we had long digested the soft porridge we'd had for supper. We would scramble and share, each taking just enough for a taste and then supplement that with water from the taps.

The bell for sleeping was 8 pm – but the fluorescent tube was left glaring and buzzing, day and night. After that bell, complete silence reigned and anybody found talking would receive *drie maaltye* (three meals forfeited). The warders watched us through the window grill and, occasionally, would shout, '*Stilte!'* (Quiet!) Eight, in summer, is no time inducive to sleep. The sun is still up in the south western part of the country. This meant that in that time of *'stilte'* bright sun rays still filtered into the cells.

Every night, we slept with hunger pangs and fatigue from the harsh, hard, back-breaking (backs we refused to bend in full view of the warders watching us) labour. We went to bed tortured by sore limbs; eyes, scratchy and teary; oozing, aching blisters; ears ringing from the cracking and hammering, and the insults.

We went to bed remembering the humiliation that had been piled on us throughout the day; the inadequate food rations; the lack of basic toilet items such as toothpaste, wash cloths, and deodorant; remembering that we had no underwear; that the only clothing we had was the bare-threaded, hard uniforms. We knew all this, remembered it every waking moment of our lives while on that island (how could we forget our living hell?) but we embodied the art of suffering which, as our colleague, Dr Neville Alexander, said, '… is comprised of learning how to suffer.'

Sometimes, I thought of the island as a place designed to test the levels of man's endurance. The glaring comparison between life on the island and life in the gold compounds didn't escape me. Like those migrant workers who toiled for long lonely months underground, our only relief lay in solitary dreams of phantom women. The seeds of future generations dried on those hard dirty blankets of Robben Island Prison. I regretted the missed opportunities of knowing real women.

18

Christmas on the Island

Our first Christmas on the island was uneventful. We had arrived on the island only two short weeks before, still in a daze, grappling with this new and hostile environment. Besides, we were also preoccupied with our appeal, the last thread of hope left for any reduction of our sentences – we certainly did not expect to be freed; we were not that naïve. Our attorney based our appeal on the grounds that we had been sentenced on the main charge of being members of an unlawful organisation and his contention therefore, was that if we were members of that organisation, it stood to reason that we would promote its objectives. Therefore, he argued, it was redundant to further sentence us to another three years.

But now it was Christmas, and there we were. Before we arrived on the island, the 10th of December 1963, we knew there were other political prisoners there. More than half of the hundreds of prisoners we found there were members of the PAC. Men like Jeff Masemola were charged with conspiracy to commit sabotage and sentenced to life imprisonment. With him were Mike Muendane, Dikgang Moseneke, Johnson Mlambo (of the water affair), the three Nyobo brothers, from Kwa-Tshatshu near King Williams Town, the Gwentshe brothers from Tsomo and many others. The Gwentshe brothers were young militant ANC cadres and constantly confronted the feared Kleynhans brothers with equal fervour. Some of these young PAC fellows from the Pretoria Region had been sentenced to natural life terms by the apartheid judges. Among those were prisoners like John Nkosi, Philemon Tefu, Ike Mthimunye and Pro Dimake. It never ceased to amaze me that anyone really expected these people to never again see the light of day – that is, outside of prison walls in their – lifetimes.

We were fortunate to have predecessors. They warned us that the situation on the island was very difficult. But they also encouraged, and prepared us to accept the fact that the suffering would never go away – it was the one constant we could bank on. Timothy Dyantyi had warned us that one of their colleagues from the Eastern Cape, Jimmy Simon had died soon after arriving on the island in February 1963. I found out some forty-five years later that Jimmy and others weren't returned home for reburial but were thrown into pauper graves near Stellenbosch. Therefore, from the onset, we conditioned ourselves to endure that suffering. The intervention on the part of our predecessors was very, very helpful in enabling us to face the ordeal that awaited us. But it also gave us courage: the very fact that they had survived all those months on the island gave us hope that we, too, would make it. And that was crucial to me because although I was still prepared to die for the cause, I had not expected this prolonged torture. A swift death by shooting in combat or through some other method or madness was one thing – languishing in prison, for years, quite another. Therefore, I was truly grateful for the support of our men on the island, for giving us the benefit of their hard-earned experience.

Obviously, no one expects conditions in jail to mirror those at home. However, that Christmas was in such stark contrast to the Christmases of my youth with their merriment and abundance of food and love. From the day the mines closed towards the end of November, our home became a hive of activity as we prepared for the big day.

On that last day at work, *Ntate* would appear swaggering on his scooter, heavily overloaded with a big bale of material for dresses to be sewn for all the girls in our church. All of the girls would be measured for the dresses, which they wore on Christmas day, boasting, 'To match!' All the households of Bekkersdal, though of modest means, found something to share with neighbours for all those heady weeks around Christmas.

But we had taken a stand: we would have no celebrations on Christmas day. We felt very strongly about that. This was, after all, our first Christmas in jail. In later years, however, this changed and we did celebrate Christmas; but not that first one.

That day, an unusual quiet lay over the island. I found a corner and sat all by myself and recalled how every Christmas morning our family would go to the stoep. *Ntate* taught us that on Christmas day, the sun dances and Christmas mornings we went to the stoep, before the sun rose, and watched it for a long time as it rose. And, indeed, it did seem as though the sun danced! Or, perhaps, it could have been my own childish hallucinations. Later in the morning, people would come to the church, built of corrugated iron and attached to our home. The service was much, much longer that day, because it was an important occasion, to mark the birth of Christ.

With a heavy heart, I remembered where I was – in a prison cell. How different, how lonely and lonesome – our decision to not celebrate seemed to make a bad situation worse. Nevertheless, I understood and supported the decision wholeheartedly.

Meanwhile, in stark contrast to my quiet solitude and the group's 'We are not celebrating' stance, the noises from common-law prisoners said there was celebration all right over there. That noise had started early. In fact, it was the IsiZulu-toned melodies and rhythmic sounds that woke us up that morning. The Cape coloured prisoners, with their guitars and drums, sang the Cape minstrel songs cheerfully. The celebrations in the common-law precinct sounded loud and wild. Some of those prisoners were A-Group and were allowed additional privileges over Christmas. Stolen liquor from the warders' quarters was often smuggled into their cells. The wild noises suggested that the excitement was much exacerbated by inebriation.

How I longed for home. I could see it all in my mind. December – the season of ripe peaches. No school. The children in Bekkersdal would raid the peach trees in the neighbourhood. We stashed ours in the coal shed outside. For those weeks, after completing our nightly chores, we would insist on sleeping in the shed, telling our parents it was cooler in there. However, once inside the shed and away from adult eyes, we'd feast on our stolen peaches.

One night, we heard a *meow* inside the shed. That stopped us and, hearts pounding, hair standing straight up, we listened; and waited. Out of nowhere, a kitten appeared. You should have seen us run. Now, sitting in a jail cell on Robben Island, I chuckled, remembering how we scurried out of that shed. You see, according to some African folklore, cats bring bad luck – especially black cats. Well, of course, we ran to the parents; where else do scared-stiff children go? The parents went to investigate; if they were scared, they didn't let on. Now I can't remember whether the cat was ever found or not, but what I do remember is that *Ntate* and *Mme* discovered the stolen peaches. From then on, we were never again allowed to sleep in the shed – heat wave or no heat wave.

As time went on, we realised that our predecessors on the island had not lied to us when they had said, at our arrival, we should get used to the hardship, it was not going to go away. To quiet our growling stomachs on the island, we discovered with time, there was not much we were not willing to eat. The bamboo *span* whose duties entailed gathering bamboo and other material that could be used for building also scouted the coast for food while they were at it. They usually brought back raw oysters which they smuggled in having just rinsed them in salty water.

We would eagerly slurp the slippery meat that resembled the entrails I never wanted to eat at home.

We were lucky, sometimes. Once, we experienced what turned out, paradoxically, to be, at one and the same time, our greatest good fortune and our worst misfortune since our arrival on the island. The bamboo *span* had come upon a dead whale – a massive creature that had been swept onto the shore. Our benefactors smuggled the whale fat stuffed in bottles for us to use as a condiment for the lunchtime *kaboe* mealies and the supper *motoho*. What a gastronomical feast we all had. But as it turned out, that would be ephemeral. Shortly after our feast, we all suffered from incontinent fatty diarrhoea. Saturdays we changed clothes. Well, come this Saturday, and the warders demanded to know what the fat residue was on the rear-side of almost every pair of pants. We denied we knew anything about those fatty spots. By then, there was no trace of our treasure. It had had a rancid odour and we threw it all away. We were so sad doing that you'd have thought somebody had died.

But scarce commodities are always prized; and food was more than scarce on Robben Island. There is no way of describing what passed for food there except to say it didn't meet any standards – be they those of health, gastronomy, or anything else that could apply.

I remember Welcome Duru (everybody called him Bra Wel), an impresario from Port Elizabeth, who had been married to Dolly Rathebe, the greatest African movie star of our time, with legendary thighs.

Dolly was from my hometown and, for that reason Bra Wel had a soft spot for me, the boy from the same area as his famous wife.

He served two years, though he did not consider himself a political activist because his protest was 'only' through music and acting on stage. In prison, he was one of the fortunate ones, a *span* tending pigs. When the pigs were slaughtered, the members of that span were given the entrails to throw away. *Throw away?* For most South African black people, this is a delicacy. Bra Wel would cook and smuggle the entrails to the prison and we'd have a real party in the cell, glad to be sharing the finger-size pieces of intestines. For, by the time all that was shared all around, who could get more than that? We were exceedingly grateful – just for a taste – and appreciated it. That is how precious every morsel was.

The day Welcome left prison, he said to me, 'You know Gaby, I want to tell you guys something. I've experienced what hunger is. I know what it is to be really hungry. From now on, I'll never again take food for granted.'

These days, free and far from the island, I'm always reminded of those words when I'm sitting with my family and I see my children grunting for this and that, spoilt for choices.

19

The melting pot

But it was not all gloom and doom in the prison. As the saying goes, 'Every cloud has a silver lining'. And what was interesting and unique despite the trials of Robben Island is that we met people from many different parts of South Africa. Remember now, this is apartheid South Africa and, for black people, the pass reigns supreme. Among other restrictions, this meant that black people did not have the right to mobility – they could not move around the country at will, so there was little opportunity for meeting people from other areas of the country.

The PAC prisoners had continued their dominance in numbers until around 1967. Around that time, *Umkhonto weSizwe,* The Spear of the Nation (the armed wing of the ANC), accelerated the armed guerrilla campaign within South Africa. Consequently, the ANC numbers began to swell the ranks on the island. Toward the middle of 1967 hundreds more ANC cadres arrived and the ANC ended up outnumbering all political parties, including the PAC. Between 1964 and 1967, there was a huge contingent of ANC and PAC cadres from the Eastern Cape: Port Elizabeth and East London. The older, more seasoned politicians were mostly ANC converts, while the younger, more radical chaps, were PAC adherents.

It was those swoops of the 1960s that created a political void, promptly filled in the 1970s by the entry, on national stage, of Steven Bantu Biko, the founder of the Black Conscious Movement (BCM).

While we were languishing in prison, the BCM came to prominence in South Africa's resistance struggle which culminated in the police massacre of hundreds of school children in 1976.

Among the newer arrivals there was a young man, Vuyani Bobotyane, who I also mentored over the years and a strong friendship developed between us. Vuyani was from East London, younger, but had not had the privilege of a high school education and he was quite thirsty for knowledge and willing to learn.

He helped me understand the isiXhosa idioms in a different way and so I took my time to assist him to learn to speak and write a bit of Sesotho and English. Later, he could write letters back home, and converse eloquently in English and Sesotho. He had learned two languages and thanked me heartily for that when I left. Unfortunately, I haven't seen or heard from Vuyani since I last saw him, in 1968, when I left Robben Island; but I have heard he was still in the Eastern Cape.

Someone else who stands out from that time and whom I came to admire greatly was Louis Mtshizane, who has since passed away. He was an extremely fiery attorney and, like Vuyani, also from East London.

Louis had a reputation for taking on the white magistrates (who were prejudiced) and demanding every right that his white counterparts enjoyed in court. Louis had defended a number of cases; the irony was that when he arrived on Robben Island he found some of the inmates he had defended while still a free man.

We had numerous other lawyers with us on the island among whom were outstanding teachers such as Reverend Stanley Mogoba and *Ntate* Rikhotso, who had been arrested, charged, and convicted of 'teaching communism and inciting students'. Some of their students at Kilnerton High School were arrested with them. Among those were Dikgang Moseneke, Anthony Suze and Owen Damoyi.

Jeff Masemola, who was sentenced to life, was also a teacher. Never afraid to challenge the warders, Jeff inspired us all. Among his many talents was that of master locksmith. Where he had learnt the art, only heaven knows. But, right there on Robben Island, under the round-the-clock surveillance, somehow Jeff managed to make a *skelm* key. This is a key that is so masterfully crafted it will open any and all locks. Imagine that! The man was too crafty for his own good apparently – or so the warders figured. He ended up in the *khulukhuts*! Whether for the *skelm* key affair or some other perceived breaking of the many rules, I never knew.

While there were a few medically trained inmates and they tried to help where they could, with no access to medical supplies *and* also tending to their own injuries, there was precious little they could do.

On the other side of the spectrum, there were the ordinary people: factory workers, peasants from the deep rural areas, particularly the Eastern and Western Cape – Paarl, (in the latter case), a stronghold of Poqo, and the extreme wing of the PAC. Incidentally, warders referred to all political prisoners as 'Pokos', regardless of political affiliation.

With such a convergence of people from across political, cultural, racial and ethnic backgrounds, Robben Island was a veritable melting pot. I had entered Robben Island not very knowledgeable about our country. I had arrived thinking I knew the suffering of our people. I had had no idea just how pervasive that suffering was. Unlike the late Attorney Griffiths Mxenge, I had not travelled the country.

He is a man that I admire greatly and to whom I am deeply grateful for having taught me to understand literature, which opened new and exciting horizons to me and provided me with an understanding of human interaction. Griffiths was an intense man who had been detained for ANC activities in Kwa-Zulu.

Tony Suze from Atteridgeville, near Pretoria, was also very giving of his time to those who had the privilege of studying.

It was around this time that I also became better acquainted with Dikgang Moseneke who, at sixteen, holds the dubious record of being the youngest prisoner, ever, on Robben Island. He preceded us, arriving there with the first group of PAC cadres. Dikgang worked in the library and was focused on his objectives – to study for a law degree, which he subsequently completed after his bachelors. After his release, he grew to become a well-known civil rights lawyer and is now the Deputy Chief Justice of our land.

For many of us, Robben Island became the cradle of knowledge and it is not the least bit surprising that so many of the present leaders of this nation are alumni of this dreaded (and dreadful) place. But mercifully, the wishful dreams on the island have become a nation's reality.

Here are the names of others that I remember well: Simon Ramogale from Thembisa – he stuttered, had an inflammatory temper and constantly fought with the warders because he didn't suffer fools easily.

Then there was the irrepressible Steve Tshwete, who became Minister of Safety and Security in the new South Africa and passed away holding that position. We stayed in the same cellblock and Steve was unimpressed with the noise I created with my trumpet. He would shout, 'Gaby, you know we are studying, why can't you find another place to fumble with that noisy horn of yours?' Like I had a choice! But that was Steve.

Henry Makgoti, from Pretoria, was an erudite man, who brought sobriety to all of us. He would become my neighbour in Mabopane after our release from Robben Island. Then there were the elders such as *Baba* Mqoma from Idutywa and *Ntate* Martin Ramogadi who came from Alexandra Township. These men were in their late fifties but endured it all – all that hardship, hard work, and demeaning treatment – with remarkable dignity.

Selby Ngendane was a member of the National Executive Committee of the PAC and one of the members of the ANC Youth League group of Africanists who, along with Robert Sobukwe, broke away from the ANC in 1959 to form the PAC. A highly intelligent man, Selby became a major influence on the island. He took it upon himself to educate us on life skills and politics, and made sure we understood the underlying politics and founding doctrines of the philosophy of Pan Africanism. In *The Long Walk to Freedom*, Nelson Mandela mentions the talks he had with Ngendane in 1967 on the question of unity between the ANC and the PAC. Mandela continues to say of Ngendane, 'Before coming to prison, Selby was considered something of a political lightweight. But in prison, he showed his mettle. In prison, one likes to be around men who have a sunny disposition, Selby had one.'

Ah, those days! As I write I feel such a deep nostalgia for that period. Sadly, many of these people have since departed this world but they live inside of me.

The teachings that I impart to my own children are teachings I received from some of these people regardless of stature. They were all my comrades and we embraced each other in a cause and in our suffering on Robben Island. Two words sum up the characters of all these men – bravery and courage. They had absolute commitment to the struggle for the liberation of our people. It didn't matter who they were, what hue they were, or what political affiliation they ascribed to – these people represented the core – the backbone of the liberation struggle.

20

The wheels come off

Six weeks after I'd arrived on Robben Island, I started to feel weak. I had attacks of aching whooping coughs, which deteriorated to a point where I was coughing blood. My movements became heavy and lethargic; my whole body was semi-paralysed by hunger and pain. I had to drag my feet just to go to the toilet. My body trembled from both heat and cold as my temperature fluctuated between the two extremes. On top of that I suffered excruciating pangs of pain on the left side of my chest.

For a while, I didn't want to show any sign of weakness. I was a man, too old to cry, I told myself. I asked *Mme* and God, in my silent prayers, to help me stay the course. Eventually, however, I couldn't do otherwise; I just had to go the prison doctor at the makeshift hospital at *Zinc Tronk*. Subsequently, I was confined there with others who had developed acute asthma. From an altitude of 1 500 feet above sea level, we had descended to the level of the ocean, which wreaked havoc with our health, compounded, no doubt, by the very poor diet we were subjected to and the exerting manual labour we did.

I remember that at about the same time, Njongo Ndungane, now the Archbishop and spiritual head of the Anglican Church in South Africa, was struggling with a nasty cough. Many others besides, people whose immune system was somewhat weakened by the conditions, fell quite sick.

The doctor who examined me – hair greying; well scrubbed, clean-shaven face adorned by an impeccably groomed black-brown goatee and moustache – had an air of disinterest and the physical profile of a Nazi doctor (or what I imagined a Nazi doctor would look like). Every time I saw him, he wore a fresh clean white shirt and blue tie under his starched blindingly white lab coat. All this and his thickset build and protruding stomach no doubt had something to do with that 'Nazi doctor' notion coming into my head.

Twice a week, this man used state money to take the trip to Robben Island, supposedly to tend to the sick. To see him do that 'tending' you'd never have guessed, if you didn't know any better, there was an oath the man had ever sworn.

The first time he examined me, gleaming stethoscope dangling from his neck, he stood as far away from me as he possibly could. His standoffish manner said he was not there to do what was in his heart, but was just fulfilling his obligation to the penal system that assigned him that task. With his mouth almost closed and his breath tightly held, he spoke to me for a little while; asked me a few questions about my health; all the while scribbling on his notepad. I told him my lungs felt heavy and I was coughing blood.

Then he gave me a bottle to give a sample of sputum for analysis at Somerset Hospital. And a few days later, the results confirmed that I was a suspected TB victim.

Three weeks later, I experienced something I'd long been looking forward to: going to Cape Town. Never mind that I would be going in handcuffs, a prisoner, and going only for an X-ray examination.

That morning, I was handed a clean uniform, a blue jersey with red lettering: Robben Island and a matching pair of sandals that – miracle of miracles – actually fit. I hadn't worn shoes in three months. The rubber soles felt strange to my feet.

I was handcuffed, escorted to the docks and into the Dias, the same ferryboat that brought us to the island months before.

This, to my knowledge, was an exceptional trip; I was the first prisoner to leave the island for medical purposes. All the other prisoners who had left before me were going to the mainland to face what were usually fabricated additional charges. Even their manner of leaving was different from mine. Here I was, leaving in broad daylight, with absolutely no furtiveness about it. Those freedom fighters had been quietly shipped out without creating any waves on the island. More often than not, they never returned (in the best-case scenario), but numerous of those court cases ended with *intambo* (the death sentence) or (there is always a middle-road scenario, isn't there) another pile of years to the original sentence – to be served at other institutions.

I was absolutely thrilled to be going to the city. And yet, at one and the same time, I was terribly apprehensive about how people – ordinary people – would react to a prisoner in their midst. But the mere thought of being back in surroundings where people were free to walk, to talk, to laugh, to feel, just to be quelled those misgivings. Greenpoint is right across the docks, where the Victoria and Alfred Waterfront is now.

Because the doctor had not yet arrived at the hospital and I had to be fed, I was first taken to Roeland Street Prison, which accommodated hardened criminals.

I was given a piece of bread, with a pinch of fatty substance, a generous mug of coffee and mug of *phuzamandla,* and enjoyed the meal, for what I got was more than I expected. Whether benevolence or ignorance was at work, I had no idea. Perhaps it was to ensure that I was stable when I arrived at hospital. Who knows? Four armed warders – two from Robben Island and two from Roeland Street Prison – escorted me back to Somerset Hospital in Greenpoint after my meal.

My earlier fears and apprehension were not misplaced at all, I realised, as I was walked through the corridors of the hospital. Patients and other people who were at the hospital for various reasons watched, open-mouthed with horror; and I was assaulted by some of their incredulous whispers which followed my back.

They all wondered why a *kaffir* prisoner was being thrown in among them. Then in the eyes of some of the African workers I detected a little sympathy. However, their eyes swiftly darted away when I tried to make eye contact. Again, I couldn't tell whether that was because of sympathy or fear.

I was surprised at just how clean and tidy the waiting room was; immaculate, with its soft seats. Later, I realised it was a 'whites only' waiting room. The only reason I was in that waiting room was to separate me from any potentially sympathetic black person. There were newspapers placed in plain view all over the place and jazz tunes played seductively on the radio. You cannot imagine the nostalgia that flooded me at hearing a few favourites. The gods were gifting me; I had not listened to the radio in almost a whole year. For that half a day, I greedily read anything I could lay my hands on. It was an intriguing day, and for a moment, my thoughts and my physical being were removed from the cruel, evil trap of Robben Island.

With a deep longing, I followed the graceful movements and exquisite gestures of the women in pretty floral dresses and gloves. I blinked at the children who were scrubbed clean and dressed in Sunday clothes.

With deep curiosity I stared at those ordinary citizens, who stared back at what must have been – could only have been – a mutilated representation of my body. From snippets of their soft conversation, I caught disconnected bits and pieces of the world outside.

All of them, black and white, bemoaned their struggle of how to make ends meet for their own families. For me, this was a painful reminder that I had another five years to serve in prison; that my family, my younger siblings, were without a provider. I was languishing in jail and they had no-one to care for them.

All the way from Robben Island to Cape Town, that whole boat ride, I had fantasised, imagined what it would be like to be close to a woman. It had been over a year since I had experienced the gentle touch of a woman, or heard the soft velvety voices of women. I was eagerly looking forward to what I imagined would be a moment of rapture. So, trust me, I wasn't going to miss an opportunity.

And, sure enough, the opportunity did present itself. I was alone with the radiographer in the X-ray room. She did her best to make sure I was comfortable. My chances were greatly enhanced by the fact that, by that time, the handcuffs had been removed and I was now in hospital pyjamas. Hey, who could even think I was a prisoner? I was certain I didn't look like a prisoner and fervently hoped she hadn't been briefed.

She was a coloured woman with a medium brown reddish complexion and small slanted eyes and must have been in her middle to late twenties. Although she was obviously older than me, I felt it was an ideal opportunity to take my chance, make an advance. I told her who I was and asked her what her name was. Of course I tricked her. I didn't tell her exactly where I came from for fear of what her reaction might be.

That was something I could not predict and so decided not to take a chance, but keep mum. Her pretty face responded with a warm smile that melted my insides. Gently, she touched my face with her soft hands and I have to say that I felt my temperature rising. That lady was very gentle with me. I felt her compassion for me, which might have been pity that she masked with her vague flirting. In that unique lilting accent of the Western Cape coloured, she told me to hold my breath. I personalised her general endearment of *skattie* (darling), which she must have used with all her patients. As I was turning against the machine, I would pretend I didn't hear her well so that she would come close to me and gently press me from behind against the machine. I felt her breath behind my ear, and I could smell her sweet floral perfume and felt the pressure of her voluptuous breasts touching me from behind as she was pressing me. I had to do all eight pictures; side, cavity, back, and front. Every time she would come as close as she could, and boy, I relished the touch of her breast against my body. My dreams did come true for that day, yet they came too quickly to an end. For a long time after that day, my night fantasies held her beautiful face and singing voice in my brain. I even envisioned her meeting me on the Cape Town docks on my release – don't ask me how, as I had not taken her contact details.

After the X-rays were completed, I was escorted back to catch the four o'clock ferryboat. Greenpoint and Sea Point, on the Atlantic coast, face Robben Island. One of the most painful things about working at the quarry was the view of Cape Town. On clear days, the whole of Cape Town would be within view from any vantage point. We could almost feel the pulse of life, imagining what it was like to be there.

The trip became an enduring milestone for me because when I went back to the quarry, for the following few days I had drawn enough strength and some understanding of what life was about as we were sweating it out on Robben Island. I could imagine and relive the experiences of those four to five hours I had spent in Greenpoint. I embellished my feminine contact in my story to the guys and became the envy of my fellow inmates.

In March, the X-ray results came back with the positive diagnosis of active TB, which, though expected, still struck me hard. As a consequence, I was immediately removed from the rest of the prisoners, and isolated at the *Ou Tronk,* to join the TB brigade. The dilapidated makeshift barracks of horizontal disintegrating wood panels and a corrugated steel roof had been used as part of four or five shacks built early in the 19th century to be used as barracks by the Cape Corps during World War II.

I was put under an aggressive medical therapy; several times a day I had to ingest pills. Like all TB patients, I was given warm long pants, socks and a blue finely woven acrylic crewneck jersey with red lettering identifying them as the property of Robben Island. These were taken every week to be washed. According to my prison file, the medical officer recommended that I be transferred to Zonderwater TB Hospital in the old Transvaal Province where Bekkersdal is located. It was common practice to isolate TB patients from all prisons across the country to Zonderwater.

For some reason, the recommendation was never followed, for which I am grateful because being sent there would have altered the course of my life. I would have been separated from my colleagues with whom I had established a great bond. At Zonderwater I would have been alone as a political prisoner and heaven knows what treatment I would have received from the common-law prisoners and the warders at that place.

On Robben Island, there was joint protest action when one of us was treated badly and occasionally International Red Cross representatives would come and examine the condition of the prisoners. These visits, including those of Mrs Helen Suzman, served as an important deterrent against excesses from the prison authorities.

The Head Warder at the hospital was a Mr van Zyl, an efficient officer who showed empathy for our condition. During my time there he was considerate and compassionate with us and he would give us an ear, listening attentively to our problems. Whenever he could, he did effect improvements. He was assisted by the Chief Warder, Mr Nel, who stared at us with his cold blue piercing eyes. In direct contrast to Mr van Zyl, he was extremely rude and impatient. He would occasionally ask us how long we'd still be in hospital, as though our condition were up to us – controllable.

I had been admitted for two weeks for TB when on the 25th of March 1964 each of us from the Bekkersdal-Randfontein group received a letter from the Office of the Magistrate of Johannesburg.

The Commanding Officer personally delivered the letters that informed us that our formal appeal for remission of sentence had been unsuccessful. The letter addressed to me read as follows:

> *The Reviewing Judge has refused to grant a certificate that there are reasonable grounds for Appeal in the above-mentioned matter.*
> *The Appeal was dismissed, and the conviction and sentence confirmed.*
> *The Appeal was withdrawn/or struck off the roll and the conviction was confirmed.*

The news came as no surprise, yet I felt a sense of utter despair. Our initial privileges as D grade prisoners allowed us to receive and send one letter every six months. My first letter, which I wrote on the 18th of March 1964, was directed to my father. I needed to reassure him that I was fine emotionally and physically, that I would survive and return home and be able to take care of him and continue my role as his first-born son. It was a very difficult letter to write under the circumstances because at the time, I was extremely ill and was almost certain of the TB diagnosis which came only six days later. I didn't know what kind of treatment I was going to receive in order to recover.

As a matter of fact, my wildest guess was that we would just be neglected; I had resigned myself to a slow and debilitating end. But I had to just hope that some miracle would happen. Given all this, I had to be careful about the contents and tone of my letter to *Ntate* and so it was with a lot of trepidation that I planned that first letter to him.

The next letters were mainly to Leopard and my sister, Semakeleng. And both replied consistently and eagerly. I remember being told I had two letters, one from Semakeleng and one from Leopard, and I was asked which I would like to have.

Remember now, these are half yearly letters. So I could only get two letters a year. Therefore the first I accepted was Leopard's and, at the end of six months, I took the one from Semakaleng. I knew they lived close to each other; Semakeleng would share whatever I said with Leopard, and vice versa.

Two common-law prisoners acted as nurses. One of these nurses was Teeza from Alexandra Township, who treated us with extreme cruelty. He never gave or showed us any empathy.

We expected more humane treatment from him considering he was an *outie* from Alexandra Township, and was a *bra*. The other attendant was Lucas, who had the characteristics of a Khoisan and had worked at the hospital for a long time. Lucas had served more than 15 years and, he told us, had no idea of life outside of prison. He entertained us with his comical antics and would, on rare occasion, bring us an odd magazine to read. Like most of the common-law prisoners, both Lucas and Teeza sucked up to their masters and would not hesitate to spy on us for trivial offences.

Together with about 15 other patients who were also infected with TB, I was to stay in isolation from the general prison population for a minimum of eighteen months. My condition had deteriorated severely. It appeared I had a particular strain of the disease entrenched in my left lung.

For me to be stabilised, the doctor said my treatment required the strongest medication. By then my frame was skeletal and I spoke with a faint rasp. Whatever treatment I was put on for those couple of months, worked. What is more, serendipitously, I was saved from the rigours of the quarry *span*.

Further blessing not to be overlooked was that, while hospitalised, we were fed a diet with nutritious components – a vast difference from the diet inflicted on those on the other side of the fence. Of course, we shared this windfall with our healthy comrades through part of the general hospital that was accessible to us.

The prisoners who came in the morning for treatment knew where to find the food packages we had prepared the night before. None had any fear of contracting TB. We could sit outside in the sun and many ventured to our side to greet us. Mr van Zyl, though in charge of the prison hospital, often indulged us and turned a blind eye to those visits and conversations. That was still forbidden even though we were sick. Any prisoner asking how I was, strictly speaking, was breaking one or another of the regulations.

'Jou broer is dood,' (Your brother has died) the prisoner nurse, Lucas, said to me one day. I heard him but I was paralysed by the shock and didn't quite grasp what he said – what he was telling me.

He must have thought I didn't understand, and said again, *'Jou broer het gevrek.'* (Your brother died.)

Alarmed, I asked, 'Which *broer*?'

'Ganja.'

I couldn't believe it. Ganja Funani Khubani was one of our Bekkersdal-Randfontein group, a vibrant, tall, and strong sportsman. It is reported that he suddenly fell ill and was left lying in the cells under guard. They all thought he had the common cold or flu. Later he was transferred to the hospital, where he died. Needless to say, Ganja's sudden death was a major blow to all of us.

That he just died, without manifesting any visible traces of disease, made me acutely aware of my own situation. I felt totally vulnerable.

Every day we heard the warders' implicit soliloquies, which we tended to ignore as hollow threats, *'Hier gaan julle vrek …'* (Here you're going to die …) Now the threats assumed new and ominous significance.

Ganja's 'official' cause of death was pneumonia, though we suspected he could have been poisoned. Ganja passed on almost a year after Jimmy Simon had passed early in 1963. Jimmy was possibly the first political prisoner to die on Robben Island during our era. Later that year, Alfred Khonza also reportedly died at Somerset Hospital.

On my most recent trip to Robben Island at the end of July 2009, I ran into families and comrades of several 1960s era Robben Island prisoners who are reported to have died in detention and were buried as paupers. During this visit, these families, led by a former cellmate of mine Timothy Dyantyi from Port Elizabeth along with Kwedi Mkhaliphi of Cape Town, had paid an emotional visit to the graves of the deceased which had recently been uncovered after years of searching for the whereabouts of their remains. Apartheid regulations at the time ensured that bodies of prisoners who died while serving their sentences on the Island were not released to their families. As a result their loved ones had been in the dark about what had happened to the remains of these men for over forty years. Deaths in detention, often in quick succession, created unimaginable anxiety among all of us. We had been told enough times by the warders that we were pigs, *kaffirs* and terrorists who had put themselves beyond the lowest limits of human consideration. As such, sick prisoners were often locked up for long periods until they visibly came near death.

One of the most memorable events for me, on the island, happened on a Saturday morning in June 1964. We had heard what sounded like an aircraft landing at the nearby airstrip and that only happened when someone of importance visited the island.

Of course, what we could never have guessed was that this plane was carrying a group of VIPs (Very Important Prisoners, in this case) whose arrest, trial and sentencing had made international news.

Within minutes, the men were bussed into the dilapidated *Ou Tronk*, where we had been isolated for some time due to our having taken ill with tuberculosis. Among them I saw a medium sized light-skinned man wearing thick-lensed dark horn rimmed glasses, and, walking by him was this tall man who seemed to have the attention of all the warders. As it turned out, those two were leaders of the ANC, Mr Walter Sisulu and Mr Nelson Mandela. From his physical stature, I knew Mandela immediately. I had seen newspaper pictures of him. He had an imposing presence and a dignity around him that was not lost even on the warders who would go around the corner and talk about him pointedly. Of course, Mr Mandela had been imprisoned on Robben Island before, in 1962. With them were five other historic Rivonia Trialists – Ahmed Kathrada, Raymond Mhlaba, Govan Mbeki, Andrew Mlangeni and Elias Motswaledi, all prominent leaders of the African National Congress.

Drawn out of our isolation, we ran to the six-foot fence that separated us from them, as they were led into cells at the *Ou Tronk*. We waited while they were stripped and accorded the customary introductory processing and made to change into the khaki uniforms of Robben Island Prison. Immediately thereafter, they were sent to work in the prison garden. Blue quarry stones were brought for them to break and crush as was customary on the island. They were given hammers and wheelbarrows as they were being led by the warders into the courtyard.

We watched with helpless empathy as Mr Kathrada was struggling to balance the wheelbarrow he was made to carry and ferry stones in. He seemed the youngest of the Rivonia prisoners.

Predictably, he tipped the barrow over and one of the common-law prisoners who worked around them tried to rescue him. Instead, it was Nelson Mandela who seized the wheelbarrow from Kathrada and pointed out the technique of handling the instrument. And once Kathy and his colleagues had gone away for their break, the prisoner was brought into the cell next to ours and reprimanded. He was sternly warned that should he repeat an act like that, he would be heavily punished. Clearly he was a distinguished and privileged common-law prisoner to have been given the assignment to work around the Rivonia Trialists. We were warned, shortly after their arrival, to 'keep away from these men and refrain from communicating with them'. Except for exchanging greetings and courtesies in Xhosa, which the warders could not understand, we were effectively barred from holding sustained conversations with them. For these VIPs, the rules were strictly enforced as they were under heavy guard all the time. They remained accommodated at the *Ou Tronk* for about a week or so and were subsequently transferred to the new *khulukhuts* which had just been completed. As it turned out, that would be Nelson Mandela's permanent home for many years to come.

By this time I had accepted the slow progression of life and more importantly, my illness. The TB became a constant reminder that I was still alive; it also gave me something other than prison to focus on, battle and overcome.

The authorities were very nervous about our condition given that, as a consequence of the Rivonia Trialists being imprisoned on the island, the eyes of the international community were constantly on Robben Island.

Soon after Mr Mandela and the other Rivonia Trialists arrived, the International Red Cross started sending delegations to Robben Island to inspect the conditions there. On the days the Red Cross visited, the prison warders would put on their best behaviour to impress them. Other eminent prisoners who continued to arrive were: Judge Fikile Bam, Dr Neville Alexander, the poet Dennis Brutus, to name a few.

Late 1965, I was granted permission to study for a Certificate in Music Theory. Before imprisonment, I had thought of taking up music as a fulltime vocation. I had already started taking lessons, both in theory and practicals, at the famous Dorkay House in Johannesburg. Dorkay had trained some of our best musicians, some of whom went into exile abroad to ply their trade. It is at Dorkay where I met the likes of the great Hugh Masekela, Kippie Moeketsi, McKay Davashe and Abdullah Ebrahim then called Dollar Brand. It was with such inspiration that I applied to the University of South Africa to simultaneously register for Music Theory, Preliminary and Advanced courses. A year later, I was awarded a diploma in Music Theory from the university. My certificate, though, was printed in Afrikaans and when I protested and asked to have it in English, the University declined my request. I may still have to claim it from Unisa!

Later, after my discharge from the prison hospital, I taught music to scores of our colleagues. I gave lessons in music theory and harmony studies. We used discarded cement paper for stationery. Because of the construction activity on the island, that was available in abundance. Often, the cement paper also doubled as toilet paper. Archie Jacobs, who lives in Toekomsrus, near Randfontein, was one of my most enthusiastic students.

Miracle of miracles, he has somehow managed to preserve his study notes, with my comments on his progress – all written on cement paper or toilet paper by hand. I did that for each of my students.

21

My B♭ trumpet

In April 1966, I was declared fit and discharged from the prison hospital. I had put on a bit of weight and was much stronger. Before the official release, however, I was sent back to Cape Town for X-rays to confirm that I had indeed fully recovered.

I had become accustomed to living a somewhat protected life in the hospital haven. During the short trip to Cape Town, however, I was reminded that I was still a prisoner as I was once again handcuffed and escorted by two warders. When we arrived at the docks, two coloured warders were waiting for us and so, now with an escort of four warders, I was whisked into a car and driven to the Westlake Chest Hospital. That was one long drive, but it gave me the opportunity to see Cape Town's unique beauty. The day was clear and sunny as we drove around the majestic Table Mountain, past the splendorous Kirstenbosch Botanical Gardens in full flower. As a township boy, I really didn't have much appreciation of the finer things in life – forget horticulture. Now, as we zipped past flowers, especially roses, manicured lawns, tendered gardens, I was awestruck. Next, there I was driving through the magnificent mansions of large estates in Constantia. Randfontein wasn't anything like Cape Town.

I photographed that day in my mind: the bright sunshine, the colours and intoxicating scents of those exquisitely arranged roses and the brief feeling of being free to enjoy such beauty.

Those flowers made such an imprint on me that, to this day, it is still with me. After I left prison, I nurtured my love for roses. There is a small rose garden in our home, inspired by Kirstenbosch.

As you can imagine, of course I was looking forward to, once again, hearing the sounds of female voices; and more than hoped for a gentle touch. And, as we drove past, I did see quite a number of women walking on the pavements. This only whet my appetite, highlighting the severe impact of isolation from society. Later on, I listened with keen ears to sounds of women, music from a radio, and people just having conversations about everyday life: how they were late for work, how the child was getting married, etc. I listened and it was overwhelming. And although people looked at me suspiciously, I listened, only to jump when I heard a baby cry. That pierced my heart. The pure sound of innocence – so foreign to me at that time – sounded too shrill to the ear that had become unaccustomed to it.

People stared. They regarded me with suspicion. I thought I looked reasonably well. Even the prison uniform I wore was not that obvious as I had been given long pants and shoes to wear for the special trip to Cape Town.

Westlake Chest Hospital was chilling. I had hoped for soothing soft hands, but the ladies there were aloof. They were decidedly not as forthcoming as my lady in Greenpoint. They averted their eyes and conversed among themselves as if I didn't exist. To be fair, however, they were professional as far as it concerned their duty. After the examination, I was treated to a lunch of soup and bread and had the pleasure of drinking tea with milk from a mug.

I also had a chance to read magazines and catch up with what was happening in the world. Then I was driven back to the docks in time for the last ferryboat back to the island, at 4 o'clock. My fairytale day was over.

My heart was heavy as I left civilisation behind. The thought that I still had more than three years to serve in prison was galling and I wondered if I'd ever get the opportunity to visit Cape Town again.

This time I managed to return with a *Scope* magazine and it had several pages of pictures of women in swimsuits. To the starving boys on the island, that made me an instant hit and the magazine quickly made the rounds in the cells. But by the time it found its way back to me, several pages were missing, including the one that had my favourite pin-up.

The X-rays showed that I had regained my strength although I was not fully recovered. This was positive news at which I rejoiced. Now, however, the gravy train was over. I was fit enough to go back to my prison cell. But the doctor specified that I shouldn't work in a 'dirty atmosphere'. Jokes aside, I really looked forward to going back. I'd left my colleagues and comrades, the Bekkersdal-Randfontein group, and although we, occasionally, managed a few stolen moment together, it just was not the same thing as being there, together, in that cell.

I returned to find that progress had been made in construction. Section A had been completed; and it had a functioning sewerage system with flushing toilets! The B block building was functioning; and the *khulukhuts* had been completed.

Meanwhile, some of my colleagues, those serving shorter sentences (like Bruce Nchoe), had already been released. Moss Mokotong and Sam Thabapelo had been relocated – but nobody knew where they'd been sent.

If much had changed as far as the buildings were concerned, that change was even more marked insofar as the prison population was concerned and I found myself in a socio-political environment totally different from what I had left and I had to undergo a second initiation as it were.

When we arrived in 1963, there were more PAC cadres and only a sprinkling of ANC members. On my return, the numbers were balanced, with the majority split among those two liberation movements. Later on, however, it was the ANC that gained hegemony.

There also existed a small number of members of the Non-European Unity Movement, including Neville Alexander, a prominent intellectual and senior member of an organisation called the Yu Chi Chan Club and National Liberation Front who had joined the leaders in the *khulukhuts*. Another man I met briefly was Fikile Bam, now a judge and President of the Land Claims Court.

One of the people I still remember vividly was the poet Dennis Brutus, who was a very outspoken activist with a high intellect. He stayed with us for some time in the B Section but was later moved to the *khulukhuts*. Many years later, in the late 1970s, I was to meet Dennis at Indiana University, in the United States, during an anti-South Africa workshop.

Throughout my prison experience, I never felt any isolation as a person. I always felt that we were there for one cause – the liberation of our people.

With time we had formed a symbiotic relationship, we concurred that the cause was beyond just apartheid, it was about us collectively fighting for equality and human rights.

Following my return from hospital, it took a long while for me to readjust to the routine of the wake-up call, the cold water splash in the Cape wintry mornings, and the orderly rush to the breakfast grounds.

Even the *mangabangabas,* the comradely seagulls who kept the time of our meals with precise accuracy, seemed to have doubled in number since 1963 when we first arrived. I could never stop marvelling at how my colleagues had come to accept them as happy companions despite the unending disruptions they caused to our conversations as we squatted on the sandy pitch to gulp and gobble the cold mealie meal porridge with wriggling maggots. The only improvement, insofar as food was concerned, was that we now had spoons to use when we ate; these were spoons we had carved from wood, using equipment from the *bouspan*.

A few years later, I was upgraded to C group level, which afforded me increased opportunities for writing and receiving letters. Our letters were heavily censored and any contravening text excised by an opaque black marker or scissors – the work of the special censoring warders. Sometimes, a letter would only show the address, the date, the salutation – 'My dear ...' followed by the tender leave-taking, 'Your loving ...' and the signature – all the contents having been excised. We used to wonder why the authorities even bothered giving us such 'window letters' as we called those instruments of torture.

The new dispensation, my C group level status, allowed me to finally write to Papai, my childhood sweetheart in Randfontein.

But she never favoured me with a response. I suspected that she feared for her own safety and bore no ill feelings towards me personally. By then I had basically stopped writing to *Ntate* because every time he wrote back, I could almost sense the emotional strain he was going through. My sister would write me long letters that cheered me up. I really enjoyed her letters because she would tell me how everybody was doing. I never wrote to my little brother, Fetsa, because he was too young at the time. Whenever I could, I wrote to Leopard because he was one resilient man and helped keep my hopes up. Leopard was without fear of anyone, not even the dreaded security police.

Our social activities continued to grow and yet the meals remained largely unchanged although, with time, there were some modifications. Once a week, we had a small piece of hake with our porridge. I always looked forward to Saturdays because of that fish!

As the years rolled by, I watched how people changed; how we all gradually matured and began to accept the reality facing us. The tedious daily routine never wore us down; we had discovered our own survival tactics. The tradition of discussion groups continued and evenings were used productively, engaging in vibrant debate that contributed greatly to the growth of my own political consciousness.

Then, in August 1967, I was declared fit enough for hard labour and was reintegrated to the quarry *span*.

I continued to cough and had aches and pains all over my body. At some point I was given a jersey to keep me warm.

Between 1965 and 1967 the prison authorities decided to relax prison conditions by providing a modicum of recreation through mild concessions that allowed us to earn or lose certain privileges as reward or punishment. By that time, many of us had been promoted to B group level status from the lowly D status that had been our lot when we first arrived.

I decided to take advantage of the changed circumstances by making a bold request to be allowed the use of a musical instrument. I waited until one Sunday morning during the routine 'complaints and requests' drill by Major van Tonder, the most enlightened of all the island's commanding officers. I stepped forward and, 'Major.' I blurted, 'I have a request to make.'

The major turned and walked toward me. He gave me one long hard look and replied, 'If you are in good standing, you are allowed to study.'

Many of our requests those days were centred on the newly-found privilege of studying in prison. Satisfied that he had adequately dealt with the expected request, the Major began walking away, resuming his inspection routine. To his surprise (and I guessed to the surprise of most of the other inmates around me), I marshalled enough courage to go for the jugular. 'Thanks Major, but …' I muttered.

Slowly, he turned and walked back toward me. 'Excuse me Major … Thanks for allowing me the study privilege, but that is not what I am asking for.'

After hesitating for a few moments, and sensing that he seemed intrigued by my forthright stance, I clarified how much I felt deprived by not being allowed to have my musical instrument with me. The musical influences of my childhood were in my blood; I craved something tangible from home – something to cling to.

Both my parents were lay preachers in our church and from a very young age I had participated in the church choir. Later I became good enough to become the choirmaster, a feature that was constantly replaying itself in my mind all through my time on Robben Island. I had already made some progress, successfully receiving a Diploma in Music Theory, earlier.

'I would highly value the privilege of having my trombone shipped to me so I can resume my music career during the remaining term of my imprisonment,' I said, to the amazement of the officer. I had nothing to lose by making this request, so I went right on, testing the flexibility of the so-called introduction of recreational facilities.

To my greatest surprise, the request was granted.

I wrote, yet again, to Transvaal Music Supply, where I had traded in my New Yorker President trombone for a Bisson trumpet shortly before my arrest in December 1962. I had paid the music store an initial amount of R12.

The agreement was that once I had paid the balance owing, I would get a new trumpet. I had been writing polite letters consistently to the store since I had been awaiting trial at Krugersdorp Prison, early in 1963, telling them I couldn't continue to pay for the new instrument. I had received no reply from them. In addition, my friend Leopard had made representations on my behalf to the store – without success. I knew for sure that the store was taking advantage of my circumstances.

But in 1967 the Commanding officer agreed to intervene on my behalf. He sent my letter with a one-sentence cover letter on a Robben Island Maximum Prison letterhead.

The cover letter, signed by him, read:

Attached hereto a letter written by Prisoner No. 837/63 Gabriel Magomola, for your information and necessary action.

And, like magic, within a month the store finally sent me a B♭ trumpet! This was October 1967.

I still have a vivid memory of the day of its arrival, which marked an important milestone on Robben Island. Prior to that, no political prisoner had been allowed a similar privilege. The irony, however, is that the country's most notorious common-law prisoners had always enjoyed the use of the occasional guitar or harmonica –

privileges we security prisoners could only dream of. Because I could only practise in the late afternoon and evenings after work, or over weekends, now, going back to the prison cell after the long hard day of work at the quarry suddenly became something I quite looked forward to. Most nights I sat in the bathroom to practise, ignoring shouts from the other inmates to, 'Keep it soft!'

I had also assembled, trained, and conducted a formidable male voice choir which performed Handel's works. We used to practise at the hall and Saturday afternoons, the prison cells became concert halls where those with talent entertained their audiences.

We delighted in music, and other choirs and choral groups mushroomed. A lively social environment emerged in the prison blocks. That was the privilege of communal living and we always wondered how our colleagues in the isolation cells entertained themselves. But that is a story I would only get a glimpse of some twenty years later, from Nelson Mandela himself!

My trumpet-playing skills grew satisfactorily and, over time, I began to receive requests from inmates to play their favourite tunes. My favourite composition was

Uza kundishiya na bani na
Uza kundishiya nabani kulo mzi wethu?

This heart rendering tune became quite popular and soon became our farewell serenade, an upbeat melody with grim lyrics I composed for those who were released, reminding them to remember the comradeship forged on the island.

It was a song dedicated to the families we had all left behind. The song asked, 'How could you leave me alone? How could you go and face the struggle, leaving me destitute?'

I'm told that long after my time on Robben Island the song was sung by various groups in that forever shifting population as some came and others left.

I have to say that my deficiency in soccer was more than adequately compensated by my musical abilities. We improvised on songs influenced by the likes of Duke Ellington, The African Inkspots and The Supremes.

The Eastern Cape lads were real maestros at the concerts; but we had our own stars such as Thomas *Mabatha* Xaba and Simpi 'The Voice' Mehlomakulu – both since deceased. They really excelled as singers. The famous Limelighters, including Sam Thabapelo, were a delight to listen to. They performed songs like Ellington's 'In my solitude … you haunt me,' – as, in silence, the spellbound audiences listened to the sweet harmony that brought a tear to many an eye.

Part 5

1967–1970

22

Goodbye, Robben Island

What will happen when we are released? What is the first thing I will do?

I am sure this it a topic that consumes most prisoners, in any jail, anywhere in the world. The yearning for freedom is very strong in almost all animals, human beings included. It should not come as a surprise, therefore, when I say most nights, on Robben Island, this was a recurring theme. I even knew what I wanted my first day out: I would go and look for my puppy love, Papai, and ask her to cook me the best meat stew she had ever cooked in her life.

Then one evening just as I was getting ready for bed, S'dumo (a prisoner turned prison reception spokesman) walked in and announced:

'Mamelani, Ziboshwa. Heyi wena!' (Listen, prisoners. Hey you, Gabriel Magomola!)

He continued calling out other names, but I could hardly hear those names; my ears ringing with that first name he'd called out – *my name*. I knew what that meant: *my* moment of departure from Robben Island had arrived.

That night, I and the others whose names S'dumo had read out, were all huddled together in a special cell in preparation for the draft to Victor Verster Prison the following morning.

My time had come. This was towards the end of 1967, nearly a year and a half before my release. We were asked to pack our belongings as we were to be transferred to another prison on the mainland.

But, of course, my departure was not something totally unexpected. I was one of the last, from the original West Rand group still on the island, as many others had already left. Also, I only had one year left to serve. But strange enough, this event, this moment that I had thought of so often, spoken about most nights, dreamed of every waking hour of the day and every night – now, that it had come, I suddenly felt it had come rather abruptly.

Therefore, somewhat confused, the following morning, we went to reception to be processed for what we all considered the final lap of a nightmare journey. Then swiftly, we were taken back to the cells to collect our personal possession. Me ... possessions? What possessions – I had no underwear, no toothbrush, no pencil or pen, no bed, no watch, no shoes, or socks. I had come to the island with nothing and was leaving as such except for my one and most treasured item, my trumpet. I also had a few books, and small gifts from other inmates.

I looked around what had been my lodgings for those five most miserable years of my life, and I saw that the place remained unfamiliar – it had not become in any way part of me, of my inner self. And I knew I would never miss it – never, for one single day, would I miss that sorry floating mass of cold concrete and stone.

I reached for my trumpet.

And that is when the reality struck me – I was really leaving Robben Island. Finally, I was leaving all this misery behind.

Then all at once, revelation came and I knew I was not totally free of Robben Island – and never would be free of it. I knew and understood that I would miss those human beings whose lives and mine had knit into one through our suffering and hope. I would miss their spirit of generosity and resilience.

They were forever a part of me just as I had become part of who they were and that would remain till we all left this earth. We were bound, one, in a singular union of spirit – a sacred union I was part of – for the rest of my life. I had come to Robben Island with nothing; I was carrying powerful memories with me, memories I would always cherish.

The pain of separation was evident on everyone's face as they sang our traditional parting songs.

I kept wondering how I was going to shut out the memories of those faces, some condemned to life in prison. There were youngsters among them, children still in their school uniforms when they were arrested in 1963. These were people many South Africans had never heard of, unacknowledged soldiers who were prepared to lay down their lives so that we could all be free. I was leaving them behind; leaving with no hope of ever seeing them again.

I lifted my trumpet. The inmates sang for me as I played my trumpet for the last time; that is, on Robben Island. At some point in our performance, I felt a tear slowly slide down my cheek. But we continued. I blew my trumpet; and the group sang. They sang. Sang as they always sang when one of us was leaving; only this time, they were singing for me:

Hamba! Hamba kahle (Go well)
Usikeleke (Be protected)
Sohlala sinawe (We'll remain with you)
Emhlabeni wethu (On our earth)

Enhliziweni zethu (and in our hearts)
Uzuhambe kakuhle, kahle (Do go well, well)
Size sibonane (Until we see each other again)

Many of those who had left before me had had a similar experience. As they walked out of the prison walls, walking to the docks, we would continue to sing. I had received letters from those released comrades stating that the last thing they remembered about Robben Island was the wailing trumpet serenade as the ferryboat left the shores of the island on its way to Cape Town. They said long after the voices had died down they continued to hear the echoes of the sound of the trumpet; it was as though that sound accompanied them as they began their journey back to their homes.

To this day, so many years later, whenever I meet those of us who were fellow prisoners, I'm reminded about that trumpet sound. Apparently I have had a lasting impact on some. Strangely, that includes even my lovely wife, Nana. In her travels, she often meets people who, when she is introduced as Mrs Magomola, ask: 'Are you Gaby Magomola, the trumpeter's wife?' She says she just laughs, knowing what will happen next: hearing, for the umpteenth time, about the trumpet. I have treasured that trumpet to this day; but will soon be handing it over to the Robben Island Museum.

By the way, I still play the trumpet at functions or moments of joy. I played it at my son's wedding reception, to the surprise of my best friends. I also played it, most recently, when David Msiza, a family friend, was getting married at the Drakensberg Resort. But the best part was on my wife Nana's 60th surprise birthday at home. The real thrill was pairing with the world famous trumpeter and my cousin, Hugh Masekela, who joined me to play a romantically soulful ballad to Nana's delight and that of the children and friends present.

On a more sombre note, with searing pain in my heart I have had to play this trumpet over the open grave of my ex-inmates, Harrison Mbambo, Victor Khabo and, very recently, Moss Mokotong whose humour and photogenic memory made this book possible. Even more recently, and I hope this is the last time I do so before the book gets published, I had to repeat this sad ritual over the grave of Benson Mnguni, one of our very own who died tragically in an auto crash in Randfontein.

My next port of call, as it turned out, was the Victor Verster Prison, about forty to forty-five kilometres north east of Cape Town. Compared to Robben Island, Victor Verster was paradise. Set against the high rocky green-grey Drakenstein Mountains, in the wine-growing area of the Western Cape and near the towns of Paarl and Stellenbosch, the area is picturesque, the views breathtaking. Ordinarily, only prisoners who were serving short sentences for mild offences and therefore viewed as posing no risk to the general community were sent to Victor Verster.

Chief Warder Nyschens, who welcomed us to the facility, gave us a quick history of the area. Nyschens was so dark he could have passed for a coloured man. And perhaps because of that, he was very conscious of the fact that he *was* white and constantly reminded us of that – lest we forgot. He was at pains to spot an air of superiority, came across as sophisticated; but succeeded only in being aloof and officious. And although we never discussed politics with him, he seemed to understand (or pretended to understand) why we were in prison and what our cause was. On other matters, however, he made himself accessible to the prisoners.

There was nothing of the fortress about this facility built, for the most part, of corrugated iron sheets and forming a rectangular block.

At first, I worked in a group in the vineyards, but they seemed to have more than enough hands there; also, the population of the prison was quite small.

Soon after my arrival, however, I had chest pains and tried to have that attended to; but each time I reported the problem, I was dismissed without receiving any treatment. Feeling a little anxious about my health, I asked to have mealie rice instead of *kaboe* mealies as had been the case at Robben Island when I was sick. The authorities said they would do that, if I could prove what I was saying was true. I mean, they put the onus on me! All they had to do was phone Robben Island. I would have thought, though, that our transfer would involve our medical records, among other details. Obviously, nothing came of my request for mealie rice – nothing could – if it depended on me, a prisoner, to do the follow up. For some strange reason, though, I was supplied with long pants. Perhaps I should have asked for long pants, instead. Who knows, I might have ended up with mealie rice!

Victor Verster Prison gave us a sense of what the life of freedom would be about. Listening to the birds in the morning and the sound of cars passing and regular people (men and women and *children*) whom we could see walk past the walls that were not very high. I heard from those who were lucky to receive visitors that they remarked that the atmosphere at Victor Verster seemed very relaxed. It was. But then, after Robben Island, my thinking was that unless one found oneself in hell, any place else would be – could only be – better.

I had a very pleasant surprise at Victor Verster when some of the Bekkersdal group passed through.

Matthews Letlake, Shakes Matsila, Sam Thabapelo and Moss Mokotong spent a few nights with us in December 1967. They had been shuffled through various prisons, a normal procedure, so that prisoners did not get too comfortable in one place; that might lead to all sorts of complications: corruption, familiarity, etc. This group had done the prison rounds: from Robben Island they were sent to Victor Verster; then off to Pollsmoor; Greenpoint followed Pollsmoor which, in turn, was followed by Bien Doon in the Free State. And here they were, back at Victor Verster – on their way to discharge – finally.

We had a farewell concert for them at Christmas.

My stay in Victor Verster was exactly what it was designed to be, a bridgehead into the next step I would take into civil life outside of prison. I had been allowed to continue with my studies, wrote my matric exams and passed with distinctions. Soon after the results were announced, I began to anticipate the next move – after all, it could not be far from happening.

And exactly one month before the end of my sentence, Joas Mogale and I were moved out of Victor Verster. The Officer Commanding, trying hard to be civil, advised us that the time had come for us to take the next step out of captivity – to our freedom.

The world outside was beckoning.

23

'By ministerial order, you've been banished'

Back where it had all started – Leeuwkop Prison – May 1969. I am 25 years old.

But this is the next to the last and final stop – home! It is a mere month before I will have completed my sentence on the 18th of June 1969.

A few days ago, Joas (Baker) Mogale and I were moved out of Victor Verster and sent back here; that is how the prison bureaucracy works. After a lacklustre journey, we arrived here to find a dramatically changed Leeuwkop Prison. Considered to pose minimum risk, we were not locked up in the maximum-security prison but in an adjacent one, for less risky prisoners.

On the first day, we were told to contact our people and ask them to bring us street clothes. The last time I had worn civvies was at Number Four Prison, July 1963 – I was 19 years old. After I had changed to prison uniform, I had given those clothes to my sister Semakaleng but, I still remembered what they were: a coat, pair of trousers, socks, shoes, shirt, underwear and two overalls. She had bound them in a plastic bag to taken them home. Now, looking at Semakaleng, asking her to bring me real clothes, my excitement knew no bounds; in a couple of weeks (months, at the worst) I would be back in Bekkersdal. I would be in civil clothes. I would be home, living a normal life once again.

Thanks, once more, to the generosity of my good friend and brother, Leopard, I not only had civilian clothes, I had real glad rags. I could see that Leopard had gone out to shop for me – specially.

Now I was the proud owner of: a pair of black pants, a pair of very expensive shoes, fawn and shiny shoes, two shirts, a Pringle cardigan, and a jacket. A gentleman, Leopard had not forgotten underwear and toiletries complete with a shaving kit for I had grown a little beard since my teenage days! I was more than ready to hit the streets – walk on them free, resume my interrupted life. Even the sullen stance of the warder who'd handed me the clothes, the day before our release, could not dampen my spirits.

'Here, these are your clothes,' this man had said rather grudgingly. For him, they were just clothes. To me, they marked a milestone.

Baker's brother-in-law had brought him a navy suit and a well cut shirt to go with it and a matching, eye-catching tie to complete the outfit. He also had a second set of clothes. Little did we realise how helpful those extra clothes would be!

However, in the manner of the workings of prison administration, Baker and I remained totally in the dark regarding how, exactly, the release would be done. But that did little to suppress our excitement. We were so near the finish line, we could see the tape. I couldn't wait to finally sleep on a bed, my very own bed, at home.

The day before our expected release, on Monday, the 23rd of July, a totally unexpected thing happened.

Two burly, unsmiling Special Branch policemen came, politely introduced themselves as Brigadier Aucamp, and his colleague, Ogies, and said they had come to fetch us.

Immediately, suspicion rose in me at this surprising development. What we found even more troubling was to have Brigadier Aucamp as our personal escort. We knew that name all right.

This gentleman was assigned the task of the overall responsibility for security matters in the country, and reported to the Minister's Council. How had two low-risk prisoners – on their last day of imprisonment – come to deserve such high honour?

The two gentlemen congratulated us on serving our sentences and on our impending release from prison. Then, just in passing, they told us that we were being taken to Pretoria Central Prison.

If we had been surprised before, the revelation confounded Baker and me even more. Both of us came from Randfontein; Pretoria was further away from our homes than Leeuwkop.

Stiff in our new clothes, Baker and I sat upright at the back as the Toyota drove through Midrand, Halfway House, and semi-urban places of no interest to us.

But something that did catch our interest was the newspaper headlines on each and every lamppost we passed: 'Apollo lunar landing!' or, 'The moon landing!' and 'Man returns from the moon!' This seemed to be the big news of the day. Clueless, Baker and I, our eyebrows raised, exchanged glances and shrugs. Although we had received snippets of the news at Victor Verster, we'd heard nothing about the lunar event.

But, from the headlines, it seemed the world had altered drastically during our prolonged absence. When we were growing up, occasionally, there would be stories of life on the moon, but nothing serious ever came of those.

We asked our companions what the fuss was all about and one of them said, 'Don't you guys know that Neil Armstrong and his crew have landed on the moon?'

It sounded nonsensical, to put it mildly. Remember now, you're talking to the real McCoys here, your latter day Rip van Winkles.

Space exploration exercises began while we were on Robben Island; we had no idea of the success of the Apollo mission. The Americans landed on the moon on the 20th of July and returned to earth on the 23rd, the very day we were being transported to Pretoria from Leeuwkop. So, I suppose one could say that both Armstrong and Magomola were on the move that day!

Baker and I were disappointed at being taken to Pretoria Central Prison.

My sole consolation was that I was in this with him, whom I had known long before Robben Island. We had first met in 1959, at the Bantu Affairs Commissioner's Offices in Randfontein. He had just finished his matric at Hofmeyer High School while I had dropped out of Madibane High. We were both at the Commissioner's Offices looking for work. Baker, who was from Atteridgeville, had come to live with his uncle, the Makgalemeles, in Randfontein and one of his cousins, Mantsho, was one of the girls I flirted with in my youth. Understandably therefore, his being my companion in this journey into the unknown was comforting to me.

Finally, our mysterious trip came to an end. We arrived at Pretoria Central Prison to find that each one of us had been put in a cell in isolation.

At lunch, we were treated to what looked like food from the warders' kitchen – clearly different from your normal prison diet. This should not have surprised us as it did; we were, after all, no longer prisoners, we had served our sentence to the last minute. Political prisoners, unlike common-law prisoners, were not allowed any remission of their sentences at all.

We had to serve all of our time to the second whereas, normally, in South African prisons, depending on the prisoner's conduct, a first-time offender could get up to 50% of the sentence remitted, sometimes even up to 60%.

Not so with political prisoners. When they said life sentence they meant life, not fifteen years.

Technically (and, legally) speaking, Baker and I were no longer prisoners. But when and how our actual release would be effected remained illusive.

Wondering but not overly worried, we told ourselves: one more night or so in another prison cell was something we could handle. Hey, this was not an issue for us. Remember, we were the big boys who had screamed: 'Six years! That's nothing! We'll be back!' Well, we *were* back. Almost. What was another night or so? *Less than nothing!*

However, to our irritation, we hardly slept a wink. The whole night was filled with a terrible noise: incessant and desperate-sounding singing; loud, bone-chilling screams; soul-wrenching prayer sessions, harrowing confessionals and agonising confessions, pleas for redemption and the remission of the most horrible sins.

At one point, because the noise seemed to be about to come right past the door of my cell, I couldn't resist but rushed to the door and peeped through the keyhole. And, a few seconds later, the source of the commotion came within view: a blind-folded man, led and dragged by several warders.

Dreadful sight? Yes. But I dismissed the whole thing as part of the torture techniques of the prison.

The next day, however, the scene assumed another meaning – a horrific, blood-curdling meaning. The light of morning brought us terrible enlightenment: the cells we'd been allocated were in the hanging section.

All those screams, prayers, confessions, and cries of utter despair we'd heard all night long were the cries of the condemned – men going to the gallows.

We discovered, to our horror, that two or three men were going to be hanged that very morning. Now, I wondered about the man who'd gone past my cell. The blind-folded man.

That is one night that has not stopped replaying itself on my mind – over and over again, those terrible sounds from the human abattoir haunt me still.

Panic struck, a moment of paralysing fear came over me. Fear and exceedingly numbing insecurity such as I had not felt in any of the several prisons I had passed through. Was our stop at Pretoria Central Prison fortuitous or did it hold (and hide) a more sinister meaning? Were we, my friend Baker and I, brought here to hang? Be hanged?

I wouldn't have put it past the blundering authorities to hang us, even by mistake – as in the case of mistaken identity or a mix-up of files. Given the callousness of our captors, wild as these thoughts were, they were not entirely out of the realms of the possible. Panic-stricken, I could almost see and smell my own blood.

At breakfast, we were told to get ready for our departure. Now, tell me it makes sense to drag us from Leeuwkop to Pretoria – just for one day. That one day, the one immediately preceding that of our release.

When I heard that, the next thing I expected to hear was that the warders had contacted our relatives and let them know where, exactly, to fetch us.

They were expecting our release. They would expect to meet us at Leeuwkop. Surely, they were told? Told where to come and get us. But I received no such illumination.

After breakfast, with very few words, two different armed Security Branch policemen led us to a waiting car and told us to get in.

We had driven for some time when I asked, 'Where are you taking us?' And before they had answered, added, 'Are you driving us to Randfontein?' I asked the second question because it was quite obvious we were not going in a south west direction at all but heading more northwards.

'Well, wait till you find out where you're going to,' one of the men said, without a backward glance as the car continued on its merry way. On and on and on, it drove – seemingly endlessly.

About two hours later we started to pass the small towns of Hammanskraal, Warmbaths, Nylstroom – this was somewhat familiar. *Ntate*'s and *Mme*'s origins were Zeerust and, later, Naboomspruit. I spent time, as a boy, in Naboomspruit, where the Venter trailers were manufactured. Soon we were passing the district of Haakdoring (Thorny Bush), in the heart of conservative Afrikanerdom. Another memory popped into my heard: this is where my grandfather spent his last days – Haakdoring.

When we were growing up, my father took his annual pilgrimage to this farm during his leave from Venterspost mine. The purpose of the trip was to visit his father, my *Ntate moholo* Gabriel, after whom I was named. *Ntate* usually took both of us children – my sister and me.

As the train chugged along, *Ntate* would tell us stories of the family. From Park Station in Johannesburg to Naboomspruit, the train ride took the whole night and we would get off in the early hours of the morning – around three or four.

Always but always, my father brought a torch or flash light. He had various sizes of those torches – small, medium size and long torches. The long torches could take up to six batteries. Those are the ones he brought along when we travelled to Naboomspruit because they gave off the brightest light one could want or need. Naboomspruit was a vast brooding darkness when we got off the train. *Ntate* used to scare us, saying there were seasoned witches in the area and he had to scare them off with the piercing light of the torch. Now, as children, there were two things we were wary of: witches and *dipoko* (ghosts). To make matters worse, we had to pass the village graveyard. *Ntate* used to reassure us, saying that ghosts were averse to light, which was why they only came out at night. Just like witches.

Once, when I was about nine or ten, *Ntate* and I went, just the two of us, to Haakdoring. When we got off the train, *Ntate* told me to be silent.

His torch illuminated the way as we walked. I carried a small bag of provisions while *Ntate* lugged a larger bag over his shoulder. As we approached Grandfather Gabriel's village, we saw a stark naked woman coming out of a hut.

My father put the light on her and she quickly disappeared into the yard and, suddenly, there was the screeching and cackling of chickens and dogs barking madly. Perhaps she had come out to relieve herself because there were no inside toilets in the area. Why would she have expected anyone abroad that time of morning? And if she went to bed naked, why would she have gone to the trouble of getting dressed, just to go outside and make a wee?

Ntate said that was possibly a witch, and I believed my father. In my mind, I knew, was certain, that I had seen a live witch. I even told Grandfather Gabriel about it over Grandma Johanna's delicious coffee.

The whole clan waited for our coming, not just Grandma and Grandpa but *Ntate*'s brothers: Uncle Jacob and Uncle Herman and their wives and children. They all waited for us and didn't go to sleep all that night, waiting. Our coming was a big occasion for the family. *Ntate* was the most educated, more urbanised of them all and his visiting them, from the Gauteng (Place of gold) mines was always a big deal.

Something jolted me out of my reverie and hauled me back to the now, to a gnarled, unpleasant now. I was coming from Robben Island, via Leeuwkop and Pretoria.

Where I was going only God knew. Our escorts would not divulge that information. They flatly refused to say anything that had anything to do with our destination. Whatever that meant, my gut feeling told me it would be exceeding folly to wait for a pleasant surprise.

We went past Potgietersrust, through the centre of town, the signs were all there for us to see.

Suddenly, there was movement in the front seats. Clearly, we saw that we were near our destination. Our escorts started tidying up, grooming themselves. They adjusted their ties, combed their hair, putting on their best looks so that when we arrived there they would look the part. After all, they were the Special Branch – the elite club, superior to mere policemen.

The final destination, I remember very well, announced itself thus: 'Welcome to the Great North. Welcome to Pietersburg.' Pietersburg, now known as Polokwane.

This, then, our destination? I wondered what all this really meant. What did I have to do with Pietersburg? Perhaps, more to the point, what did Pietersburg have to do with me?

The Toyota stopped at the Pietersburg police station and we were escorted to the reception.

'Well, guys, this is your final destination,' said one of the escorts adding, 'the last but one.'

What, in God's name, does he mean by *last but one*? I wondered, but said nothing. Where, exactly, would be our last – very last stop? And why? What about home?

Most of the policemen at this police station were African. They welcomed us in Sepedi and we could tell they were expecting us. From their stares we saw that we were a curiosity. They would later tell us they had never come across people from Robben Island before; and they had been told that we were highly dangerous communists. They had also been told we would have a bad influence on the community, and should be treated as though we were contaminated.

One of the African policemen came to talk to us in SeSotho, '*Barena* – Men, you're welcome here, we know why you're here. So, *khululekani* (feel free) …'

Feel free? One thing was reassuring though, we were not processed on our arrival. We were not handcuffed, were not counted, tagged and issued with prison uniforms.

This said, loud and clear, we were no longer prisoners. So, yes, we *could try* and feel free. But what about going home? Why were we here?

We sat down on the bunks he offered; and tried to relax.

The police tried to engage us in conversations but we remained reticent, we had already spent years on Robben Island and our discussions were always self-censored for fear we could be victimised. For private conversations, Baker and I communicated in the code language of the island, understood only by the two of us.

Someone went to buy us a packet of fish and chips and half a loaf of bread. He also bought some cigarettes for Baker.

Baker and I were soon consumed with the newspapers we had brought from Pretoria Central Prison. We read every item that had anything to do with the lunar landing, trying to understand where it all started, how the Americans were able to put man on the moon. And the words of the astronaut, Neil Armstrong, that this was one small step for them, but a giant leap for mankind, are imprinted on my mind. They struck me then as relevant to me and my situation; I knew then that we were taking our own leap into the unknown. Yes, it was very sad and extremely disappointing that we were not going home, as was by now quite apparent. But there was a certain amount of anticipation of adventure of the immediate future. Whatever awaited us, wherever that would be, was not prison. Indeed, that element of the unknown added an air of intrigue to whatever awaited us.

Although I told myself all this, reassuring myself and trying to keep my spirits up, both Baker and I could not help being not only puzzled and irritated but also very concerned; uncertainty gnawing at us non-stop.

We asked to make phone calls to let our people know where we were. That was instantly denied. We were told that at an appropriate time we would be able to communicate with our folks. The officer in charge brusquely told us that he had no control over our situation. 'Talk to the two gentlemen who brought you,' he said.

But that twosome had already gone. We were still puzzling over these developments when a tall and athletic gentleman in a brown well-cut suit arrived. This suave man spoke to us in a bizarre Afrikaner accent but good English intonation and charmed his way into our conversation.

He was very good with words and possessed a spontaneous sparkling grin. A well-groomed gentleman, looking contemplative, he constantly polished his trim brown moustache which matched his immaculate sideburns. He was speaking to the police in somewhat good Afrikaans when Baker suddenly sprang his good English on him and asked why we were there. A look of surprise came over him then, and, after a slight pause, he turned away from the policeman with whom he had been talking. Then, looking us straight in the eye, the debonair gentleman said, 'You have been banished.'

And, for the first time, we understood our fate. Meanwhile, the policeman to whom our informant had been talking, just seconds before, had suddenly found things to do behind the counter.

We were banished. Stupefied, we just stood there, at a loss for words.

Slowly, my confusion turned into bitter despair at the bitter dose we'd been given.

Meanwhile, where the two Special Branch men who had brought us here from Pretoria Prison had been reticent, the jovial messenger suffered from no such handicap.

He informed us that our banishment was to an area outside Pietersburg and we would be transported there later that day.

Clarity, at last!

Banished – that was the official legal term. By ministerial order, it was declared that we couldn't go back to the Bekkersdal-Randfontein area where we came from. We were deemed a bad influence on the community.

According to the Minister of Justice, we, unlike other prisoners, had not shown remorse or repentance during our period of imprisonment. Therefore, we needed to be ostracised from our communities until the authorities were satisfied that we had fully repented. We learnt later that some of our other colleagues had been scattered to all kinds of remote areas. Eret Radebe was sent to the Transkei (Eastern Cape); Peter Mazibuko was banished to Pietermaritzburg and Boxy Ramphomane to Mafikeng. There was no perceptible logic to this madness.

That banishment was quite a nasty surprise. When we were sentenced, we were not advised that we would serve a further period of banishment. It was an arbitrary decision of the Minister based on reports and advice he received about our conduct in prison. Unwittingly, we had joined the distinct honour brigade of men like the Nobel Prize laureate, Chief Albert Luthuli, former President of the ANC, who had also been banished.

True to the words of the Suave One, we were handed over to new authorities with our belongings, thus noted: R3.14 for Baker and I, mistakenly noted as Derrick Bila, was accredited a net worth of R1.09. My *reeks* (serial number) for tracking by the security police was 784.

Then finally, later that afternoon, our final destination had a name. We were told that we would be taken to the Chloe sisal project, about fifty kilometres north west of Pietersburg, not far from the Botswana border.

I was outraged. I had long passed that initial stage of irrepressible emotional disappointment. The unexpressed rage of six years burned my face, made my scalp itch and stiffened my neck painfully. We persisted, seeking answers. At that point I hardly cared what was done to me; I had long passed the point of fear. I was willing to confront even a myriad of further charges, which the police could just trump up. I was old enough and had been through enough to articulate my fury with authority and no longer the eighteen-year old boy they had seized in Bekkersdal. I told that white officer we had served our sentence to the hour and the minute.

We had had our punishment and it was grossly unfair of them to extend our punishment beyond what the magistrate had meted out to us in July 1963. He told me he had no authority over the matter. 'I'm just carrying out instructions from the Minister,' were his exact words. Where had I heard that before? I blew my top.

'To hell with the Minister,' I shouted. I no longer cared about consequences and continued to vent my anger volubly.

Obviously, I had no access to the Minister though my existence was inextricably linked to his whims. We'd never met him, yet he determined how we breathed, where, when and how.

The days and nights of my dreams – my huge hope – were there within grasp, and they were snatched away with such inconceivable cruel disregard for me. And I had no means whatsoever to defend myself unless I wanted to die. So, I raged and vented my outrage.

Before we left Pietersburg Police Station we each had been rationed with a meagre month's supply of food. A bag of mealie meal, a couple of tins of beans, cans of corned beef – a dozen each – dried vegetables, dried beans, salt and a few condiments. At the end of the month we would be paid and would, therefore, be self-sufficient, we were told.

'What kind of work are we going to do?' I asked.

'You're going to pick sisal from plants and have it processed,' came promptly from one of the policemen.

What was there to say?

Shortly after that, we left the Pietersburg police station. For a while, we drove in utter silence.

At last, we enquired what the logic of this step was and the African policeman who was driving us to our final unwanted destination told us that it was a directive from the Minister. I demanded to see the banishment order, because normally there would be such an order, signed by the Minister of Justice.

But the policeman said that the official restriction orders would be served on us when we arrived at our destination, that is, when we were in the judicial area of banishment.

We were utterly disappointed, disillusioned, and devastated. We were no longer prisoners; but neither were we free. Not really.

During that tedious drive, I noted every ascent, plunge, twist and turn of the road to keep my mind from exploding. We skirted past *kamolokeisheneng*, past Seshego, the township outside Pietersburg, which was still under construction. We drove past a small village we later got to know as Blood River. We went down to the village of Moletsi and kept on driving – on and on and on, till we were driving past PAX High

School. There, nostalgia hit me. PAX had been my first choice of high school – way back then. I pointed this out to Baker and he replied that he too had wanted to study at PAX. But he said this in such absent-minded manner, I guessed he was not really paying attention, most probably also lost in his own thoughts.

After an hour and half of driving mostly on the bumpy gravel road, creating an unending spume of dust behind us – marking the miles away from civilisation and our hearts' desire – the driver told us we were approaching our *new* final destination.

24

Chloe sisal plantation

Upon arrival at this quaint and rustic place called Chloe, we were introduced to a man referred to as *Molimi* (the farmer) who seemed to have been in his mid forties. We later learnt that his real name was Meshack Khabo Mabuela. He was quite pleasant and courteous; a humble man – a typical old-world being – with an amiable disposition. His face was scarred by the harsh unforgiving hot and dry Northern Transvaal sun and he had a missing upper front tooth and a sparse moustache. *Molimi* was employed by the government to teach peasants farming methods at the Chloe sisal project. This was the gentleman who was going to be our supervisor during our period of banishment and to whom we would be accountable.

One of the policemen read out the banishment orders. Now we all knew what was expected. It was no longer a secret, known only to a select few but Baker and I were in on it. We knew how circumscribed our life in Chloe was intended to be. I was left with a hollow feeling in the pit of my stomach for, in many ways, this was a more isolating life I was about to live – anything more different to the freedom I had harboured in my heart for so long would be hard to imagine.

After that, *Molimi* sat us down and, over coffee, welcomed us to Chloe. He expressed the desire to work with us harmoniously. And, I must say, he lived up to his words. For the whole time we were there he remained pleasant and never displayed any animosity towards us.

The policeman had left. *Molimi* then explained that he would be taking us to our accommodation.

He himself lived in a brick and mortar house with corrugated iron sheet roofing instead of the mud huts usual in the area. He explained why we were there and that we were not the first people to be brought to his area. He had, in the past, received people with political leanings who had seemed to be a bad influence on their communities, and there were a couple of *rondavels* that had been built in that area to house people who had been banished to Chloe.

Molimi was quite observant and sensed our curiosity. He explained that Chloe was ideal for restricting political offenders. Firstly, it was far removed from the cities and, most importantly, it was isolated and unscathed by civilisation. There was no electricity, no running water and no communication system of any kind.

After coffee, *Molimi* transported us in the back of a trailer and reminded us we should keep a box of matches and candles because it was dark in the area and crawling insects and lizards abounded.

All three of us went first to my one-roomed *rondavel*. *Molimi* was ready with his candle. After our eyes adjusted to the light, I saw a makeshift bed, a cabinet with old mugs (some of which didn't have handles), two spoons and a knife.

We could tell it had just been cleaned, but a faint dark smell of dusty lifelessness lingered. There was a woman outside, waiting for an order from the farmer to go home.

Molimi said Baker's house was two kilometres from mine. By this time, night had fallen and it was still pitch dark. Nothing stirred. The only signs of life were the howls of animals and the chirping crickets. That was a bit unsettling for us, city born and bred, so we thought we would share my *rondavel* – at least, for that first night.

Somewhere in the middle of the conversation the farmer told us that the last person who had lived in this *rondavel* was a Xhosa chief from the Cape, one of the opponents of the creation of the Bantu homeland in Pondoland. He, too, had been brought to Chloe because he had been troublesome for the government. The chief had lived there for a couple of years. Then, one morning, he was found dead inside that same *rondavel*. That put the scare of God in me, I can tell you. Had I made it out of Robben Island just to, possibly, die in this accursed desolate place? Then I told myself that I was too young and I was resilient enough and I just had to muster my courage. And having survived all those near-death spells on Robben Island, I knew how much I could withstand. And I knew I still had some reserve resolve in me.

After that, we went to Baker's rondavel. However, as we'd agreed earlier, he did not stay but returned with me. That night, he spent the night with me. There was no restriction on that.

The restriction orders were read to us and those could not be questioned. For two years, we would not be allowed to go back to where we came from. We were not allowed to go anywhere beyond five miles of the farm, our place of work and residence.

It was not a house arrest but a banishment order. We could lead a semi-normal life except for the fact that if we wanted to go to Pietersburg, we had to get permission from *Molimi*, who would go to the local chief, then go to the magistrate in Pietersburg who could grant us permission at his discretion. There was quite a bureaucratic maze to negotiate regarding what we could and could not do. Overall it meant our lives were still under the total control of the government. We were spared house arrest which was meted out to some of those released.

People such as those lived stringent, monitored lives with unbelievable limitations – such as the number of people they could talk to at any one time! That fate was awaiting my friend, Dick Moseneke.

So, finally, this was it. We knew the worst. Had seen it. Were in it. The bleak prospect that, for the next two years, was to be our life: Chloe sisal plantation.

To remain sane, I accepted that this was the truth – my reality – at least for the next two years. However, it was also clear that I had reached the end of that horrid life of being counted, tagged, shipped, and moved; assaulted, starved, insulted and manacled.

And, for that, I was truly grateful.

The following morning *Molimi* gave us a briefing. Baker and I were introduced to what would be the routine. We assembled at the collection (and drop off) point in front of one house where, along with the local peasants, both men and women, we were fetched by two trailers led by a tractor driven by *Molimi* and driven to the sisal plantation for the day. The sisal plantation fields were just over three kilometres from the assembly point.

We jumped into the long dilapidated trailer to sit on the bare rusted and dusty steel. Both of us looked decidedly out of place in our expensive, brand new city clothes. Baker wore his pin stripe suit and white shirt with expensive black shoes. We bobbed up and down on the trailer, acutely aware of the stark contrast between us, our clothing, and that of our abjectly deprived fellow workers. These people were so impoverished that not one of them (men, women and children) wore a pair of shoes. They were covered in tattered rags resembling clothes. Everyone marvelled at our big-city clothes; in fact, no-one expected us to be sitting among them.

The workers thought we were some officials from the government offices and accorded us that reverence. Unbeknown to them, we were going to be treated in exactly the same way as them.

Molimi tried his very best to be civil to us, although he had to be mindful of the orders he'd received from above.

We drove for two to three kilometres on a narrow winding road flanked by wide interminable stretches of cotton fields. Guided by our fellow workers, we got off the trailer when they did.

Baker pulled out a cigarette, lit it, shook his head and, with his typical wry laugh, said, 'Jackson,' (that is what we called each other) 'we thought Robben Island was bad … but this, here, is the beginning of a new chapter!'

I just gave him a long stare but said nothing. I was busy wondering what our next step should be. I knew right then that at some stage we were going to have to run away. How far was the Botswana border? There was no way I could countenance anymore of this continued torture; not for two whole years!

We discovered then that Chloe plantation was worse than what any punishment the authorities could have conjured up. Chloe was a burning, parched, semi-arid undeveloped piece of farmland in a poverty-stricken part of the Northern Province, miles and miles from any town. Most of the residents of Chloe were illiterate peasants who eked out their living from the crops. The sisal plantation provided the only employment there was in the area. They were paid minimal wages, barely enough to live on. Obviously, items such as deodorant and shoes were luxuries out of their reach.

Because of the scarcity of running water in the area, hygiene standards were extremely poor.

It was hard to believe that we had been dumped in the middle of nowhere, without any warning. For us to make a living out of those miserable conditions would be impossible. Although we were in mid-winter, the heat of the day sun was unforgiving and I wondered what the summers were like. Chloe reminded me of the slave camps I had seen in the movies of the Deep South in the United States. Not a school, church or any public building was to be seen, just scores of men, women and children going about eking out a living. When we learned, later, that the plantation was the government's trust land, we immediately suspected that this plantation was the origin of the sisal mats used by the Prisons Service Department as bedding for prisoners. It made sense.

Molimi invited us to his tiny office and told us he had instructions that we should be taught how to reap the sisal cotton from the plants. We then learned how to package it in sacks, wheel the full sacks to a designated part of the field and arrange them into a certain format. From there, the sacks would be taken to warehouses to be bailed in preparation for processing.

On the first day, we didn't work hard, we watched. Everyone was kind and we were told to observe. Those poor people were compassionate and felt that it was unbecoming of the authorities to expect people like us to work under such conditions.

But the day, under the oppressive heat, went by very quickly and we returned to our new homes intact. We huddled back into the trailer to be dropped off at *Molimi's* house. Tired goodbyes and waves were exchanged with our co-workers who disappeared to faraway villages.

Molimi kindly advised us to wash our hands in his house before we left; he knew there was a scarcity of water where we were going. There were water drums left outside for us and we'd been given makeshift plastic basins for bathing. To augment the rations we'd been given, we had also purchased toiletries in Pietersburg; but water was still an issue.

Another problem was clothing. I only had one set of clothes and both of us had to make do with one set of underwear each, which we washed every night. We had not expected this detour at all and no one in our families had expected us to be five hundred kilometres from our homes after release from prison.

From *Molimi*'s place, we walked to my *rondavel*, which was closer. Dejected though we were, we nonetheless found a way of jesting about our new state. At my *rondavel,* we shared a can of beans between the two of us. This was our very first supper as free people; forget 'the best meat stew' cooked by you know who. I would have jumped for chicken feet or tripe!

We made jokes about our encounters during the day and we reminisced about our night at Pretoria Central Prison.

We were still stuck in the newspapers – just marvelling at the entire change of people, the dress code, everything seemed to have altered. Bellbottoms were in; both men and women looked bizarre in those billowing pants. The men looked awkward and resembled females in flowing pants and high heeled shoes. At first we were amused by the outrageous dangling earrings which were the size of bracelets and thick wooden peace signs dangling against chests. What had this world come to in the last six years! I felt like a Rip van Winkle come to life in the remotest part of the world.

Strangely, the last thing we spoke about was, I suspect, the one uppermost in the minds of both of us: WOMEN! It had been six long years and more since we had been in female company and we were eagerly looking forward to the earliest opportunity to remedy this. Needless to say, none of those women in the trailer would suit our needs. Their movements were unattractively languid as is customary in rural areas. They spoke in timid voices with unhurried, drawn-out diction I knew I would never get used to. We were looking for something we had imagined and romanticised about for six years: poised, sophisticated, professional women we saw in the township and on the covers of *Drum* magazine. That was what we yearned for. Our challenge was where and how to begin the search with these ridiculous restrictions inhibiting our movements. After much discussion and fantasising, we hatched a plan. We would find out where the nearest school or hospital was. We were nervous about going to townships given our circumstances; but there was nothing in their terms of banishment about entering a school or hospital. The loophole was a Godsend. That taken care, of we called it a night and Baker left for his own *rondavel*.

From the next day on, the routine was the same repetitive process, quickly boring. Once we knew what to do we couldn't hold any further sustained conversations with the workers, we were simply lifetimes apart. They kept a guarded distance from us as well, so it was just Baker and I. Occasionally *Molimi* would join us to find out how things were going, how we were acclimatising.

One night *Molimi* invited us to his house, and asked his male servant to slaughter a chicken for us. That night, we had our first sumptuous dinner in years. The chicken was served with rice, cabbage, beetroot, and we all sat around the table. *Molimi* wanted to know more about us, how we had ended up on Robben Island and what had earned us the distinction of ending up in Chloe. It had been a long time since he had seen any politician sent to Chloe understandably, he was curious about us, our case.

We laughed about where we were, and he reassured us that he didn't think we'd be there for the two years, things would change, he said. He made it very clear that he was not part of the repressive system of punishing us, although he was not necessarily on our side either.

We appreciated his frankness.

A few days later, our enquiries produced fruitful results. We were told there was a mission hospital called Nobel, between fifteen and twenty kilometres from the plantation. The workers told us, '*A se ko khole, ke haufi nyana*' (Don't worry, it's not too far. It's just around the corner.) Ten kilometres was nothing for people used to walking long distances to the store or to the bus stop, to anywhere and everywhere.

The first Friday working at Chloe sisal plantation – like desert travellers lost in a sand storm, the day couldn't come to a close fast enough. Baker and I were almost out of our minds, delirious with anticipation – enough *was* enough. We were going out. We were on a hunt because we were burning for decent female company.

After work, we went to our *rondavels*, spruced up and brushed our shoes. Looking our best, under our peculiar circumstances, off we went. *Molimi*'s people had given us directions and we had a ready explanation for our being out of bounds, should the need arise: we needed medical attention. We thought that would be a good response in case we bumped into *Molimi.* After all, nothing in the banning order had said we couldn't go and see a doctor.

At three, sharp, we set off. If I were to perish in Chloe, at least, let that be after I had touched a woman.

I wouldn't say the hospital was not far, but there was will enough in our hearts to walk twice that distance. A little short of two hours' walking, we saw smoke billowing from a protruding boiler chimney, a good sign.

We were near civilisation! Our resolve rekindled, we walked a little faster.

Finally, there it was – the hospital. Before we approached the gate, we dusted our shoes, adjusted shirt collars, and combed our hair in an attempt to look businesslike. At the security gate, we told the guards we had come to visit people in hospital. Playing it safe, we signed in false names in the visitors' book. And we were in!

As soon as the guards were out of sight, ecstatic, we hugged each other. Then, as though that were not enough good fortune, we had hardly walked fifty yards when we saw two women coming towards us. I quickly assessed the situation.

'Jackson,' I said to Baker, 'you go for the taller one.'

We met the two young women and greeted them and, after introducing ourselves – again giving fictitious names – politely asked if they could help us find someone we were looking for. A white lie, of course, but we needed to start somewhere. The two ladies exchanged glances and then talked things over between them.

The very sound of their voices got me so excited I wanted to scream, 'Halellua!' I looked at Baker and saw he was just as excited. I wondered whether these women didn't see through our fake calm. Could we really hide the sea of feeling coursing through our veins? I had my doubts.

The taller of the two was Madire. She turned to her friend, Maphefo, and said, *'Mokhotsi, areye reobabontsa.'* (My friend, let's go show them the hospital.) So they turned around and we followed them back into the hospital. They wanted to know where we came from. *'Letswa borwa na?'* (Are you guys from the South – Johannesburg?)

We said we were. It was clear that that put us several notches up in their eyes. Moreover, we couldn't tell them we were what the villagers called, 'the men who work at sisal plantation'. I quickly replied, *'Ja, ja, retswa borwa.'* (Yes, yes, we come from the South.)

A mischievous smile passed between them and one said, *'Relebone.'* (We saw that.) By our city look, we had successfully led them to come to the conclusion – even before we lied about it – that we were from the big city.

These clean, well-groomed and cultured Pieterburg girls led us toward a spot near the reception. Sounds of Afro jazz music came from a radio somewhere nearby. They showed us to some sofas and asked us to wait for them and disappeared inside.

Wide-eyed, Baker and I looked at each other. We jumped up, hugged and slapped each other's backs like naughty schoolboys after scoring a goal. This was a major achievement. But there was a little problem. We were *platsak* (broke). *Molimi* had given us R5 each (which in those days could stretch far) to replenish our supplies; but we would only be paid at the end of the month. What if these two women suggested we go out? How would we entertain them?

We waited, our anxiety mounting with each passing minute. What if they were playing games with us and did the disappearing act?

Then, a thought struck me. 'Jackson,' I said to Baker, 'I think we should make our visit here seem formal. Let us register with the admission clerk as outpatients.'

Baker agreed with my proposal and we promptly went to the receptionist and presented ourselves as ill and seeking an appointment with a doctor.

The receptionist introduced herself as Mahlodi and duly registered us and arranged for a day of consultation. Meanwhile, the girls were making their way back and they had changed into pretty dresses, obviously to impress us. Would they have gone to that trouble were they not interested in our company? And that was exactly what we had hoped for.

As soon as Maphefo appeared, I felt something happening to me. She had a trim, neat body and the looks to go with it. My heart beat accelerated. Baker was acting cool and we had to be that way to dispel any kind of notion about who we really were.

The girls came and sat with us. They invited us to drinks, somewhere in the residences

Of course we obliged.

The occasion seemed like some kind of celebration, a party. We sat and watched and didn't dare dance, scared we'd make fools of ourselves. The music was a strange American pop infused with jazz.

Almost all the people there were doing what was called the monkey dance in the 1960s. Watching the complex and confusing uniform steps was enough for me. I decided to mind my own business and avoid going on the floor where, no doubt, I'd not only make a fool of myself but reveal more of myself than I cared to.

I had my first beer – a Carling Black Label. And, deliberately, I drank it very slowly – to savour the taste. We had told ourselves we wouldn't have more than one beer each, for fear of getting drunk and, like the monkey of the folktales, letting the secret out of the bag in front of the whole village. But, in no time at all, I became alarmingly light-headed. Startled, I thought, Gaby, things have really changed in your system, *mfana*! Before Robben Island, I used to consume gallons of the stuff, with hardly any effect all.

Then, before we knew it, it was 10 pm and we were worried about finding our way back in the thick of night. We asked the girls to walk us to the gate and lied that someone would come and fetch us. We promised to return and they gave us their contact details and, we each got goodnight kisses.

We went back to Chloe with new confidence; we had asserted our manhood and had been affirmed. Neither one of us had gone to any extremes, for one of the things we had learned in our political schooling was that we should respect our women. Besides, even had we forgotten those lessons, how could we have gone any further?

This was, after all, our first meeting with these young women; never mind that, for Baker and me, it was, for years, the first encounter with women – barring my brief adventure at Greenpoint Hospital.

Some time during the walk back, I heard Baker say, 'Jackson, I am not sure, but suffice it to say that it was a magic moment for me.'

I knew what he meant. I had had a similar strange and somewhat nostalgic sensation as my friend planted her soft lips on mine.

For once, we forgot about our personal tragedies, buoyed by the lingering exhilaration of those magic moments. We chuckled. We laughed out loud as we reminisced about the escapade. It was a moonlit evening and we could see the gravel road very clearly demarcated from the bush.

'How close did you get with your buddy?' we asked of each other. Because, at some time during the evening, we had separated, each pair going its way after the girls had suggested 'we all take a little walk'. It had been during that walk that there was ample opportunity to steal a few private moments. And I have to admit that the first touch and feel of warmth of this woman's bosom on my own, was like going through a very hot shower. I don't know where sweat came from. Maphefo, from e-Kasi, where she had been born and raised was a very even tempered person with an easy smile.

Going over the evening, talking and thinking about it, we both knew we had to repeat the visit – as soon as possible.

The following morning, we were back to the ugly reality of our existence, back on the trailer. Now the contrast between the people around us and the people we had seen at the hospital was even more acute, more stark; it emphasised the misery of our condition.

And, my resolve to escape sharper, I swore anew that I wouldn't be long in Chloe, despite the twenty-four months the banishing order stipulated. The Botswana border was only 150km away, we had been told. More and more that border beckoned mightily and I said to Baker:

'Jackson, you can stay, if you like. But I'll find a way out of here.' And I meant what I said – meant it with all my heart. It didn't matter what it took, I would escape. Leave the Chloe sisal plantation. As soon as do-able.

The end of August brought our first pay day. We were each paid R12. I bought another pair of underpants, a pair of khaki pants and a tee shirt of suspect quality, the fabric being light and hard to define. But that was adequate; I could stretch my meagre earnings. The remainder, I saved for contingencies.

On our third visit to Nobel Hospital, Maphefo and I ended up in her room, an outcome she seemed to have planned. Her room-mate was out for the afternoon and early evening.

Before I knew it, I was undressed and she expertly led me with her playful soft caresses. Nature took its course as I rediscovered moments of pure ecstasy that surpassed, by far, any wet dreams of the past six years.

A few months into our Chloe sisal plantation stay, I had not only had it, I was bordering on madness – sheer madness. One day, I told Baker that we should write jointly to tell the Minister that unless he removed us from that place or ordered us out, we could commit acts for which he would not be able to hold us responsible. And we were prepared to commit the kinds of acts that could have taken us back to Robben Island. At least on the island we'd had intellectual company and we had friends around us, something we were sorely deprived of in Chloe. When we left Robben Island and all those friends, we'd believed we would be joining our families. That had not happened. So far, the only positive thing in connection with my banishment was that Sam, from our Bekkersdal group, had sent me a set of decent clothes via the post office: two white shirts, a pair of trousers and some underpants. Now, at least, I had a change of clothing.

Also, by then, we had ceased working on the plantation itself – a kind of promotion, if you like. Now, we worked as clerks.

We processed workers and performed a social-worker role, counselling and coaching.

The people warmed to us, especially to Baker, who was an extrovert and had fantastic interaction skills. For him, those people would even defy their masters.

Baker had the gift of speech – he could speak Sepedi fluently.

However, as things turned out, we didn't have to commit any crime to get attention. After four months of our nocturnal trips to Nobel Hospital, our visit yielded more than just leisure; we were also blessed with something we had not planned at all. Apart from our ladies, we were introduced to a man called Otto, an administrator at the hospital. He was a handsome young man with boyish looks who reminded me of my brother, Fetsa. He was of medium build, had chubby cheeks, soft skin, a well-manicured medium Afro and spoke quietly.

Otto had a very soft spot for us and much admiration for what we stood for. We kept warning him not to get too close to us because, with time, the Special Branch might hear about our friendship and that would prejudice him one way or another. That didn't seem to bother Otto at all. Instead, he got involved in our plans of how to get the hell out of the purgatory called Chloe.

Otto introduced us to a well-known physician who was also the district surgeon for the greater Pietersburg area. Dr Makunyane seemed to be mildly curious on hearing about our circumstances. He asked to see us and then gave us an appointment two days later.

We felt honoured and thought he would examine us to find out, without prejudice, what medical deficiencies we might have acquired during the period we spent in prison. My medical history was not a happy one and I still had pains on my left side where I had been kicked. The occasional dull pain on my chest also continued to bother me.

In two days, we met Dr Makunyane in his office. He closed the door and motioned us to seat ourselves on a sofa. Soon, we were served tea.

'So you guys were on Robben Island? I'd like to hear more about that,' he said then added, 'First of all, young man, why are you here? You look like you've just come out of high school. Why are you in Chloe? Why are you working in that farm?' Dr Makunyane looked at me squarely in the eye as he probed.

We thought Otto had given him the background. My response was long-winded.

'We'll go back to that,' he said, and insisted, 'I want to know why they brought you here.'

We didn't know who he meant by 'they' because as he was a state official, it was difficult for us to separate him from officialdom. Dressed in a white coat with a stethoscope around his neck, to us, he was officialdom.

But soon, his forthright manner disarmed us and although we had thought we'd hold back, I told him: 'We've been victimised, Doctor. After having served our time in prison, we're now receiving further punishment, far away from our families and loved ones. We are puzzled and need some answers.'

Then the good doctor wanted us to start from the beginning. Baker jumped in at this stage, he was a fantastic storyteller, and had a knack for detail. He started by lighting up his cigarette, to which the doctor said, 'Please do not smoke in the surgery.' He seemed to be a smoker, though. One could tell by his teeth and his lips, which bore the smoker's trademark burn marks.

Baker told the whole story of our journey from Randfontein police cells in 1963 to Chloe, in 1969.

The doctor listened very patiently; I could tell he was making mental notes. He looked back at us and said, 'Are you telling me that you guys spent six years in prison?'

We nodded simultaneously, as we said, 'Yes sir.'

'I'm going to an official meeting. I'll be back in thirty minutes,' he said, and left.

When he returned, Makunyane seemed to have made up his mind and, to our relief, said, 'I'd like to make sure that you're well taken care of. I'm going to make it my business that you're uprooted from this place, and I'll use my discretionary judgement to do so. First of all, my professional duty says that you need to be examined thoroughly and placed under observation.'

My initial thought was that he would examine us, admit us into a hospital and while we were there sometimes call on us. But the real shocker was yet to come. Dr Makunyane then said: 'I'm writing a letter, immediately ordering you out of Chloe. I'm taking you to the city hospital in Pietersburg, where you'll be under my personal care. And I will write to the commissioner of prisons, or whoever has authority over you.' He knew that his medical authority would supersede anybody else's view, including that of the Security Police.

And true to his word, the doctor wrote the letter for both of us and he advised us that we would be fetched the following day from Chloe and so we shouldn't go to work that day. He told us to give another letter to *Molimi*.

After that meeting, what do you know? We even forgot about the girls!

We raced right back to the plantation to pack our scant belongings. Though extremely excited, we didn't talk much; we just thought 'let it be true'.

Still incredulous, I said to Baker, 'I told you we're going to get out of this place, Jackson.' That was barely six months after we had arrived in Chloe.

That evening, we delivered the letter to *Molimi* and told him that my TB seemed to have recurred.

Molimi was genuinely concerned that I had lapsed into illness and he felt guilty that he wasn't around to see me to the hospital. We assured him it wasn't his fault at all. We held no grudge against *Molimi*. He was a respectable man, and had integrity. He did his job well, kept a distance from us as he had been told, but treated us with respect.

The following morning a cream-white ambulance bearing the distinct International Red Cross markings arrived complete with twinkling red siren lights on top. It was from Pietersburg Hospital. The two attending paramedics assisted us to loosen our belts and remove our shoes. Then we were given medication and told to lie down on fully equipped stretchers covered in fresh white sheets. I thought that the doctor had exaggerated our condition, but we were told he had instructed the staff that we were not well and to be picked up in the ordinary manner in which patients were collected.

And that's how we said goodbye to Chloe.

Even as the ambulance drove off and away, I knew that I would never come back to that place; and this was just before the end of 1969. My wishes had been granted, my prayers answered, we were not going to spend Christmas in Chloe!

I remember the dust rising behind us as we were driving back to the city where we had landed in July and to which we were now returning – Pietersburg.

To me that journey was a symbolic return to my family, where I came from. It was also a symbolic return to the road to our liberation. I felt as though chains had been taken off me and I was heading back to my freedom. For the first time since I had left Robben Island, I allowed real hope to come and stay in my heart.

When we arrived at the hospital we were seated on wheelchairs and wheeled to admissions, according to Dr Makunyane's instructions. He certainly was doing everything by the book! But the best was yet to come. We ended up in a private ambulatory ward, with two beds, just to ourselves. We were given brand new pyjamas, obviously taken out from some warehouse, and were provided with sandals and green gowns – as if we were being prepared for surgery.

Baker and I were lost for words. Dazed, we just obliged, followed the instructions of the pretty women in starched white dresses. That's all we could see. We had thought we'd seen pretty women at Nobel, but these were women in the city of Pietersburg. They came from all places. Some were trainees; others, staff nurses; and others still, auxiliary nurses – all dressed in pristine white dresses, performing their duties with military discipline, but all of them wore smiles. And they were smiling at us, were not clinically impersonal as the nurses I'd come across at Westlake Hospital.

I knew that we had arrived in paradise. I was grateful to God for creating the perfectly curved, beautiful, soft, kind, considerate species called Woman. That was the beginning of another journey.

The doctor arrived the following morning and subjected us to a rigorous battery of tests, including taking blood, urine samples, blood pressure, just about everything you can think of.

After a couple of days, we found out that this man was actually a political activist in his own right. Dr Makunyane had been a member of the ANC for many years and he couldn't be bothered in his own mind that we'd been incarcerated for PAC activities. All he wanted to hear was that we had been working for the liberation of our country. And he kept saying, later, as we got to know him. 'I want you to understand that I'm treating you as I would treat soldiers at war or, soldiers who'd returned from war.'

The red carpet that Dr Makunyane accorded us, the treatment and the comfort levels we found ourselves in, were beyond our dreams. He said, 'I'm going to keep you here for as long as I deem fit, whether it takes days, weeks, or months, but as long as I'm not satisfied that you have regained all of your health, I'm not letting you loose.'

Shocked by the fact that our families who had been expecting us on the 25th of July had no idea where we were, the good doctor contacted them on our behalf. That was the greatest gesture of humanness he could've extended to us. That act certainly went well beyond the call of duty.

For two months we were well-nourished, and had two warm baths a day. Our test results didn't show anything seriously negative. My chest X-ray results did, however, depict the devastation caused by the pulmonary TB bacteria to my left lung. For the time being, however, I had put all of that behind me as I relished the clean white sheets, the soft Edblo mattress and the guaranteed nourishing three meals per day.

In all the time we were at the hospital, we only received one Special Branch visit and there was no evidence that they lurked anywhere around either.

They seemed to have accepted what they realised they could not change. In Dr Makunyane they had met more than their match.

As things panned out, we spent Christmas 1969, in that hospital.

25

This could be a new beginning

Word spread quite quickly. In no time at all, Baker and I started receiving visitors from the greater Pietersburg area, people who had heard about the two ex-Robben Islanders, under restriction in the area and currently at Pietersburg Hospital.

Just outside of Pietersburg, there was a university that had been started a few years earlier for Africans – The University of the North, also known as Turfloop. Many of the students who were cutting their teeth in politics came to visit us at the hospital, and we made some very interesting friendships. They were keen to hear how the hundreds of prisoners we had left behind were coping. There was a huge amount of curiosity about Robben Island and some of its famous inmates, people such as Nelson Mandela, Robert Sobukwe and other political leaders who were still languishing in prison.

That's about the time we met Moon Masemola. *Bra* Moon was a couple of years older than us and he was to become a major pillar of support to us in the period shortly after our release from the hospital. He and his family lived just outside New Look Township between the old location of Seshego and the city of Pietersburg. Mrs Masemola lived in the mission house of Khaiso College, a reputable academic institution for African boys. Moon, or Gulch as we called him, was a father, a socialite, and a respected leader in the area; always willing to walk the extra mile to assist others.

At the beginning of 1970, we were discharged from the care of Dr Makunyane. We had gained considerable weight – our tight clothes told the story.

After our release from hospital, *Bra* Moon generously invited Baker and I to live with him while we were finding our feet. Like many others, he had great sympathy for us and our circumstances. Gulch never came across as a man with strong political views, but he was a decent human being. We accepted his offer. Taking our meagre belongings with us, we left the hospital and went to stay with this family. Baker and I looked very different from the people who had entered the hospital a few months earlier. Dr Makunyane had made sure that not only were we professionally taken care of, but that our physical and psychological health was monitored, and regularly reported to him. He also used his influence to ensure that we were not harassed by the police. Then we were left to slowly assimilate into general society. So much for the twenty-four months' banishment!

Upon our discharge, Dr Makunyane's home, in New Look, was also open to us. Though not ostentatious, his place was evidently the home of a man of standing in the community. It was made of face brick. The furnishings were tasteful, but not in any way extravagant. He was raising his own young children in that house, two of whom became very well known and befriended us in later years.

Seipati grew to follow in her father's footsteps, becoming a specialist physician while her brother, Thabo, was made Executive Mayor of Polokwane after the demise of apartheid. I have often shared with them how their father was helpful to me at a very difficult time in my life.

Moon Masemola knew and was friendly with the Makunyane family and lived very close to them.

He was a senior officer of the provincial government at the time. Mrs Masemola, a nursing sister, was a very loving woman who treated Baker and me as though we were part of her family, making sure that we were well taken care of. She cooked the most delicious meals for us and made sure that our clothes were washed and ironed. She did all that, always with a pleasant smile on her face. *Bra* Moon's family were an incredible support to us. I'm not sure how we would have coped had that family not volunteered to take us in. *Bra* Moon was also of great help in our reorientation to our new life, making sure that, gradually, we got to understand how things worked in these changed circumstances. There were many things we didn't quite understand. During our absence, the music had changed, so had the dance style, and the dress styles. On top of that, the tempo of urbanisation had increased very rapidly in that time.

Very quickly, Pietersburg became home to us. Masemola helped to induct us and introduced us to several community leaders who were quick to embrace us.

We were also assisted with work and soon procured jobs and the meagre income we earned was of great help in creating some sense of stability and independence. Slowly, we were rebuilding our lives.

Baker started sneaking home to Pretoria soon after our hospital discharge. After a few trips back and forth, he finally took the big leap and permanently disappeared from Pieterburg. I was more cautious, and it was months after he'd gone before I decided to visit home. I also decided to do so without obtaining permission from the District Magistrate as we were required to do. This was not a light move, but I had taken it after consultation with Moon and our confidants. I was, notwithstanding, somewhat nervous at this bold step but prepared myself for whatever consequences.

My biggest concern was my family, especially my younger siblings. I had not seen my brother at all since my release and Semakeleng only briefly and always in the company of others. These two had been constantly on my mind while I was in prison. I'd heard that both of them no longer lived with my father. Since *Ntate* had remarried, they had found the new home uncomfortable and left. That caused me great distress; I couldn't understand how they could be left to their own devices at that tender age, particularly my brother who was in his early teens.

Finally, I made the trip back to Bekkersdal. That was a journey that I had been looking forward to for a long time.

No one can predict the future but the evidence presented to me in the course of that visit was revealing. Immediately, I could see that in my nostalgic dreams on Robben Island, I had greatly idealised the township of Bekkersdal. The idea of Bekkersdal that had sustained me through the hard, arduous life in the island prison was not the reality that met my eye. Physically, Bekkersdal had not changed in any significant way except for a few rows of identical new houses. The roads remained unpaved, covered by the red soil that came from the deeply eroded land nearby, land gouged by the summer rains digging deep fissures, disfiguring it. No development had taken place. There were still no running toilets. *Samponkaans* still came whistling to collect the night soil buckets.

What is more, the happy bountiful energy that we had left behind in Bekkersdal seemed to have dissipated. The lack of access to opportunities – a lack suffered by the community I came from – was nearly complete and completely devastating. As I looked at the defeated shadows of the faces of those that I had left behind, they seemed to have aged ten to twenty years prematurely.

Evidence of that accelerated ageing could be seen all around: some had lost their teeth while others had gone prematurely grey. I could clearly see the tragic truth on people's faces, where nothing but absolute misery was stamped.

That horrific truth was stamped on their gaunt faces, faces devoid of hope, faces where lived eyes that reflected aborted dreams – eyes that said hope was not the only casualty there; life itself was tenuous. So many people had passed away. Only the witty and strong-willed could survive my hometown, Bekkersdal. It dawned on me then, looking at that devastation, that had I not been condemned to Robben Island, I may have ended as one of these statistics: the dead. Or, worse still, one of those living dead, living but destroyed forever. Those who could had moved somewhere else before they too became smothered by the gold dust of the mines. The sad truth is that the end of apartheid came too late for most black people, not only in Bekkersdal, but in most parts of our land.

That change, that downward spiral, had also scarred my home. My home was no more. The home I went to was not the home of my Robben Island dreams, not the home of my growing up, not the home from which I was arrested. No. I went to an unfamiliar home on Kgomo ya hlaba Street, because my home, the home of my dreams, had been taken over by other people after my arrest.

Weighty regret came over me at the realisation of what we had lost. I was filled with searing remorse for the unrealised hopes my father had for my future and for leaving my siblings alone and unprotected.

Disappointment had taken its toll on *Ntate* – physically and emotionally. According to my wishes, time should have stood still.

It was sobering to see that *Ntate* had also aged, and aged greatly – far beyond his years. His face gaunt, he seemed to have grown shorter. His hair had turned all grey and was not as immaculately groomed as I remembered. He no longer wore his spectacles which had given him an intellectual look. *Ntate* had lost the sparkle, the aura that he had commanded in the 1960s up until 1963, when I was arrested. However, the one thing that my father seemed to retain still, something he never lost, was the respect he commanded from the people around him. He was an impoverished gentleman. People still spoke of *Ntate* Magomola as that great man who knew how to rally and unite and pray for people with his oratorical gift.

And that pleased me immensely. It also gave me solace that he was still lucid; not all was lost, after all.

His smile of recognition had not changed at all, seeing me brought shining warmth and a startled pleasure to his face, an expression I remembered from the days when *Mme* was still alive. His pleasure eased my soul, a little.

Ntate, it seemed, had not been able to maintain that beautiful home of ours. My father had been psychologically crushed, he was never able to cope after my arrest, I was told. Leopard told me that *Ntate* lost his job soon after my incarceration. That must have been harsh on him; he was a proud man who stood erect. *Ntate* had lost his glamour and elegance, which remains immortalised in my parents' sepia wedding photograph.

In behaviour, he'd also changed and had become a man who was no longer the naturally restrained person he used to be. The pain of my loss had turned my father to drinking and, at times, heavily. Not the kind of drinking that got him to be reckless, but it just took a toll on his frame. He had lost his strength to keep our branch of St Johns alive.

He had become temperamental and abusive, according to reports. My sister told me after my release that we'd have to do something about my father because the circumstances with his new wife were far from pleasant.

Four of my fellow inmates had returned to Bekkersdal by then – Sam, Matthews, Moss and Shakes. Most people in the community were welcoming while to others, we were contaminated and they kept a healthy distance from us for fear of reprisals from the Security Branch. My primary objective was to find my brother and sister. Family members, neighbours and the people from the church assisted me in locating Fetsa and Semakeleng. Since my arrest they had been shuffled from place to place, depending on the generosity of people from our church and relatives. Though willing to accommodate the destitute, most people had to deal with their own destitute conditions and could ill afford extra mouths to feed.

Semakeleng had been forced to quit school prematurely because she couldn't afford the fees, uniforms and books. She was fortunate to be living with *Ousie*

Josephine then, a friend of the family who has since passed away. May God rest her soul.

My brother had stayed there briefly but being the man he was, he had moved on and sought accommodation elsewhere while they were waiting for me. When I found both of them, my two siblings, I felt a sense of major achievement. We hugged, laughed, cried and spent hours trying to catch up. This was the moment, I told myself; a moment of glory and triumph. Over six long years I had prayed to my Maker to protect and preserve me for this one moment, and it had come. After spending a couple of days with my family on the first visit since 1963, I knew that my world was coming together.

For a man of my reputation, finding reliable employment was almost like a pipe dream. During that time, I earned a meagre income from a clerical position at the local township manager's office.

I remember once I applied for an advertised grade two clerical position at Turfloop University. One of the academics, Professor Muxe Gessler Nkondo, who empathised with my situation later shared with me how the selection panel pondered over my resume. My CV could not fully account for the six year vacuum of my imprisonment. I covered this gap by stating that "peer pressure" had prevented me from taking up employment during that period. Very funny, they thought, but hey, how could I openly state my case to a state-sponsored institution and win?

I told my brother and sister that I would come back to fetch them since I had found a job and, a few days later, I returned to Pietersburg.

Through the intervention of a well-known businessman in Pietersburg, Mr Bomonyane 'Bom' Thema, I was allocated one of the newly constructed municipality houses in the new township of Seshego. It was a typical small four-roomed government house for which I paid nominal rent. I had nothing to my name. I would have slept on the floor were it not for the sparse furnishings that were provided by Bom and his family. They gave me a medium-sized bed, blankets and sheets plus the bare essentials, complemented by my addition of used oil drums, upturned and used as stools in the kitchen. Someone in the neighbourhood donated a rickety Ellis De Luxe coal stove that kept me warm in the winter. That's how I started my new life in Seshego.

Bra Moon continued to offer his unconditional assistance and friendship. Another philanthropic civic leader, Mr Jackie Tema, later joined in adding a wardrobe and a dressing table. By the time my siblings arrived, I had acquired imitation leather chairs and a coffee table in the lounge. Sadly, both Bom and Jackie have since passed on. May God bless their souls.

My stay in Pietersburg was, however, not going to be a long one. I was very fortunate to have been adopted by those three gentlemen. Moon Masemola and I started to get quite a number of visits from the students at Turfloop University and one, in particular, that I became close to was a guy called Bobo Kgware, a boisterous character, a very loving man, great fellow and good company. Bobo was the son of Professor William Kgware who was the Principal (the first black Principal) of Turfloop University. A strong adherent and loyalist of Steven Biko's philosophy of Black Consciousness (BC), he and I occasionally travelled together through Gauteng on his way to his parent's home, in Thaba Nchu, near Bloemfontein. Our last trip on the train to Johannesburg was very rowdy. Overnight in the train, we had both imbibed a bottle of brandy and we were as drunk as skunks. Sadly, that would be the last evening I'd spend with Bobo. After we arrived in Soweto, Bobo told me he would be visiting with his friends and would put up at Fancy Mosala's place.

Fancy was a successful businessman who owned a Volkswagen dealership in Soweto. I proceeded to visit my folks in Bekkersdal. A few days later, I read in the newspapers that Bobo had been killed after he had arrived at his home in the Free State. The circumstances were not quite clear.

Another person who consistently provided me with substantial material support, even after my wife and I were married, was my cousin Simon Magomola. Our paternal grandfathers were brothers. Simon, or Sy as we called him, just took on the duty of looking after me when I was released from prison. Between him and Leopard, they bore the burden of sustaining me. Sy would fill his Valiant with groceries and travel all the way to Pietersburg almost every month end. He and his family lived in Zone 9 Meadowlands, a resettlement of old Sophiatown in Soweto. He was a tall man with a Mohammed Ali build and enjoyed a good fight. Sy, belligerent in attitude, had a thunderous temper and would pick a fight at the drop of a hat. I was constantly trying to intercede between him and people with whom he had got into arguments. Because of his towering height and great strength, he won most of the fights.

Sy was also a compassionate and genial gentleman always ready to rally around the neighbourhood whenever required. With the passing of time, Sy's health weakened and all attempts to save him were unsuccessful. Finally, in 1989, he lost the battle to cancer.

I was later able to fetch my sister and brother from Bekkersdal and bring them to attend school in Pietersburg as I had promised. I was not earning a lot of money working for the municipality; it was barely sufficient to buy groceries, and to generally sustain us. Occasionally, we visited home to be with my father and my stepmother. Meanwhile, the security apparatus never let up; they kept watch from a distance; yet they never once entered my house to confront me on any issue.

I continued to make steady strides in Pietersburg. By that time I was formally dating Connie Ngomane, a staff nurse at Pietersburg hospital. I had met Connie during my days under the care of Dr Makunyane. We became very good friends and Connie occasionally came to the house to bring me medication, cook for me and wash my clothes. Over time, a strong relationship developed between us and both my brother and sister got to like her very much. In fact, it was almost a foregone conclusion that I was going to make Connie my life partner. I had also started studying for my Bachelor of Commerce degree through distance learning with the University of South Africa (Unisa) thanks to a bursary granted by the Institute of Race Relations.

Part 6
1970–1976

26

Unstoppable, a new man

Towards the end of 1970, I increased the frequency of my clandestine trips to the South. I had hatched a plan to return and my resolve to do so was unstoppable. After a series of meetings with the Pietersburg District Magistrate, I was finally granted a conditional permit to return home and this received a stamp of approval from the Security Police. With great relief, I began my move and aggressively applied for a real job in Johannesburg.

I went back and scrounged on Sy's place and his wife Paulina and the kids made sure that I lived comfortably while I was job hunting. I eventually accepted a position as a stores cadex clerk at an auto dealership in Germiston owned by the Ephron brothers, a well-known Jewish family in Johannesburg. While I enjoyed the assignment, I resented the harsh treatment the black employees of that firm received from some of the managers. Meanwhile, the job was paying me well and I had made good friends with young Phillip Ephron. The son of the eldest of the brothers, Phillip was a liberal chap who in his youth saw through the fallacy of racial domination. His liberated mind made it possible to later make friends and business partnerships across the racial divide of the country. His intervention gave me an opportunity to find my feet and take a new view on life.

Meanwhile, I kept the house in Seshego because the Polokwane authorities had made it very clear that, like all Black people, my sojourn to Johannesburg was temporary. I would have to return to my 'homeland' of Lebowa sometime in the future. At month ends, I travelled to Seshego to check on my siblings, and to give them money for miscellaneous expenses and groceries. By then, I had obtained temporary accommodation in Katlehong Township so as to be close to my place of employment.

By this time, my good friend Baker had moved to Attridgeville, near Pretoria and, occasionally, I would pay him a visit. On one of those late Sunday afternoons on my way back home, I waited at the Pretoria Station for the train heading for Johannesburg. From across the platform, I spotted a beautiful young woman standing by herself, clutching her handbag tightly. She had a flawless mocha, creamy complexion accentuated by two beauty spots on her left cheek and upper lip. My mind raced very quickly, I had to be very creative, so I walked towards where she stood on the platform. Little did I know that this was the beginning of a lifetime affair.

Soon the train arrived and both of us found seats in the same coach. I felt quite relieved I had bought an upper class ticket that day.

As fate would have it, I found a seat right across from the young lady and caught a whiff of the scent of her perfume. Her outfit was meticulously selected, complete with matching jacket and a well-tailored top, a dashing short skirt that reached to just above the knees. She wore white pantyhose.

Whenever I looked up at her (my mouth must have been agape), she would pull down her skirt so that it would cover her knees as far as that was possible. She never for one moment looked at me directly. Her hair was styled in big curls, just like the glamour girls on fashion magazines.

She seemed engrossed in her own business, though her eyes now and then darted curiously to the headlines of the newspaper I was reading. When she became conscious of the fact that I was targeting her, she seemed annoyed. I tried to be calm. I pretended to be absorbed in my *Sunday Times* but, occasionally, took furtive glances at her when I thought she was not watching. I was lost for words to approach her.

My only hope was that she would ask to borrow my newspaper; she looked like a woman who would be interested in current affairs. I flipped the paper, trying to wet her appetite but she continued to ignore me.

Notwithstanding my great interest, the evening before had taken its toll and I fell asleep. When I woke up, I asked her where we were. She told me we had just passed Germiston Station, where I was supposed to alight.

Eventually, I mustered the courage to ask this woman if she was comfortable; she gave me a splendid, slightly shy white teeth smile and said yes, she was comfortable. I introduced myself and asked her what her name was.

'Sophie,' she said. 'Sophie Mokwena,' she quietly muttered.

That was a good sign I thought to myself, that she had my own mother's name. 'What do you do for a living, Sophie?' I asked.

She confidently told me she was a domestic servant and worked for a family in Johannesburg, where she was headed.

I gave her another look but could not see a maid in her. After some hesitation I offered her the newspaper, which she gladly accepted. And I knew I had made my first move.

We only had ten minutes to Johannesburg Park station, the terminal point of the train. As we arrived in Johannesburg, she handed me back the newspaper and I asked, with hope, anticipation and some trepidation, if she would mind if I bought her a cup of coffee and a sandwich. I shook my head with disbelief when she accepted my invitation. Electrical jolts of pleasure threatened to stop my heart.

Sophie had just about the most incredible body and I estimated her age to be anything between twenty-one and twenty-three years, but I wouldn't dare ask her.

I noticed she didn't have a wedding ring except a nice dress ring on her right hand.

As we walked to the exit, I admired her dainty hand gestures; she was what I would call the classic, sophisticated lady. The one original I would have invented myself. I couldn't ask for more.

I could tell she was impressed by my invitation. In those days it was not common for young, African men to ask ladies out for coffee. We had not been socialised into cafes and restaurants. My cousin, Simon, was a senior clerk at the ticket sales office at Park Station and it was he who had introduced me to their beautiful private lounge, furnished with spotless deep sofas and tables covered with bright white tablecloths with green trimming, tables set with silver forks and knives.

My wife would later tell me that was what bowled her over; but charm helped as well. The food presentation was quite unbelievable. I was able to spot a table for two. I ordered two cups of coffee and sandwiches with ease, as if I had done that many times before.

For that moment I was a good-looking man of style. We continued to talk about a variety of other things. I became enthralled in our conversation; we went from one topic to another. It was a meeting of the minds. Sophie told me she was a voracious reader and I was impressed with the vast knowledge she exhibited. When she asked me what I did for a living, I hesitated for moment. Then, I said, 'You know Sophie, I'm actually between situations.'

She insisted, looking at me straight in the eye, 'What do you actually do Gaby?'

I bit my tongue slightly, stalling to find the right combination of words to sound knowledgeable and impressive. Suddenly, the words rolled out of my tongue, 'I'm a researcher for a research institution and a sisal plantation project.'

She nodded in approval, obviously intrigued, especially by my knowledge of space technology. I had taken quite an interest in the lunar mission and had read anything and everything on it to catch up. After that she didn't probe very much. She was contemplative; her sombre eyes kept studying me when she thought I wasn't looking. Occasionally she would give a demure enigmatic smile. She was not very obliging, though she was not exactly indifferent.

I wondered if she had seen through my whole façade.

On the way out, we passed Simon's ticket window. He was not only a relative but a good friend and confidant. I wasted no time introducing Sophie to my cousin Sy who seemed impressed by my new friend. Spontaneously, we held hands as we walked toward the taxis to transport her to her destination, which at that time I thought, but couldn't accept, was a suburb in Johannesburg.

I recall very well the bus station was at the Diagonal Jeppe Street corner. She walked towards this bus with quite a number of nurses in uniform. The bus sign read Baragwanath Hospital. I asked her again what she did for a living. And she gave me this long smile before telling me Sophie was not her real name.

She said her name was actually Nana-Girl Matlala and she was a student nurse at Baragwanath Hospital in Soweto. Once a month, they received a week-end off, and she had just been to visit her family in Atteridgeville.

It could not have been more opportune. I knew I had arrived at the right station, at the right time, and I didn't want to betray my excitement at the discovery. She told me she had never had an opportunity to talk to someone that she was meeting for the first time for such a long time.

I felt quite flattered. 'Well,' I said, 'We could do it again.' I gave her my telephone number, which she seemed happy to have and waved her goodbye as she got into her bus. I retraced my way back to Park Station, everything in the world forgotten. My steps were light, propelled by the diamonds in my shoes.

As things turned out I waited anxiously for the call for a few days, and around the third day I got the long-awaited call from Nana. She said she had arrived at the hospital safely. I promptly asked her whether we couldn't meet on her first Saturday off. Before she could say no, I invited her to meet me in Germiston. After a pause, in which I could imagine her frowning, she capitulated. After the call I began to sweat, because I had told her an outrageous lie that I was conducting research. I could tell she had assumed I was a university student.

And she had mentioned that she liked to go out with men who were educated and ambitious, certainly not with a warehouse attendant.

She was going to be a staff nurse and would not wash greasy overalls for the rest of her life. My resolve to better my situation grew even stronger.

I made sure that she arrived in Germiston after work and I met her at the station. We went over for light refreshments and that became the beginning of an eternal romance for me. During those days, Africans weren't allowed into restaurants; the Johannesburg station concession café was an exception.

For the most part, black people were only allowed to buy from a cafeteria through a dark side window and sit under a tree somewhere or on a bench marked 'Non-whites only' to enjoy the food.

Out of habit, I bought a half a loaf of bread and a packet of fish and chips. Suddenly ravenous from my jumping nerves, I asked her to join me. Her eyes dilated but she joined me only to drink from the curvaceous bottle of Coca-cola.

For me it was the normal thing to do, but I didn't realise I was being crude, exhibiting behaviour that was unbecoming of an intellectual researcher. Obviously, I had been removed from society for too long and my behaviour on the day betrayed me.

To place a woman, a young student nurse, on the pavement and ask her to join me in crushing half a loaf of bread with fish and chips was a most unsophisticated way of hosting and it nearly cost me what I had worked and hoped for, for weeks. To this day, my wife reminds me often enough about how I made her eat bread on the sidewalk of a busy road. She confessed later that she did find my professional deceit innocuous.

After some time, I got to meet her parents. They still lived in Pretoria and we would visit them from time to time during our courtship. As we became closer, I took Nana to meet my father and step-mother in Bekkersdal.

Ntate was just enthralled. He couldn't bring himself to call Nana by her African name. To him it was beneath a staff nurse to be called Nana, he insisted that she should be called Anna. I suppose many people of that generation were highly influenced by the persuasive colonial mentality and my father was no exception. Around Nana, my father was the gentleman of old, the man that I remembered.

He was courteous and pleasant to her and for the remaining days of his life, in his eyes, she could do no wrong. He would not even let me say anything that sounded like a reprimand against (or criticism of) her. Nana was the best for his son.

It came as no surprise to both sets of parents when we announced that we were planning to get married.

True indeed, on the 1st of November 1971, Nana and I walked into the Magistrate's court in Ga-Rankuwa, near Pretoria, and emerged as husband and wife. Nana wore a pink tailored dress and a coat, the fashion of the day. I wore a pinstriped banker's suit Simon had helped me select. We didn't have a traditional white wedding. However, we did have a celebration, hosted by Nana's maternal aunt, Ethel Selloane Leisa, in Soweto. Our joining was celebrated by Simon and his wife, Paulina, and my numerous cousins and friends. All of Nana's friends, fellow student nurses from Baragwanath, also attended.

It was Nana's final year at Baragwanath Hospital and she was starting a new life with a new husband.

In December, as soon as she had completed all the formalities of her qualifications, we went to Seshego in Pietersburg.

We spent Christmas night on the train to Pietersburg. In those days the journey took the whole night, we only arrived in Pietersburg at 10 am, and eventually in Seshego by midday. It wasn't an easy trip for Nana at all. The combination of the merciless dry heat and the pregnancy was uncomfortable for her.

My wife would be seeing my house for the first time. And, more importantly, would be meeting my brother and sister. Semakeleng is three years older than her, and my brother, far younger. My one apprehension was how they were going to react to my new love for they had become quite fond of my previous girlfriend, Connie. They didn't know that I had been seeing Nana while I was staying in Johannesburg.

As I expected, when we arrived at Seshego, my sister was taken aback. She wasn't welcoming, because her first choice of a sister-in-law was Connie. She was more mature than Nana and older. They could relate more to her as a sister-in-law as opposed to Nana, who was much younger. By then I had made up my mind that I had to extricate all of us from Pietersburg. The slower pace of life in Seshego had offered me the cushion to recover from prison and to reintegrate into society safely. But the time had now arrived for a new beginning and Pretoria was beckoning.

27

Picking up the pieces

Nana had a married sister, Doris, who was married to Job Mosieleng and lived in Ga-Rankuwa, near Pretoria. So she would partly stay with Doris and partly with me while we searched for our own home. Fortunately, that search for a house in Pretoria was quickly rewarded, thanks to the kindness of the Mabopane Township Manager of the time, Mr Phalatsi.

Mabopane, where we found our home, was a construct of the apartheid government, erecting new black cities for the so-called homelands, the Bantustans. Located some forty kilometres northwest of Pretoria, the township was designed to house most of the people who were being relocated out of Atteridgeville, which was seen as too close to the city.

It was relatively easy to find housing in Mabopane because the government of the day was encouraging black people to populate all those homes, which had been built by the state to promote its designs of racial separation. And the idea was to give credence to the concept that Africans were accepting having to move into their own homelands.

Mr Phalatsi, like most people that we met, listened attentively to my account of events since my release from Robben Island in 1969 and my banishment to Chloe.

Before I could even finish retelling the tale of our banishment, he stood up and said, 'I'm going to make sure that by the end of this very day, we have found you and your wife a place to live in this township!' After that he ordered us into his car.

We drove around Mabopane, viewing several empty homes in the newly-constructed township. Finally, we found a house on a large plot of some 1 500 square metres which he had reserved for a municipality official.

He asked us if we were interested, and recommended that we should take it because there weren't that many houses on stands that size.

With alacrity, we accepted the offer. Our own home! Very pregnant Nana and I could barely contain ourselves. Our baby would have a home of his very own! Of course, the house would be rented from the municipality; it was not a freehold title. All the houses were identical; that was the pattern of old South Africa. The unpaved gravel streets had no names either.

In 1972, it was very difficult for black people to find housing. Newly-wed couples would either stay with their parents or, at best, they would rent what we used to call two rooms and a garage, additions erected by home owners for extra income. Others went so far as to divide the garage into two, one side for sleeping and the other used as kitchen and living area. It was virtually unheard of for black people to rent living quarters of their own. The law didn't allow Africans to own immovable property.

The working conditions ensured they couldn't even were the law in favour of such frivolity. Inadequate town planning meant there were long waiting lists for the township houses we were allowed to rent and priority was given to large families. Don't ask me where those people were supposed to live, start and enlarge that family before they would be considered for a council rental!

We felt immensely fortunate. For us to have all four rooms and a whole big yard to ourselves was magic.

There were two bedrooms, a lounge and a kitchen and a small bathing area of one and half by two square metres, with no bathtub or sink, just a toilet seat with the expectation that the person leasing the house would improve it with a tub and add amenities such as a geyser for hot water.

While waiting for the essential improvements, we had to make do with a primitive sheet metal basin that was large enough to stand in while bathing. First of all, we had to boil the water in a kettle on a coal stove, pour the hot water into the basin and mix it with cold water. Then we squatted down into an uncomfortable position to wash our faces. Thereafter we soaped the body and rinsed it by standing, both legs in the basin, and running the washing cloth down the body or, alternatively, squatting down to have a bath by splashing the water all over the body. Needless to say, the latter could be quite messy even to the initiated.

It was common that in most African homesteads there were no separate bath areas; people had to wash in the bedroom with no privacy unless you took turns. This is still common practice in many homes although improvements are being rolled out as part of the democratic government's reconstruction and development programme.

To establish ourselves and to keep up with our new-found prosperity, we bought some furniture. Nana worked as a nurse at the Atteridgeville Hospital, forty-five kilometres from Mabopane. She had to commute back and forth on a daily basis. It was not easy for her because she had to work shifts, and the morning shift was the most difficult as it started at 7 am which meant that she had to leave the house at 5 am to catch the bus that would get her there on time.

Before we were even settled, it was time for the arrival of our first baby. Our son, Thabo, was born in March 1972.

I worked as a trainee accountant in nearby Rosslyn, for a company owned by the Raimondo family and I had just started my second year of university study, by correspondence, so the job was interesting and in line with what I was studying. Later, Nana secured employment at a nearby hospital and things were looking up for us although the living conditions were far from luxurious.

I dedicated myself to my studies, driven to obtain respectable results and complete my degree on time. Mabopane was not exactly a shining example for drawing inspiration from and the reasons are found elsewhere in this narrative.

I, however, found myself in the company of several other neighbours, friends and work colleagues who were equally driven and shared some of my own frustrations. A few of these stand out and these include my dear friend, the departed Oscar Motsepe who was a senior lecturer at one of the country's top universities. His wife and partner Mosima Ellen was helping raise their girls in nearby Ga-Rankuwa but unlike me, Oscar had the advantage of stature in the community and was possessed of an engaging personality. Through his ingenuity, he networked me into some of the more influential Pretoria groups and I got acquainted with people such as the uniquely gifted entrepreneur Walter Dube, Dr Banzi Nkomo and others. As fate would have it, Oscar later attended Purdue in Indiana just a few miles from Ball State University where I had graduated a few years earlier.

I had an eight-to-four job, like everybody else. I'd arrive home at 6 or 7 pm and when it was time for Nana to prepare for bed at 9 pm, I would sit in the lounge and take my Unisa guide books and read until about midnight and only then go to sleep. Next morning, I'd wake up early to go to work. Often, I would have to do this by candle light as power was most unreliable.

Even on weekends, when we had guests as it often happened, I would follow that routine. Or I would wake up at 3 am and study, a blanket over my shoulders to keep warm; the homes were poorly constructed and not energy-efficient. When Nana woke up I would make coffee for her. If she woke up before me, she would make some for me. Thereafter, we would get up and wash, getting ready for work.

A year later, I purchased our first car for R200. It was a little white Ford Cortina that filled me with pride and a huge sense of achievement. I could fetch Nana from the hospital in the afternoons; she didn't have to face public transportation after a gruelling day. She still had to take the bus in the mornings though, but this was a great improvement.

Nana had always wanted a daughter. When we had Thabo, she often commented that he was my child. When we found she was pregnant again, Nana was very excited, and hoped and prayed it was a girl. She would go into long spells of imagination on how she would dress her girl in beautiful colourful clothes and how she would create hairstyles. Her prayers must have reached the right audience for we were, indeed, blessed by the birth of our daughter, Dineo-Amara on 15 February

1974 at Kalafong Hospital, near Pretoria. The baby had her mother's looks with my mother's cheekbones and tapered face and chin. When I came to visit them for the first time, the nurses were excited because they had known my wife's wishes. Nana could not wait to take her baby girl home.

I marvelled at how maternal Nana had become. From the sexy girl on the train, in just three years, she had become an extraordinarily mature woman with a great womanly body, who talked about her children as if she had always had them.

That was the beginning of our new lives: the Magomolas, raising Magomola children. Robben Island was receding into the background as I continued to pick up the pieces.

We developed a circle of friends, young couples who, like us, were starting life and curious and trying to make the most of our lives in the township. With them we embraced our new life as husband and wife with abundance. In the process we discovered the simple pleasures of life and the proprieties of society. With laughter and new experiences, I found life warm and comfortable – for the first time since my teenage years – so rudely interrupted. We were encouraged by the beautiful generous souls we found ourselves surrounded by, interesting family and friends who, for the most part, have remained in our lives.

One of the things that I had not lost sight of even as I was going through this exciting stage of my life was the fact that I had left some good friends back on Robben Island. I had made a commitment, as we often did when we were released, that I would keep contact with those I had left behind. One of my very good friends, someone with whom I had developed a strong relationship, was a young guy from Nana's township, Atteridgeville. That was Dikgang Moseneke, whom I fondly call Dick. Dikgang worked in the library on Robben Island and once, he brought me a copy of Karl Marx's *Das Kapital*. For some inexplicable reason, the authorities allowed that in our library. With the help of Klaas Mashishi, another intellectual from Pretoria who had majored in English at Fort Hare University, I could understand some parts.

Over the years on Robben Island, Dick and I developed a close friendship, and one of the things he said to me just before we parted was, 'You know Gaby, I'm gonna ask you a favour when you go back home. We've shared lots of moments here. After your release, I'd like you to find me a female friend with whom I could keep contact until I am released.'

Dick was serving ten years. His request could have sounded flippant, were it not for the seriousness of the circumstances. I understood very well how important it was on Robben Island to receive letters from people outside and since we had been upgraded from level D to level B and some to A, we were entitled to write and receive an unlimited number of letters.

A year or so after we had settled in Mabopane, Dick happened to be reading *Drum* magazine in his prison cell when he spotted a feature and the photograph of a young woman from his hometown, Atteridgeville. The Robben Island prison regulations had been amended to allow for 'non-political' feature magazines to be made available to inmates. He promptly sent me on assignment to track down the lady. As fate would have it, this was someone I knew well as a friend of my wife's. In fact, this lady was one of Nana's nursing colleagues who had attended our wedding function.

I faithfully passed on her address to my friend who wasted no time in contacting her. They finally connected and their friendship grew into courtship after Dick's release, four years later. One of the greatest joys of my life was to have Nana and I attend and celebrate their wedding, shortly after my graduation from the University of South Africa. Dikgang is now Deputy Chief Justice of South Africa.

Very recently when Dick or more formally, Judge Dikgang Moseneke, was installed as Chancellor of the University of Witwatersrand, he quipped about his time on the infamous island and how he and Khabo met. Nana and I in the audience could not help chuckling.

28

Searching for a career

Mabopane was where we brought up our children in the early 1970s. Despite the thriving community of a good mix of young progressive professional Africans – nurses, teachers, doctors and lawyers, a sense of deprivation still prevailed, further aggravated by the clear and visible contrast between black and white life and living. A low-level white worker, say a railway policeman or a foreman in a factory or at the offices of the municipality, would live closer to the city in a house three times that of mine. He would own property twice what I rented and could only rent but not own, all the roads around him tarred, the amenities supported, a city hall, clinic and first-world schools at his disposal. At the end of the year, he could afford to drive to the coast in his own car with a caravan (which were popular in the seventies) trailing behind. We had none of that, and I had almost completed a university degree.

Day in and day out, on our way to and from the city where we worked, going by bus or taxi or whatever other transportation was available, we would cross and recross the white suburbs, the glaring disparities inescapably in our faces. Apartheid ruled that whites should enjoy superior privileges just because of the colour of their skin.

In 1973, I left the family-owned paper and pulp company in Pretoria and joined one of the larger firms, the Swiss-owned Ciba Geigy in Spartan, just outside Johannesburg, again as an accounting clerk. But this time, I reported to the Chief Accountant, Mr Bassi. That was, by the days' standards, a very prestigious opportunity. The Swiss were trying hard to crack the delibitating job reservation restriction and I was the first black professional at this firm to be brought into the corporate head office among a sea of white faces. It became obvious that this was a delicate experiment and I felt like the proverbial guinea pig. However, I was cautiously well-received by the majority of the people there. It was quite intriguing that while we had that comradeship and professional fraternity on the job, come lunch-time, I would have to walk to the inferior lounge facilities designated for African employees who were, for the most part, lowly unskilled workers. I shared this dilemma with two other colleagues, Moses Simelane, the Personnel Officer as they were called those days and his deputy, both of whom were responsible for human resource development for African employees. Like me, they were professional and were subjected to the odd embarrassment of being herded into the blacks only cafeteria at lunchtimes and during tea breaks. The travel to and from work took its toll on us. All of the senior African employees lived in the so-called black townships outside of Pretoria.

Simelane lived in Mamelodi, about twenty kilometres out of the city while my Mabopane home was located some thirty-five kilometres north of Pretoria. My combined daily commute amounted to four hours; two each way. A notorious piece of legislation known as the Influx Control Act prevented us from residing anywhere near our place of employment.

I often wondered how all this went down with those who were trying to effect social transformation. However, despite such hiccups, the results of attempts such as these of the Swiss firm and others like it, attempts to react to their conscience and make a small contribution at breaking the walls of apartheid, should not be underestimated. I used the opportunity at Ciba Geigy to destroy the myth of black inferiority by excelling professionally and engaging the minds of those who were cocooned behind the walls of apartheid. This, I believe, is a yardstick by which we should measure ourselves as to whether we are good for the task at hand.

Today, I am generally impressed by the young professionals from disadvantaged backgrounds who occupy positions of trust in the private sector. I often wonder how much they understand the collective responsibility they have to push themselves harder to make it easier for those left outside the door.

Later, another black accountant was employed alongside me and slowly, the impact was felt. I always understood that these were small steps but, in the larger social context, huge milestones.

My Swiss colleagues attended my graduation ceremony which was held in a dilapidated community hall at Ga-Rankuwa outside Pretoria in April 1975. They had to obtain a special permit, like all whites, to enter a blacks only designated area. By decree, the University could not have its graduation ceremony for all students at the same venue. Whites held their grand march at the University's beautifully landscaped grounds in Pretoria with all the essential amenities while African graduates had to make do with what confronted us on the day. Mind you, black students and white students shared the same professors and paid equal fees. Many of our fellow white students were acutely frustrated by the treatment we received. Apartheid rendered things senseless. We took all of this in our stride and kept the bigger picture in mind. It was important, I thought, to focus on my desired achievements; thus far, I had not let adversity deflect my attention from my long term objectives.

Ntate had come from Bekkersdal for the graduation ceremony to join our celebrations. Nana was dressed in a turquoise caftan with a long skirt decorated in green velvet patterns. She was gorgeous. My two children, Thabo and Dineo (whom we affectionately called Amara) were in their Sunday best.

My uncle, John Modisane, and my aunt Mannini, my cousin Simon and his family, as well as Leopard Mosito, joined other family members and friends to witness an event that had never before happened in our entire extended family.

The graduation ceremony was held inside a small dingy hall. Because of the size, each of the graduates was restricted to only three or four tickets for guests who could enter the hall. At that glorious moment, only my wife and two other people were allowed in to watch me receive the laurels, a mark of an achievement that would create an enormous platform from which I would henceforth operate. The rest of our guests anxiously waited outside exposed to the chilly dusty wind. There were no television wide-screens for the people to savour the moment with us. After the ceremony, we marched outside to receive good wishes and congratulations from all of the well-wishers.

This difference in the graduation ceremonies of black and white Unisa students was symptomatic of our society and it reminded me, as though I could ever forget, of how precisely my life was prescribed, proscribed, and in every-which-way curtailed by the government.

Another constant irritant in black life was housing. It fuelled the anger in me that even though I had served my time on Robben Island and in Chloe, trying to better the situation, still, the absolute best I could ever get was Mabopane. Resplendent besides Venterspost and Bekkersdal, where I had started off; slightly loftier than Seshego, where I had stayed for a short while; and downright opulent compared to the Chloe sisal plantation – it just didn't reach the standard I was aspiring for.

It was not what I had gone to Robben Island fighting for. It definitely was not worth the pain.

I had gone to fight for the ability to select where I wanted to live, the freedom to take my children to a hospital where they would get the best treatment, and the ability to select the best schools for them. The conditions under which we, black people, lived – were forced to live under even in the seventies – were despicable and I decided I wasn't going to subject my children to that. We would have to leave the country, and a scholarship was the only feasible way for us to achieve that. I decided I'd apply for one.

Another reason why I decided to apply for a scholarship to leave South Africa was that I was forever hitting my head against the wall when looking for professional growth. The anger was building up inside me and was reaching explosion point.

Many people were leaving the country to join the liberation movements, via Botswana and Lesotho. I did not contemplate such a move; I had a new family and couldn't see myself leaving them behind. And I wanted to further my studies.

At the end of 1974, barely five years after leaving Robben Island, I completed my B Comm degree, which I had pursued part-time over the years. I had married, had two children, had a little place I could call home, and I had a job and a car. I could hold and keep my head high.

When my father passed away, in July 1975, many of our friends humbled me by sharing our sorrow and coming to Bekkersdal to help me bury *Ntate*. I was fortunate that my father had witnessed my graduation from university, barely three months earlier. But by then, *Ntate* was just a shadow of the great man I knew when I was growing up. He wasn't having a good marriage and I believe my father was neglected. He seemed to have lost his spirit.

To me, however, he was still the father that I adored and my heart ached for there was something about him that just wasn't right. What I didn't know, and discovered much later, was that my father had liver cancer. He was only in his middle fifties. A family friend and member of St Johns Church from Bekkersdal, Sister Gladys, came to Mabopane to alert Nana and me about *Ntate*'s health and insisted that we fetch him from Bekkersdal. She was concerned about his state. We went to Bekkersdal and had to overrule our stepmother's wishes to take him to Baragwanath Hospital in Soweto. Instead, we had him admitted at Ga-Rankuwa Hospital, where he peacefully passed on.

Ntate was buried in Bekkersdal, close to my mother, Matlakala. Yes, at the same cemetery where, eons ago it seemed now, we had held our clandestine meetings to overthrow the government. I wore my black university gown as a tribute to the man who had charted the way for me.

People spoke well of him and I learned then that there is no greater pride than the knowledge that your parents – the people you looked up to – are also respected by people in the midst of whom they live.

Ntate's death marked the end of an era for me. May the good Lord forever bless his soul! I'm consoled that he died before I left for the USA and have often wondered what would have happened had he died while I was away. Not only would it have been financially difficult for me to return, but I might not have been allowed to go back to America by the Security Branch. It is strange how everything does work out for the best outcome, although this is not always easy to grasp at the moment, especially when high emotions are involved.

Then, one day, I saw an advertisement for scholarships to study in the United States. I gathered and filled out the necessary forms and motivated my application by stating that my long-term objective was to become a competent business person, with a career starting off in accounting. In this process I was greatly assisted by Fundi Denelane, a charming lady with whom we had an excellent relationship. Fundi worked at the US Embassy in Pretoria and is a lifelong friend to Nana and me. The application was a wild shot. I have always placed very high goals for myself and that was one of the highest goals I had ever set.

My ambition to become a successful chartered accountant in South Africa was totally frustrated because of apartheid laws that reserved certain jobs for a particular racial group. I had knocked on the doors of the top six accounting firms and, sadly, each one of those firms turned my application down. Without spelling it out, the implication was that the web of related legislation made hiring me simply impossible. But the world offers life choices and it is often so much more difficult to discern and grab such options if blinded with anger. It becomes much less easy when you are younger because of the distractions around you.

Now that I fully understood this, it became clear that my aspiration to become the first black chartered accountant in South Africa would not be accomplished. I was compelled to look for alternatives but, within the context of life then, these were not in abundance. I have always thrived on treading new ground and took this on as a challenge.

Most of the black professionals at the time worked in the teaching and nursing fraternities and fewer still were doctors, engineers or attorneys. That was not what I aspired to.

I was single-minded about what I wanted and got to appreciate that my entire career objectives were thwarted. For the time being, I was fooled into believing that I had reached the end of the road.

However, two months after I had sent off the application forms for the American scholarship, I was called to the Embassy and told that out of hundreds of applicants, I was one of ten successful candidates.

The news numbed me. It was something I was not quite prepared for, and it ushered in a new reality in my thinking. To have been selected as a recipient of the prestigious Fulbright Scholarship evoked a deeper understanding of an inner strength, of my inherent and untapped capabilities. It reminded me of what I had known from the time I started school. I was sharply reminded that it was not an accident that I had always topped my class. This new achievement drove me to dig deeper inside me for hidden talents and to use that as my defensive armour in future battles. This is the selfsame armour I have carried with me into my adult life and it has helped me scale the most daunting heights.

The Fulbright Scholarship is the US government's flagship programme in international educational exchange. It was proposed to the US Congress in 1945 by the then freshman, Senator J. William Fulbright of Arkansas. The programme's purpose is, 'to promote mutual understanding between the people of the United States and the people of the countries of the world'. It was unimaginable for me, coming from where I came from, the depths of hell itself, to be declared a Fulbright grantee.

That night, I broke the news to my wife. Nana stared at me with disbelief in her eyes and asked me to repeat what I had just told her.

While it seemed a distant dream to her, this was not the case with me. I had dreamed, planned, organised our exit and, as a result, I was ready.

A letter from the US Cultural Attaché, Merryll Miller, followed soon after the interview. But the spadework was just about to begin; and problems loomed large. The big imponderables were firstly, whether I, a former Robben Island prisoner, would obtain a passport; secondly, whether the Special Branch would stand by and watch me slip out of their clutches and, thirdly, (and that was a big one), how would I finance my family's travel to (and maintenance in) the States? But the warrior in me said it didn't matter what it took, I would do it. I was going to the United States and, by hook or by crook, I was taking my family with me.

The passport application was facilitated for me at the US Embassy in Pretoria by a person whose diligence and passion is legendary among those South Africans who have had the good fortune to interact with her. Gill Jacot Guillarmod was a programme officer at the Embassy and had learnt all the tricks in procuring travel documents for difficult cases such as mine.

First of all, she gave me the counselling which I required, and got Nana and me to understand that they would stand by my family after I had left.

When my passport arrived, Gill offered to keep it at the US Embassy. A visa was procured on time and the date of departure set. Despite the uncertainty, I stayed calm and looked forward to the big day.

D1(a): A youthful Nana shortly before our marriage

D1(b): My parents-in-law, Asaph and Machipu Matlala outside our Mabopane home, 1972

D2: Our wedding day, accepting congratulations from the presiding Officer, Soweto, November 1971

D3: (above) Toasting the marriage with my cousin Sy Magomola on Nana's right and Matsatsi, Nana's cousin

D4: (right) My sister-in-law, Doris Mosieleng in a warm pose, 1987

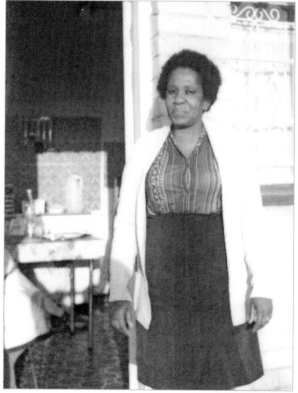

D5: (left) An elated Gaby with Nana holding newborn baby, Dineo-Amara, at my Unisa graduation day, April 1975

D6: (below) Family and friends came to wish me well after my Unisa graduation, 1975. Many were seeing me for the first time since my arrest in 1963. The tall heads at the back are that of my cousin Simon and Leopard Mosito, who was later killed by the apartheid police in 1989

D7: Standing outside our first 'matchbox' house in Mabopane, Pretoria, 1974

D8: Nana posing in front of our car, Mabopane, 1974

D9: My son Thabo enjoying his traditional wedding with his bride, Mosima, in the midst of family and friends, 2002

D10: (left) Gaby and Nana's daughters Naledi and Dineo at home

D11: (below) Our first family visit to Robben Island in 1995

D12: My granddaughters, Boitumelo and Botshelo, posing with their parents

D13: Moon Masemola, facing camera. He adopted me after the apartheid government 'banished' me to Polokwane shortly after my release from Robben Island

D14: My childhood friend Joe Seremane to whom I was manacled en route Robben Island. Esther, his late wife, next to him

Part 7

1976–1982

29

You're a free man, Gaby

The mid-seventies were a period of youth awakening and rebellion in South Africa. In the absence of lawful political activity as a result of the banning of the two principal liberation movements, the ANC and the PAC, the Black Consciousness Movement grew rapidly to fill that void. We all felt the tensions accelerating, particularly among those of us who had been on Robben Island. Yes, we were not as active in politics as we had been in the 1960s; however, it was impossible to live in a place like Mabopane, Ga-Rankuwa, or anywhere in the country if you were black, and not feel deprived. Correspondingly, the authorities were becoming nervous and more vicious by the day.

By sheer good fortune, I was to meet the man, Steven Bantu Biko, who had become a political thorn in the flesh of the apartheid regime. Since 1969, while I was in exile in Pietersburg, I'd heard about the eloquent, intelligent and humble man from people like Bobo Kgware, an extremely active, anti-order, anti-establishment, rebel himself.

I was introduced to Steve Biko by Reverend Maurice Ngakane, a Pastor of one of the churches in Mabopane. Maurice had warned me two days before that Steve Biko would be visiting and invited me to lunch with them.

Steve was a big man with an imposing presence. We spent the afternoon together and I told him that I was going to America and he congratulated me on that achievement.

Two years later, to my horror, I learned that Steve Biko had been brutally murdered by the dreaded Security Branch. We held a memorial service for him, in New York, which was attended by many South Africans living in exile, including Steve's old friend, Donald Wood, who had travelled from London, for the occasion.

On the 16th of June 1976, what began as a mass protest march by students in Soweto against the use of Afrikaans as the medium of instruction exploded from the accumulated outrage into burning of government buildings and trains in Soweto.

The police response was reminiscent of that of 1960, in Sharpeville. They fired teargas at the protestors who responded by stoning back. The police then opened with live ammunition that resulted in the deaths of hundreds of school children. The well-documented Soweto uprisings raised tensions to levels never experienced before in modern times in South Africa. During this period, my wife worked in the operating room of Ga-Rankuwa Hospital. Almost daily, she would return home in tears, and would relate stories of children they had admitted to hospital with torn off flesh, their young bodies riddled with police bullets. The injured would come from the casualty department straight into the operating room. The working conditions at the hospital were becoming unbearably heavy and so was the tension, Nana would tell me. These developments were throwing my imminent departure plans into total confusion: the date had been set and classes would be starting soon.

According to our plans, my family would follow me soon after we had sold all of our assets, hopefully raising enough money for the airfare. This would be a task facing Nana without my assistance and I wasn't sure if she would cope. I enlisted the help of family and friends and in the end, felt assured that they would succeed.

But more importantly, my faith in Nana and her abilities was unshakeable; and my siblings had grown into their jobs and had moved on in life.

Finally, the day of my departure dawned and found me mentally well-prepared. Nana, the children, friends and relatives arrived ahead of me at Jan Smuts (now OR Tambo) Airport and anxiously waited and prayed for a smooth departure. Perhaps my family and I had not felt the looming presence of the Special Branch as heavily as we did that day.

The plan was that I would arrive at the airport shortly before the plane took off in order to evade the Security Police. I didn't have my passport on me, our friend and facilitator at the US Embassy, Gill Jacot Guillarmod, still had it in her possession.

There was a strong feeling that the security police were around there somewhere just waiting to pounce on me as soon as I arrived. All over the country, the Security Police were pouncing on people, particularly former Robben Islanders who were wrongly accused of having created the tension that led to the Soweto uprising of 1976. Many I knew personally had been detained and, quite a few, re-detained. But I had to gamble to end up in that Pan American jumbo.

A few minutes before the gates closed, I was whisked in by friends, checked my baggage and Gill handed me my passport to have it examined for clearance visas. Once that was done, I turned to my family and after emotional kisses and hugs, disappeared behind the turnstiles. Fortunately, most people on the flight had already gone through the check-in point. I went through the glass doors into the customs passports control area with no hurdles. In thirty minutes, my check-in was complete. I could still see my folks from a distance as they waved and I responded by waving my white handkerchief back at them.

I waited anxiously for take-off inside the enormous Pan American Boeing 747. It had not even occurred to me that I had not been in such a big aircraft before.

All I knew was that I was in safe territory. My heart continued to beat like a drum even as I met the six other Fulbright Scholarship winners on board. We all shook hands and embraced like old friends.

However, my heart was not really in that aircraft. To tell the truth, I was oblivious to my surroundings, thinking about my family, my loved ones whom I had left behind in the most unceremonious way. I felt like I had been booted out of my own country, wandering into alien space. I sat in that aircraft and swore silently at the police, at the government, at the entire system of apartheid. Before long we were given clearance and the aircraft taxied away. But still, I felt vulnerable and could not wait for the plane to actually pull away. The South African authorities were a law unto themselves. They were known to go to extremes to prove a point. It wouldn't have surprised me at all if the Security Police had actually followed me into the aircraft, ready to pounce on me and yank me right out of that plane.

Suddenly, I thought about Monty Seremane, Sam Thabapelo, Benny Ntoele, Mark Shinners and Eret Radebe, who had all been re-detained for questioning. It was an eerie repeat of the period of nasty surprises of 1963. Then, I thought about Baker and wondered if he had also been nabbed. I also thought about my extended family and friends in Bekkersdal-Randfontein, people I would probably never see ever again. I couldn't help but feel deep regret and some guilt for being in the momentary secure safety net, due to Nana's generous spirit and the support and assistance of those around me.

Then the plane took off.

As we soared into the clouds, I was suddenly filled with a sense of adventure.

But at the same time, I also felt that I had a duty to ensure that those I had left behind would in the future benefit from any contribution I could make.

It was the 21st of August 1976 when we took off from Jan Smuts Airport, now renamed OR Tambo, heading for the USA via Rio de Janeiro. The news of our beloved country sent us off with heavy hearts. We read the headlines in the various newspapers: 'More children arrested!' we read in the *Star*, while the *Rand Daily Mail* announced 'More are dying at the hands of the police'. A visibly emotional passenger handed out badges to mark the massacre of the children in Soweto. We pinned those badges on our lapels to pay tribute to those brave children who wanted to liberate us only armed with rocks and rubbish bin lids for protection. I didn't feel the journey at all but slept through the whole ten hours. I was too tired, too emotionally drained to do any otherwise.

I woke up when we arrived in Rio. It's not only the beauty of Rio and the sandy beaches of that city including the Copa Cabana which struck me. Nor was it the Sugar Loaf Mountain, which was awe inspiring on its own. What did was the novel experience of seeing people of various colours and hues mixing freely on park benches, restaurants and public places. And, of course, I was thrilled to be stepping on the same ground as the greatest soccer player of our time, Pelé.

For the first time, I experienced the depth of the subjugation of the human mind and how it manifests itself at times. My short stopover in Rio opened my mind to the damage apartheid had caused to my psyche. While physically miles away from home, I still felt a measure of vulnerability.

I had not been to a beach before in my entire life. And there I was walking on a world-renowned beach, Copa Cabana, with my new friends. For one moment they left me alone with hundreds of foreigners, all of them speaking a language I couldn't comprehend, and all people of mixed hues.

I just sat and watched in awe as a new world unfolded right before my eyes. But I still felt a sense of discomfort even in that freedom. I was in a world away from the Special Branch, away from apartheid, away from artificial restrictions; but my mind remained under arrest. Years of indoctrination and oppression cannot be easily cast aside like a pair of old slippers. I just kept walking, I couldn't find a place to sit down and relax. My knowledge of Portuguese was limited to a few swear words I had learnt back home. People lounged under the shade, relaxed and sipping their tequilas and mixed cocktails. I must have walked two to three miles when it occurred to me that I was unconsciously looking for a 'black's only' spot on the beach. Suddenly I snapped up as it occurred to me then that, 'Hey, you're in a foreign country and, by the way, you're in a free land. You can sit wherever and do whatever you please.'

And when the strangeness of the thought struck me, I felt a yoke slide off my shoulders. 'You're a free man, Gaby,' I exulted. For the first time in my life, I inhaled the whiff of freedom all around me. What a shame that I had to be in a foreign land to feel like a member of the greater human race. People here were laughing, talking, walking around and shouting and their smiles and greetings encompassed even me in that festive spirit. I sat among them, a feeling of exhilaration spreading through me. At that moment, I began to celebrate my own freedom albeit solitarily. After that initial celebration, I walked with my head truly held up high.

30

Midwest, USA

En route to the Midwest from Rio de Janeiro, we flew through New York City. I had the exciting experience of being whisked by helicopter from John F. Kennedy to La Guardia Airport for the connecting flight to Cincinnati. With a whole day to wait, I decided to explore New York. In my dreams I had identified the Statue of Liberty, Harlem and the United Nations building as the priority places of interest. When I saw the massive transit system, I thought I would struggle to find my way back from the Statue of Liberty, which was on the other end of the island of Manhattan.

The heat was unbelievable, suffocating; but my curiosity overcame my reluctance and I ventured forth despite it. Without much difficulty, I got to the Upper Westside, on 125th Street, Harlem. As youngsters, we knew that Harlem was where 'Negroes' lived – confident, fast-talking, well-dressed, sophisticated, and light skinned with naturally long soft hair, talented black people we wished we were. However, on the real streets of Harlem, I saw many faces that resembled black faces at home. In the olden days, where we grew up we used to see 'All negro cast' films such as 'Stormy weather', starring Lena Horne. I felt as if I was cast into one of those old movies of the sixties – just being there, walking on the sidewalk of 125th Street.

For a long time, I just stood, there watching all the black men and women; some of whom looked like what we called coloureds back home. How they interacted, and for the most part not understanding properly the way they spoke, was a very interesting phenomenon.

Their language sounded like music but I had difficulty understanding their accents. They stepped in rhythm. All types of musical melodies – gospel, jazz and rhythm and blues blasted out of apartment windows and store fronts onto the street. A man blew a trumpet on the street accompanied by a saxophonist. It was truly surreal.

I had read much about Harlem and had formed my own mental images and had always thought that Harlem would resemble Sophiatown or townships like Lady

Selbourne, outside Pretoria. The Harlem I saw was a different sight. I was able to quickly locate the famous Apollo Theatre, and was disappointed that it did not look well cared for. Still I was thrilled and I couldn't wait to write home about my adventure.

Directed by friendly street vendors who seemed enthralled to meet a 'brother' from South Africa, I then took a bus to midtown Manhattan. Within an hour, I was in the United Nations building, barely able to suppress my excitement. I had read enough to know that a number of African states had become members of the UN. It was in these chambers, I reflected, where Prime Minister Kwame Nkrumah, the Osagyefo, strode with pride in his native Ghanaian kente robes.

As South Africa continued to be a political hotbed, it continued to occupy the minds of the General Assembly of the UN. In my naivety, I had thought that just walking around the buildings I would see some of the well-known political figures and observe the Security Council in session. I hoped I would have an opportunity to voice a first-hand account of my experiences as I had just come out of South Africa (not to mention that the Soweto uprisings were still continuing).

Disappointed, I spent quite some time in the areas where the public was allowed, as I found out there were restricted areas, where only accredited delegates could go.

In the afternoon, I went back to the airport, with mixed feelings about New York. It had been brief and hard-hitting. The highlight was, of course, just to walk on Broadway, about which I had heard so much. Down Broadway, I walked till I got to Times Square and went and stood right at the intersection of 7th Avenue and 42nd Street. Within a short space of time, I had seen more than I had thought possible – sightseeing in New York – a city that I had long looked forward to seeing. Quite content at what I had achieved, I then rushed off to the airport.

Soon thereafter I was on a plane heading for the Midwest where I had been placed to attend Ball State University in the town of Muncie, Indiana. With no direct flights to Muncie, I had to fly to Indianapolis, Cincinnati or Chicago. I chose Cincinnati, where I had arranged to meet Victor Khabo, a friend from Atteridgeville.

Victor, sporting a disconcerting combination of Western and African attire, welcomed me jubilantly. He wore a dashiki shirt and an Eyre's and Smith black chequered cap and, in no time at all, quickly ushered me out of the airport building. I had last seen Victor in 1973, when he left for the States.

We collected my baggage and made our way to the carport, where Victor proudly showed off his huge American convertible saloon car which he called *sphengu-phengu*. A student car, with a few knocks, it reminded me of our own township taxis.

On the way to the city, Victor never stopped asking me questions about people from the Pretoria area, although, now and then, he punctuated his questions with comments on the sights of the city of Cincinnati. From some of his questions, I gathered that my friend was terribly homesick.

As can be imagined, my eyes kept growing bigger and bigger at the scenery and I was only half listening to what Victor said. It began to sink in that I was really in the dream – I was in America!

We entered the campus of the University of Cincinnati where Victor was studying for a Masters degree in economics. Without any waste of time, we proceeded to the students' apartment complex. It was very decent by any standards, but especially so to one coming out of a township home, in Mabopane. The grounds were covered by a well-manicured carpet of green lawn. Black students and white students mixed freely. They walked together, talked in groups, and it all looked very relaxed. Some sat cross-legged under the shade of big lush trees. I marvelled at what I saw.

Victor lived with his wife, Mokgadi, and their lovely little daughter, Naledi, who looked a year older than my Dineo. He provided a six-pack of Budweiser beer, which tasted watered down, but my friend kept pumping me with it. His wife also had a few things to ask but couldn't get a word in, totally overwhelmed by her pushy husband. I stayed with them for a week before Victor drove me to Muncie, some 100 km across the state of Indiana.

Driving there over smooth highways, I was quite surprised by the vast tracks of rows of lush cornfields that we passed.

Like most people in South Africa, I had expected the United States to be completely made up of tall imposing futuristic buildings. I had not expected the rural countryside, which is quite predominant in the Midwest. It was only later that I understood the importance of agricultural activity and that the people in the Midwest were quite passionate about land. That was the breadbasket of the US. The state universities in that part of the world had very vibrant agricultural departments, something we, in South Africa, could learn from, I thought.

We arrived in Muncie, Indiana in the middle of the afternoon. Basically, a college town, Muncie was very small in comparison to Cincinnati.

Firstly, we identified the International House, where I had been told to report to Mr Kirk Robey (the West Africans called him 'Kark Ruby'), the Director. He was a tall man, with a reddish complexion and a mop of brown hair over his forehead and he wore a wool of red beard. He received me, together with all the other foreign students, for orientation just before classes began, in September, for the Fall semester.

I had already made contact with a white South African student, Steve Daneels, who had studied at Stellenbosch University, in the Western Cape. He had been introduced to me by Kirk Robey through correspondence. Steve had enlightened me about Ball State and American universities in general. I recall in my correspondence enquiring about what Ball State was like; he spoke about it in very humble terms. In contrast to his briefing, my first impression was that of an incredibly beautiful campus. The surrounding lawns were carpet-like in the bright summer sun. Stately ancient trees provided shade and were bordered by carefully arranged flowers.

I only understood Steve's assessment of the college many years later, when I visited Stellenbosch University, a white university in South Africa, which like all others, were by far superior to those built for non-white students. To him, Ball State seemed like an average institution compared to Stellenbosch, which is an old university that has catered for the elite of Afrikanerdom going back generations.

A number (if not all) of the Afrikaner presidents, prime ministers and *volks* leaders of South Africa graduated from Stellenbosch. I was grateful to him for he had helped to set my mind at ease.

A few days later, I was introduced to my host parents, Newby and Joyce Dixon, who were part of a web of foreign students' host families. I was to stay with the Dixons for a while, to help orientate me about living in America: the culture of the country, the city and the state, and the university surroundings. The time with them was time very well spent, indeed. They made me feel welcome in their home and allocated one of the bedrooms – quite comfortable and pleasant like the rest of their home – for my use. The Dixons seemed like a modest middle class family, considerate, hospitable and eager to assist. However, they possessed a limited understanding of Africa and, as I was to find out with disappointment, so did the majority of Americans I met later.

The Dixons were retired people. Mrs Dixon was generously proportioned and wore large faded grey spectacles that seemed to cover most of her face. She had a big smile and a fantastic sense of humour. Mr Dixon, probably in his mid-sixties, had a teacher's disposition and appeared more rigid. We sat down and they inducted me into how things worked in the United States.

What they showed me first was a flushing toilet inside the house and Mr Dixon demonstrated to me how to flush it.

Next, they walked me around the kitchen and Mrs Dixon showed me and said in a clear calculated diction, 'Gaby, this is what we call a refrigerator. It cools the food. You can put your food in here, and you can come back days later, and your food will still be fresh. We call it the refrigerator. Anytime you take things out of here, make sure you return them. But you're free to use any item of food that you see in the refrigerator.'

Thereafter, they showed me the television and how to operate it. And that was the one thing we didn't have back home then – if only they had known. Finally, they took me back to my room and showed me where the light switches were, and showed me everything that would make my time with them enjoyable.

As soon as they left me to rest and closed the door, I just threw myself on the bed and cracked up. I thought it was very funny. I came out of a city much larger than Muncie but to them, I was just an African boy who desperately needed guidance.

The Dixons understood that I had come a long way. They wanted to give me time to let the fatigue wear off. It was July in America, very hot and very dry in Muncie though not as humid as New York. I rested and woke up a couple of hours later in time for dinner. Guests and some neighbours had come to meet me. They were also very generous and some had bought me presents. Everyone wanted to know what life was like in Africa and particularly in South Africa.

Mr Dixon particularly seemed to have a large appetite for knowledge about Africa and especially South Africa's policy of apartheid. He took time explaining American anti-segregation laws and the civil rights movement to me. He wanted to make sure that I knew that black people in America had full citizenship rights and assured me that I shouldn't expect any discrimination in America – it was a free society. He went out of his way to make sure that I understood that there were great opportunities for anybody in America. I was told that America was a land of opportunity, where people from all over the world came to seek a better life. He really encouraged me and taught me quite a bit about life in general. In many ways, he reminded me of my own father.

Then came dinner. We sat around the exquisitely set table, complete with glasses for red and white wine, and glasses to serve soft drinks and juice. Mrs Dixon had prepared turkey and vegetables. Grace was said, after which I again received a lecture, this time, on how I could just use the fork only and dispense with the knife – that was what most Americans do, I was told. However, they still wanted me to understand the protocol of knife and fork and how to use the napkin at table. To make sure I didn't stretch over the table to reach for anything, I was told that every time I needed something on the other side of the table I should ask my neighbour to pass it on. All these were things I already knew.

After all, I had a dining table at my own house and in my parents' home, long before then. I politely made them understand that I knew how to use a knife and fork, which came as a big surprise to them. They thought it was something that I had been taught perhaps as part of my orientation. But I was spared the question which I later encountered from numerous Americans – to my utter horror and shock – whether I had bought my clothes when I stopped over in New York. Quite a few people laboured under laughable perceptions about Africa.

My host parents were really keen that I was as comfortable as could be. While we ate, I answered many questions about South Africa.

What seemed to intrigue them most was how I was able to procure a passport because they thought that black people were devoid of any rights. Although things were very bad at home, something I couldn't deny nor wished to defend, I was puzzled by the extremely exaggerated distortions of South Africa's reality I often encountered.

Americans themselves were just emerging from an era of legislated segregation and a painful history of racial prejudice. I noticed many misperceptions, which I planned to correct when I was more comfortable. I also found myself duty bound to make sure that they understood that one had to go through due process when applying for a passport and a visa, just as one would in America.

And I had to get a visa for the States just as they would if they were visiting other countries. It took me time to set the record right and I found that they were keen listeners.

The dinner was delicious and crowned by a generous helping of ice cream. Later, I excused myself to get some rest. Suddenly, I felt as if I had been thrust into the world of *Silas Marner*, one of the prescribed readings for my high school exams. Inevitably, this experience took me back many years, to Robben Island. I was surprised and somewhat disappointed that the world's most advanced nation had people some of whom were frightfully ill-informed about the rest of the world.

A few weeks later, when I told an administration officer that I was from South Africa, he asked me whether that was anywhere in the Middle East. And I said, 'South Africa is in Africa.'

And, 'Oh, oh!' the man said, 'I know where that is, you know? You're from Africa. I'm met a guy from Africa the other day. His father is a chief. He's from Lagos, Nigeria, you must know him? His father is a very famous chief.'

I had heard those kinds of stories and thought they were myths. I explained to him that actually Africa is quite a vast continent, like America, and Nigeria is some eight hours away from South Africa, by plane, and halfway between Johannesburg and London.

Then, just when I thought I had clarified matters and he really understood, he replied, 'Oh, it's really a pity that you don't know my friend from Lagos, because his father is a very wealthy, influential chief, from one of your tribes.'

I gave up.

I missed my family from day one; it was plain lousy to sleep on a bed on my own. I missed my children's voices. I wrote long letters to Nana, almost every week, to give her an account of things as they unfolded for me and I wanted her to cling on to hope. Although I didn't know where the money would come from for their air tickets, I was also clinging on to that same hope. They just had to come.

One evening, Mr Dixon asked me why I didn't phone my family. I tried to explain to him that we didn't have a telephone at my house. That, of course, just reinforced the stereotypes they held about Africa. I had to be careful how I broke that kind of news to them.

A few days later, Mr Dixon took me on a tour of the town, including McDonalds and the other fast-food stores, while cautioning me about American junk food. The hairstyle of the day, for both men and women was the Afro. In South Africa, we always admired the sophisticated looks of most African Americans and their innovative hairstyles. I discovered, for the first time, that African Americans took great care to groom their hair, treated their skin with moisturisers and manicured their nails, something that even men did.

What a shocker! After only a little while, I thought I would also relax my hair – you know? – to blend in. For starters, I used a store kit. The instructions seemed simple enough. However, on the first few occasions, I over-processed my hair. Instead of slight curls, it came out almost straight. I had just been overpowered by technology. With time, I learnt to visit a hairdresser, something I never thought I would ever do as a man. Little did I realise how important grooming was for a successful career in business. This habit became even more pronounced in New York when I joined the banking fraternity. You had to look the part to succeed in selling your product. I carried this brand image to South Africa when I returned and was often criticised for trying too hard to mimic Americans. Of course, to-day's young successful business executives have learned to benchmark themselves and most have adopted the 'dress for success' look. Perhaps, I was a little ahead of things.

Early September, my classes commenced. My stay with the Dixons had come to its designated end and I moved into a dormitory to share a room with Larry Mack, a young boisterous fellow from Miami, Florida. I remember the day I moved in. After the introductions at the door, everyone left and Larry let me in and asked me to pause while he prepared to officially welcome me. He then turned his back on me, pulled his pants down, bent back a bit and slowly pulled down his pants to 'moon' for me.

I did not know how to react except to sheepishly laugh it off. I later found that to be a common practice, particularly with freshmen in some colleges in the US.

Larry and I would sit down over some beer and converse about any subject. From him I learned a great deal about the America of my generation. He seemed to have come from a very successful family.

We co-habited in our small room harmoniously, except at night, when Larry snored – I am talking chainsaw here. When he started it would seem like a huge diesel truck was coming from around the corner. I dreaded the nights because I couldn't sleep. His bed was right across from mine. I would wake him up. Larry thought I was just as good a snorer myself. We would tease each other and complain in the morning about our loud nocturnal habit.

Before I went to the United States, I had my own perceptions about the country, things I had gathered from reading newspapers and magazines. I knew, for example, about America's advances in science and technology, and was impressed by the ease of obtaining information and assistance. I had expected new knowledge but didn't realise that I would experience lifetime learning. My interaction with African Americans was something I had particularly looked forward to and I was struck by my first impressions.

First of all, they seemed to live in a world of their very own.

On initial meetings I could never predict how the discussion would progress after I mentioned I was from South Africa. While a few displayed ignorance of our country, I found that many were politically astute, knowledgeable and very passionate about events in South Africa and the world as a whole. They even had access to information about my own country to which we, as South Africans, were not privy; that made their analysis and perspective of our situation all the more fascinating.

A phenomenon I found particularly perplexing, and which I noticed immediately after my arrival at the University, was that almost everywhere on campus, African American students tended to congregate by themselves.

This happened in the student centre, the sports grounds and the dormitories – everywhere – except in class, where there was intermingling and sharing by all participants. I had naively perceived America as a society that had achieved racial integration, unlike where I came from. Ball State University was a traditionally white university with a minority of black students who constituted, it seemed, no more than 5% of some twenty thousand odd students. That also was a shock for me, considering I had always been part of the majority; to find myself in the minority was an unnerving experience. This phenomenon of voluntary segregation by African American students just added one more dimension to the general disquiet and puzzlement I felt.

I had thought that they would celebrate their recently achieved liberties and integrate fully with their white counterparts. I had a sense they didn't want to be assimilated, though I learned with time that African American parents preferred to send their children to historically black colleges. My mind found it difficult to accept that. Back home, the opposite was the case. The Government had forcefully removed us from 'open' universities and built patently inferior institutions so as to promote the concept of 'separate but equal' development. We called these 'bush' universities and were vehemently opposed to them. How then, I asked myself, could African Americans prefer historically black universities when the civil rights struggle was about a free, open, and integrated society?

So I made it my business to speak to friends to find out from them what I might be missing in the equation. Across the hallway from us, were two tall guys who came from Arkansas, in the South.

One of them, J.W. Mason, got to be quite close to me. They all had a keen interest in South African politics. J. W. and others took pains to explain the historical perspective that led to what seemed, certainly to me, to be very odd behaviour – voluntary separatism. They took pains to make me comprehend what was to them, a natural development. I got to learn the esteem with which historically black colleges were held particularly in African American circles.

A large number of African American leaders, from across the spectrum, had themselves been educated at those institutions and had made great impact on the greater society.

We had many discussions about the anti-apartheid struggle in South Africa and the US Civil Rights Movement. We noted the similarities and differences in the two historical movements. I was learning.

31

American discoveries

Only a few weeks after my arrival in the US, Victor took me on a trip to Chicago, two hours from Muncie. There I met South African exiles as well as students. I also met African-American friends of these compatriots. A debate soon arose about what it was like for me, newly arrived from Africa, to be there. What were my experiences of America?

I seized the opportunity to probe what had, from the start, struck me as odd, the voluntary separatism of African Americans. I said that, in my view, they were rejecting a hard-won victory.

An African American professor in our midst opened my eyes, in various ways, regarding this issue. First, he asked me whether in the few months that I had been there, I had noticed any racist tendencies from white citizens.

I actually hadn't, I responded. I added that, if anything, I had experienced a spirit of embracing from Americans of all colours. I had a white host family and there I wasn't experiencing what I would call racism. On the face of it, everybody seemed to be open-minded. Yes, the patronising attitude of my host parents was a little worrying. I never thought of it as racist; it may have had something to do with their ignorance and stereotyping of Africans in general.

The professor listened patiently and remarked that I had not lived long enough in America to comprehend the complexity of their situation. He gave me another look and concluded, 'You need to spend more time in the US to understand what we mean.'

That was the first time I heard of the term subtle racism. I was told to be a little bit more observant. And, true indeed, when I talked to African American students who came from various parts of the US, I kept hearing that, 'You, in South Africa, come from an environment of ruthless repression and segregation which is enforced. There is no legislated segregation in the USA, but it exists.' Many described it as an insidious overhang that shadowed black people wherever they were.

That unsettled me.

My interaction with Americans was not limited to black people only; I had made it a point to learn and to open up my world. I wasn't sure whether or not my embracing white students and professors (who were always so willing to assist and converse) would be seen as a betrayal by my new friends.

Then I started to read and understand African American literature; and that helped in opening my mind even further. I was growing in all sorts of ways – both expected and unexpected.

Back home, I had studied by correspondence for my Bachelors degree and here I was, for the first time, living in a dorm.

Almost all the students were much younger than me, except for J. W. and his friend; both had worked for some years before graduate school. What intrigued me most about our residence was that it was a co-ed. Ball State University was a typical traditional Mid Western State College, and here I was, weeks out of South Africa, where I lived a life of absolute and total separation and, suddenly, I am thrust into an environment of total integration of both races and genders.

After Thanksgiving in November, Larry and I parted ways. He relocated to another room and was replaced by a Tanzanian student. Larry was a great roommate coming out of a liberal background but I am not sure how comfortable he was sharing a room with an African. I thought I got on well with Larry, although we had our differences on hygiene standards in the room and we were both expressive. I was not sorry that he left me to join his friends and I thought I would get on even better with a fellow African. But I didn't quite hit it off with this man. He had some serious negative views about South Africans in general. I was quite puzzled by his behaviour and could only come to the conclusion that he had probably had a bad experience with some of the many South African refugees in Tanzania. I ignored his hostility, especially since I only had to endure that until the end of the semester. So I carried on with my business, and let him be. We parted company soon enough.

However, my problems were not confined to roommates only; the studies were far from easy. Victor Khabo would visit almost every weekend. He compounded the situation because while it was nice to have him around, little studying took place then. Victor had superior intellectual prowess and he seemed to have the ability to just grasp things much faster than I could. Advanced in his Masters degree, he was about to graduate. He was extremely homesick. He would look through my clothes and pick those he liked. 'These clothes are fresh from home,' he would lament with painful longing. His old beaten up convertible was a useful mode of taking us around and I remember this one Saturday, a group of us were travelling to a party out of town. On the way to Gary, Indiana, where the party was going to be held, we stopped to refuel in a town called Marion, Indiana. The beer consumption had been excessive along the way and I stepped out to look for relief. I was the new arrival and was still feeling my way around. I walked around in great anguish and pain searching for a concealed corner around the building. One of the guys in the car noticed my discomfort and asked, 'What are you looking for?' I was about to do what we black men commonly did back home, pee against the wall.

'Listen! You're in America, boy. Why don't you use a toilet? They catch you doing that here, and they might deport you!' from inside the car, the guy screamed at me.

That was a light bulb moment for me. Right then and there, it occurred to me that know what? I was allowed to use any facility! Back home we weren't allowed to use rest rooms at most fuel outlets and, consequently, relied on crude alternatives to respond to nature's calls. Sadly, that is a practice that is still very much with us, more than a decade after desegregation. You still find people stopping close to highway walls, peeing against fences and against the tyres and wheels of cars. While this disgusting practice has decreased, it is a habit that still lingers uncomfortably among many of us. That man dragged me from the corner and said, 'Go, go, go and find yourself a proper toilet. You'll get yourself in trouble!'

That's how deep and cruelly the subjugation and conditioning of the mind reaches.

At the same service station, I had the most striking experiences – seeing a white blond woman working as a garage attendant. Back home, that was a job reserved for black men. As I marvelled at this woman pouring petrol into our car, my mind still reeling from my recent bladder experience which almost got me into deep trouble, these anomalies told me I had prayed, worked, and fought to achieve my dream. Little did I realise that perhaps the greatest feat wouldn't be the degree I would get but the discovery and healing of my damaged soul. How was I to put myself together – mend myself?

Amid all these goings on and learnings, with me thrust in the Midwest and the days dragging on and on and on, I missed my family more and more. My wife was struggling to raise the money to come over; and I told her to sell everything in the house. The most expensive item was the car, which we had just finished paying off. Used car dealerships were offering her ridiculously low prices. Her own words were, 'They're trying to steal it from us!' Finally, she sold it to her cousin and my friend, Baker Mogale, for a marginally higher price, which was all he could afford. She had sold all the furniture except for the bed she and the children slept on for half of what they were worth. Finally, she was able to buy the tickets for the US. We decided to sublet the house to relatives until my sister and brother were mature enough to take care of it and take it over.

Only then could I have full empathy for the anguish of the men on Robben Island who had to leave their families and I remembered how Magalies used to taunt them at Leeuwkop Prison about their wives. Now I began to feel the full impact of his cruelty.

But, if anything, my suffering strengthened my resolve. Whenever I felt overwhelmed by my studies, I reminded myself how fortunate I was to be where I was, with an opportunity to further improve myself. And that spurred me on and I stayed in the library for long hours to maximise the opportunity.

Time was getting tight, Christmas, fast approaching. Soon after Thanksgiving, I felt the excitement of the holiday celebrations in the streets.

I had already registered for an apartment at Schidler Apartments, for married graduate students, in anticipation of the arrival of my family. The next challenge was the furniture.

Many African students relied significantly on thrift shops for clothes and to furnish the apartments. I found the concept of thrift shops in America such a joyful convenience because, generally, Americans tend to get tired of things after a while. There is just so much wealth and goods under production all the time, people often just get tired of what they have and throw it away or donate it to thrift stores, many of those managed by the Salvation Army. The beneficiaries ended up being people in distress and charitable organisations. I bought a lot of my own clothes from thrift shops and furnished my apartment the same way while waiting for my family.

I'd also learned from the other students at International House that I could accumulate goods at the end of the semester. When students graduated, there was a tendency to dump things – furniture, beds and televisions – clothes even. I discovered, very quickly, that America is a prodigious throw-away society. It shocked me, actually, at the end of the first semester, to see how graduating kids would walk out with radios, TV sets and other appliances and just put them on the sidewalk to be collected by whosoever would find use for them.

By the time Nana and the children came, we had a bed, dining and living room furniture from the Goodwill and Salvation Army Stores, and a TV set donated by the students. I was anxious to know how Nana would react to my acquisitions.

On the 13th of December 1976, with great excitement, Victor, his wife Mokgadi, and I were at Cincinnati Airport to meet my family. Despite Victor's incessant talk, my mind was galloping a mile a minute as I wondered how my children had grown in my absence. Not that I was really concerned for I knew they had a caring mother and were well looked after. I was also imagining what Nana would look like. Had she gained some weight? Had she become a little bit older? I knew she was very fashion conscious and wondered what she would be wearing.

Then I saw the plane land and my anxiety shot up; but within a few minutes, there they appeared. I rushed to them, picked up my two children, gave them big hugs. Dineo (Amara) was two years and nine months, she still stumbled on her steps and was animated with exitement to see me. Thabo could speak Sesotho fluently with amazing maturity for his almost five years. After that, I went to my wife and gave her a big squeeze. We must have made the loudest noise at that airport, that day; but, my golly, I had just been reunited with my family!

32

I stumble into banking

Nana still says she cannot remember being so cold in her life; although I had warned her, she was totally unprepared for the extreme windy chill of the Midwest. They had left bright sunny South Africa in the middle of a beautiful warm summer and, what is more, even the winters we were used to were mild and only required that one put on a jersey or a light overcoat. Also, they were exhausted from the long trip; it had been hard and exhausting for Nana, travelling as she did, with two children. That had kept her so busy she even missed the thrill of flying for the first time.

The drive from the airport to Muncie was a big disappointment for Nana because all she could see were unending cornfields. That was definitely not the America of her grand expectations; there were no blinking colourful neon lights.

We reached home. Finally, I would hear the verdict. To my utter delight, Nana was hugely pleased with her new home. So were the children although, I suspect, if we lived in a cave the TV would have more than made up for that – as far as my children were concerned. Remember now, this was their very first contact or experience with television.

I was glad they liked the apartment. They all clapped and squealed and the children ran up the stairs of the duplex to see the two bedrooms upstairs.

The fridge was full of food, Nana noted; and my kids had never seen television before in their lives. The first thing they did was to sit in front of that television, and that would be their life for the next six and half years in America. I didn't have classes for a while, so we spent some quality time together.

With no more cares about a far-away family, Indiana suddenly became a bright, thoroughly enjoyable place from that point on.

We spent Christmas with the Dixons, who had cooked a bountiful Christmas dinner for us. Nana had her own experience of the Dixons as I had deliberately not said anything to her about them except that they were my host parents. She found them affable, warm and welcoming. Not too long after the introductions, Amara had dropped a few crumbs on the carpet and Nana tried to collect them with her hands.

'Don't worry! Don't worry!' Mrs Dixon cooed, adding, 'I'll show you what we do in America.' She then went to fetch a vacuum cleaner and enthusiastically sucked up the crumbs; exaggerating the motion for what she believed was Nana's benefit.

Mrs Dixon had generously bought our children Christmas presents – a toy car for Thabo and a doll for Amara. Before handing Amara the doll, she asked permission from Nana to do so, believing Amara had never seen a doll before and the sight might scare her. Nana was more amused than upset and we laughed the faux pas off.

Every day of our lives seemed like we were waking up from a train ride on a long unending journey. Before I graduated from my Masters programme, and thanks to the kind intervention of Professor Louis Hoskins of Earlham College, Richmond, Indiana, I had secured an internship at a large Midwestern Company in Columbus, Indiana. Thus, after I graduated, we relocated to Columbus, Indiana, where we were to stay just over a year.

The weather continued to be a challenge for us. In many ways, I was learning to deal with life's challenges and equipping myself for what was going to be an irrevocable change in my life.

Although Nana was a fully qualified nurse, in order to practise in the US, she had to pass the Board Exams. So she undertook a course of studies towards that goal.

Occasionally, my wife would go away for months on training and leave me alone with the toddlers. With no other choice, I learnt the act of being both a father and mother. The latter role was a challenge and it is during these times that I got to understand what I believe we men don't fully comprehend. To be a mother, wife and professional woman is a daunting task. I had to experience the patience and resilience required (and taken for granted) of our womenfolk in the raising of children, particularly in that environment where you have to pick up after yourself.

Very quickly, I taught myself cooking, vacuuming floors, frying pancakes amid dealing with screaming children while faced with the daily pressures of a demanding work situation.

'Please make us some waffles, dad,' the kids would say.

'I don't know how to guys, your mom isn't here you know?' I would protest.

'Read the directions, dad! They are on the back of the box,' the young one would insist.

Every night after dinner, I bathed and prepared them for bed and then read them stories.

In the morning, I would wake them up, make sure their faces were washed, that they had eaten a cooked breakfast, teeth brushed and, the most challenging task – braiding Amara's hair and fastening appropriate accessories at appropriate positions – and done to mademoiselle's satisfaction. Then, on my way to work, stop and drop

Thabo at school and Amara at kindergarten. I have not even mentioned the other chores such as shopping, housekeeping, laundry and occasional trips to libraries and centres of learning for additional interests and development. I had my hands fully occupied and, needless to say, all this created an immeasurable bond with my children – for which I am eternally grateful.

Snow blizzards rendering roads unusable for days are not uncommon in that part of the world. We were close to what is called the Tornado Belt of the US and, occasionally we had physical drills about what to do when there was the threat of a twister. It was most unsettling to watch how gale force winds assaulted people, destroyed properties and took away people's prized possessions.

Back at work, I felt I was progressing extremely well. It was at Cummins Engine, where I learned first-hand to work with foreign currencies and obtained my first practical lessons in financial analysis. Part of my responsibilities was to determine the impact of currency fluctuations on our profitability. Cummins had a global presence and our foreign subsidiaries often operated under volatile currency movements which caused distortions on our reported earnings. I had my first exposure working for a female boss, who was highly respected by her peers and senior management. My confidence was sharply enhanced by the ability to compete in spite of my background. To some around me, I was viewed as an enigmatic entity, with a strange accent (perhaps, some saw me as a freak).

To compete, I read every financial publication I could lay my hands on and never stopped asking questions.

My quest for new knowledge was insatiable; I had already, by that time, set my sights high. It is at that stage that I began reading biographies of great achievers and Muhammad Ali, Duke Ellington and Louis Armstrong stood out as heroes to emulate. One of the lessons I learnt in America was that to be at the top of the heap like Elvis Presley, Duke Ellington or Michael Jordan, you had to be the 'best of the best'. The level of competition was extremely high and only those who truly excelled received recognition. I knew my own limitations, but never underestimated my unmeasured inner strength. I reached deep down; and my best surfaced. This is not something I told myself; but when I was recruited by the largest and most successful American bank (the largest bank in the world, at that time) I could no longer deny something staring me in the eye.

In 1978, Citibank was on a nationwide recruitment campaign for corporate bank trainees and it is during that search that I was picked. This was a great blessing because it granted me that much needed extension to stay on in America almost (hopefully) indefinitely, but more importantly, to give me a career almost immediately and to look after my family. I would never, in my wildest dreams, have thought of myself as a prospective banker.

Years later, I was interviewed by a magazine in Oslo, Norway, while on a business trip. I was asked why I had opted for banking as a career and my response, about which I'm often reminded by a very successful young South African businessman who shares the same office building with me, Mxolisi Mbetse, was that, 'I stumbled into banking'. And that is the truth, thanks to Citibank.

That employment agreement was in itself a milestone event because it marked the beginning of a major turning point in my life.

E1: In Rio de Janeiro, Brazil (Copa Capana Beach) on my way to the USA to study, July 1976 (where I 'discovered my freedom')

E2: My first day in New York, August 8 1976

E3(a): International Student Director Kirk Robey (far left) with the 1976 intake of Ball State University foreign students

E3(b): Newby and his wife Joyce at Schidler Apartments, our student living quarters in Muncie, Indiana, 1976

E4: (right) Joyful moment after receiving my Masters at Ball State, Muncie, Indiana, 1977

E5: (below) Receiving congratulations from my late friend, Dr Victor Khabo upon graduating from Ball State, 1977

E6: My Indiana host mother Joyce Dixon and Nana wish me well

E7: (above) A winter morning outside our residence in Columbus, Indiana, 1977

E8: (right) Nana and family friend, Oscar Motsepe who attended Purdue University in Indiana, enjoy a friendly embrace, 1980

E9: Nana's graduation from New York (Hunter College) at Madison Square Gardens with Thabo and Amara, 1981

E10: Childhood friend, Leslie Mampe and Steve McDonald at the latter's home in Washington DC. Steve previously worked for the US Embassy in Pretoria

E11(a): Our first encounter with the South African music icon Hugh Masekela, after his concert in Cincinnati, Ohio, May 1978. Victor Khabo stands between Nana and Hugh and his wife Mokhadi is on extreme left

E11(b): Nana with famous composer/arranger Caiphus Semenya (on right) in Harare, Zimbabwe on their 'Buwa' music tour just before 1994. South Africa's famed trumpeters Hugh Masekela and Dennis Mpale on the extreme left

263

E12: Growing up in Manhattan, Thabo and Dineo-Amara, 1981

E13: My son Thabo embracing his sisters, Naledi and Amara after graduating from Clark-Atlanta University

E14: Sharnia Buford and wife Phylis at their Westchester, NY residence. Tab was assigned to work with me on the rehabilitation of the The African Bank in the 1980s

33

'Welcome to New York City'

My first interview, at the end of 1978, was at the head office, 399 Park Avenue, in New York City. I was interviewed by Bene M'Poko, who was an assistant Vice President for the International Corporate Banking Division (ICB), which was located on the 5th floor of the building. At the time of writing of this book, Mr M'Poko is the Ambassador for the Democratic Republic of the Congo (DRC) in South Africa.

Bene M'Poko was a fellow African from what was then Zaire; he had been living in America for many years and was a seasoned banker. I found the environment highly intimidating and only the welcome of the interviewers reassured me, which helped me give of my best. I was then subjected to a few aptitude tests and, thankfully, found suitable for placement.

So, early in June, 1978, we set off for the Big Apple. We sold our sturdy Oldsmobile, the gas guzzler Nana drove, and I drove my small Pinto, all the way to New York. But, we began our journey in Chicago, our favourite city – the windy city, to bid farewell to our friend Professor Sithole and family; Uncle Collins Ramushu and the community of friends of Chicago, a group that had received us well and made us feel at home in the Midwest of the United States. After the one-day stop, I took Nana and the children to O'Hare Airport, saw them off, and drove towards New York with our belongings.

Nana and the children were flown business class by Citibank. From La Guardia they took a taxi to St Regis hotel, on 55th and Park Avenue.

I drove as far as Pittsburgh, where I spent the night with another South African Fulbright scholar, Victor Mkhize from Kwa-Zulu and his wife. Nana and I had agreed that I would check on them, later that evening. When I phoned New York, I found my wife in absolute awe; totally overwhelmed by the St Regis. Up till then, the most expensive hotel my family had ever stayed in was a motel. And the biggest thing Nana just had to tell me was her surprise at how expensive it was. They had just been billed $60, for a meal for three. This was a fortune for us; we spent that amount for the family groceries, for two whole weeks. Nana wanted to check with me if they could continue to eat at the hotel and I assured her, 'That is part of the package, my dear!'

I set off quite early the next day and it was still morning when I arrived in New York. I drove around the huge city, surprised I was able to navigate my way around. My only reservation, as far as traffic and driving in New York was concerned? There were just too many taxis; all I could see were the ubiquitous New York yellow cabs. The drive from Chicago had exhausted me and as I drove around, looking for parking, the combination of heat and humidity didn't help matters.

I walked into the large lobby of the St Regis, one of the most expensive and luxurious hotels in Manhattan, renowned as a favourite home away from home not only for top business executives but also for people of stature and the affluent of New York. I was just a boy from Bekkersdal via the laid-back Midwest, and there I was, rubbing shoulders with all the sophisticated men and glamorous women of New York, all decked out in evening wear.

Right in the centre of the lobby, there was a grand piano that the pianist intimately caressed, making it give out the most melodious tunes.

I knew then that I had arrived in the America I aspired to see. That was the New York that I had read about. The America that everyone in South Africa and the world referred to when they said 'in America, the streets and pavements are made of gold and diamonds'.

A bell porter came to fetch my luggage. For me, that experience was a first. I'd never before had a white man pick up my luggage and take it to my room.

When I got to my room, Nana said, 'Well, welcome to New York City.'

The suite was luxurious – a pleasant surprise, indeed. Obviously, Citibank wanted us to feel very comfortable. I had already mentioned to Bene M'Poko and Maria, the two people who had interviewed me, that what reservations I had expressed had nothing to do with the job but arose out of the insecurity I felt for myself and, more important, for my family.

They had, I suppose, gone out of their way and secured me that kind of hotel, located just a few blocks from the famous Central Park and, of course, on the most expensive boulevard in America, 5th Avenue.

Our move from Indiana to New York City was a glamorous whirlwind. We felt we had arrived in America. Before that everything else was preparation. Now I had a real job, a glamorous well-paying job. Why, on my way to the hotel I'd even bought a copy of the *New York Times*, as any businessman in New York does on a daily basis. Nana was excited; we knew this was the real deal. We had to pinch ourselves, a few times, just to make sure it was not all a dream from which we'd wake up and find ourselves back where we'd just been so thrilled to have left.

The musician that night was Roy Ayers, who seemed to have been the house entertainer at St Regis, frequently featured in the entertainment pages of the *New York Times* and *New York Post*.

And across the road, on 54th Street, there was a famous jazz club, Eddie Cavels. That's where I got to meet Joe Williams, just a couple of weeks after our arrival in New York. I couldn't believe it. It was just a marvel to talk to the legend of jazz, someone who had recorded and performed with the likes of Ella Fitzgerald, Louis Armstrong and Duke Ellington – the same Joe Williams that every jazz fan around the world had listened to. After every set, Joe would sit with us and crack jokes in his gravelly voice.

At the same jazz club, I also met the great trumpeter, Roy Eldridge, on another occasion. There was a piece written about him in the *New York Times* and he signed an autograph for me when I told him I was from South Africa and I played trumpet as well. He struggled with where South Africa was, like the average American. We always had to go out of our way to explain to people where, exactly, Johannesburg or even South Africa was. Often times they would know where Pretoria was; don't ask me why.

The following day, giddy with excitement, we took a walk on the streets of Manhattan. Inside the hotel, it was comfortable because of air conditioning. But as soon as we stepped outside, we were hit by a wave of hot steamy air. Immediately, all four of us were dripping in sweat.

I cannot describe the surprise and the anxiety of just walking the streets.

I had never seen so many people in my life, just walking casually, seemingly without a care in the world. Also striking about New York was the diversity of the people and of the languages one heard spoken.

We liked the food, the variety of restaurants: Chinese to Greek, Indian as well as European cuisine. A big surprise for Nana was the discovery of a store that existed just to sell candy. Then, a block away, there was another store where the only thing they sold was ice cream; it was funny to watch grownups lining up just to buy ice cream for themselves. For us, that was a treat for children – and a rare one, at that. If I stood in any line to buy ice cream, that would be for the children, not Nana and me. The long winding queues of people patiently waiting for a movie was another spectacle for us. We had come from a city in South Africa where everything seemed to be rushed; we rushed for our packed buses and taxis to work, pushed each other in the supermarket to be on time for a long ride back home, and generally had to ensure things were done and prepared for the weekend funeral of a friend or a relative. There was little time for leisure back home. Not when one had grown up and left one's childhood behind. During childhood, yes, one played about. But grownups had no leisure to speak of and no leisure time even should they have such a strange notion in their heads.

As for my job, I kicked off with a number of meetings. I was introduced to my new colleagues, and I was told that I would receive ten months of intensive training in corporate banking from the Bank's college in Long Island City, just outside of Manhattan.

I was one of a group of 30 plus new MBA recruits from various parts of the US. Upon successful completion of the course, I would work in the International Corporate Bank Division.

The training was in itself a test of endurance and got me to stretch my own boundaries once again. I had to compete with a select group of Americans who had received training from top business schools and had made banking a career choice.

We were trained by seasoned bankers and a lot of the study tutorials were based on Harvard Business School material of the case studies of large corporations. It was quite important for me to succeed as my extended stay in the United States was, in the main, dependent on my new job. My student visa had expired and my immigration status had been readjusted by my employer. It was far too early to contemplate a return to South Africa; I realised that my future was unfolding right before my eyes.

My family remained at the St Regis hotel for two months while we looked for a suitable residence. House hunting became quite an assignment. We had a choice of living on the Eastside of Manhattan but were concerned by the congestion. Our biggest consideration was a place where our young ones could move about freely, in a safe environment. New York was intimidating; we had come from a small Midwestern town with friendly and helpful neighbours.

While we were looking for housing, I met up with Beverley Hawkins, a former colleague from Cummins in Indiana and she had friends from her home state of California, who also had two small children. Over dinner with Nana, Beverley recommended that we talk to this couple, who lived in a place called Roosevelt Island, just across the river from Manhattan.

Roosevelt Island proved to be just the ideal place for a hectic New York executive who also needed a nice quiet neighbourhood to raise a family.

Located on the East River between Manhattan and Queens, the island is accessible by an overhead tram from Manhattan. This was extremely convenient for me as my workplace was only four and a half blocks from the 59th Street tram station. Living on Roosevelt Island was an extraordinary stroke of luck. We later found out that many of its residents were diplomats, working at the United Nations, which was right across the island. Also many top business executives, Broadway entertainers and famous personalities had made this place their residence of choice, primarily because of its ideal location, country lifestyle and proximity to the city.

Roosevelt Island was the beginning of my family's life in New York. It was completely different from Indiana. I had impetuously disposed of the Pinto and purchased a new Toyota Celica, to keep up with the affluence level of New York.

That car remained parked in the common garage for all residents of Roosevelt Island at the entrance. I brought it back with me to South Africa, years later, because we'd hardly used it in New York for all those years.

The social life in New York was hectic; but we enjoyed it tremendously. We found out that this city was home to scores of South Africans exiled over years and years. Many of these lived on the West Side of Manhattan while others were scattered in various parts of the Bronx, Brooklyn, and Queens. This is where I met an old friend, Thohlane, who was studying at Columbia University. He and Prof. Herbert Vilakazi were helpful in introducing us to countless other South Africans.

Both lived not too far from the church where most famous people used to go to, 114th Street, the Church of St John the Divine.

That's where I met Max Roach, the great jazz drummer one Saturday afternoon. I related to him the strange incident of how his album, 'Freedom Now Suite', was used as evidence against me in my trial which led to my being jailed on Robben Island in the 1960s. The investigating police officer was so excited that he had discovered this evidence of my leftist leanings; the fact that I had an album that was recorded in America, and had something to do with Sharpeville, to him, was a great discovery.

With disbelief in his eyes, Max introduced me to his band at the end of the show and related my story and we took a few pictures together. Two other close friends, Rhodes Gxoyiya and Sam Shakong, shared an apartment on 96th Street on the upper west side of Manhattan. This block of apartments had been quite popular with South Africans in exile. I was told that Mirriam Makeba had lived there before moving to West Africa prior to her marriage to Stokely Carmichael. *Broer* Aubrey Nkomo and his wife Barbara also lived there. Ambassador Barbara Masekela, Hugh's sister, Andrew Lukhele, a Harvard trained academic and Steve Matseoane, a clinical professor of Obstetrics and Gynaecology in the faculty of Medicine at Columbia University, New York and also a Director Emeritus of Obstetrics and Gynaecology at Harlem Hospital, were all residents in this exciting part of New York City. Later, we were joined on Rooseveld Island by Motlatsi Motsoasele, and his wife Malesiamo, both citizens of Lesotho. Motlatsi was employed by the United Nations and was one of my earliest friends when I arrived in the city. Our families grew quite close and it was with great sadness that we learned of the loss of this family's second eldest daughter, Lerato, in an auto accident in New Jersey, years later.

Living on Roosevelt Island had an almost unreal Hollywood type of feel for me. It is difficult to describe the giant leap I had just taken.

Many a time I would take a walk along the banks of the East River and try to reconcile the life I was living with the pain and suffering I had endured, particularly in my late teens and early twenties, as a prisoner in perhaps the toughest jailhouse in the world. How then was it that my fortunes had turned that radically in just a few years? Is there a message that was being conveyed to me by some invisible force?

I could not find a rational explanation for my drastically changed circumstances, especially in the face of the worsening situation back home.

I remember another friend, playwright Mfundi Vundla, who also lived on the Westside, saying to me, 'You know, Gaby, you've set a benchmark that is difficult to achieve.' He repeated that to me many years later, after we had both returned to South Africa. Mfundi is the older brother of Peter Vundla, the well-known businessman who also studied in Columbia before my arrival in the city. I had known Peter since my high school days, at Madibane High School, in Western Native Township, back in the late 1950s.

New York was known for its abundance of jazz clubs. One Sunday afternoon, Mfundi, who shared my love for jazz, invited me to a club where a women's only band was playing, in the Bronx. We drove over in my Pinto. The food was great, the music fantastic, the company was most engaging and, inevitably, we over-stayed. After 1 am, we decided to return home. I dropped Mfundi off at International House, near Columbia University and crossed over to the East side, on my way to Roosevelt Island.

I was driving through Queens when I suddenly noticed a woman in bright shiny evening clothes with a mass of dishevelled hair that looked like a wig. She seemed to be struggling on her spiky stilettos.

As I approached, she signalled for a lift. I thought she was from a date that had gone bad as she clutched her bag and seemed very frightened. The street was quiet, given the time of night. I stopped my car and she asked for a ride to the Diners restaurant nearby, which I knew was quite close.

The woman jumped into the car quite ungracefully and I noticed that besides the deep voice, her limbs were quite masculine. Before I could utter any niceties to cover the distance, the person who I thought was a woman turned out to be actually a man disguised as a woman. He pulled out a knife and while I was still baffled, he stabbed me on the side of my stomach and tried to get control of the car.

So I stopped and he tried to stab me again on the lower abdomen but I blocked the knife so he cut my hand and blood just gushed out. I didn't even feel the pain then; I was still trying to figure out what was happening.

He demanded money. I could see he was highly strung on drugs. I tried to calm him down by talking to him and once he found out that I lived on Roosevelt Island, he started cursing and called me a fat cat. He was extremely agitated by then. Next, he told me to drive back on the Queensborough Bridge and on to his house in the Bronx where he said he was going to kill me. Queensborough or 59th Street Bridge links Manhattan to Queens. By that time, I was bleeding profusely, trying to steer the car using one hand and blocking the knife he was pointing at my abdomen with the other hand. He yelled at me to stop the car on the bridge and ordered me to get out. Clutching my bleeding stomach, I stumbled out. At this point, he asked me if I preferred to die by being thrown over the bridge, into the East River, or if I would rather go to his apartment I guess to meet my fate there.

To buy time, I opted for the latter and said, 'Let's go to the Bronx.' My idea was to delay him and, hopefully, get a chance to escape.

Once we got to Second Avenue, I ran a red light and I was closed in by two cabs. When the furious drivers came out, my captor ran out of the car. I was rescued and taken to New York Hospital, where coincidentally, my wife was employed. Fortunately, she was not on duty that night.

I found the whole episode both painful and ironic. I had come out of South Africa and had been schooled in the notorious West Rand and Newclare where there were fierce roving knife-wielding gangsters yet I had never been mugged or stabbed. As fate would have it, I got stabbed in New York City and I still carry the scars from that night. A few months later, a friend bought me a T-shirt marked, 'Native New Yorker'. This was supposed to be confirmation of my newly-acquired status, after the mugging. But I only found the humour in the statement long after that harrowing incident.

I had surely come a long way, I thought: from Robben Island to Roosevelt Island had been one long freaky leap. However, there was still a lot to learn.

With the guidance of our friend, Nonceba Lubanga, Nana identified Hunter College, which is part of the City University of New York, as ideal for her to study for a Bachelor of Science degree. Professor Herbert Vilakazi stepped in and walked my wife, personally, to help her gain admission to Hunter College. Then he took her by the hand to the UN to make an application for a scholarship that would provide for her tuition and a monthly stipend.

Herbert Vilakazi is the one person who became, arguably, the biggest influence to date on us and a host of other South Africans who arrived in New York destitute. He was well known for his generosity and preparedness to assist others in need.

Many exiled South Africans, we later found out, lived under trying conditions in this city. My wife and I often had to reach out by providing all manner of assistance. This was nothing new but part of the African tradition of caring for the extended family. Our gestures were later rewarded by the professional growth we witnessed later as some of these young people matured. Many of them have returned home and have taken on role modelling positions in their chosen fields. These include Pearl Luthuli who has assumed a leadership position in the media industry; Duma Ndlovu the creator of a long running soapie on our national broadcaster, Papi Molotsane, former head of the New York Securities Exchange listed Telkom, Tau Morwe, head of the National Port Operations and several others in our public service. Unlike some of us who had been blessed and had the option to return home, the situation for exiled refugees in the States was not always exactly a bed of roses. Some, like Reggie Nyovane could not make it and succumbed to severe levels of depression. The sustained displacement from their homeland became too hard to endure.

34

A look into the future

After I had completed the training at the Bank's college in Long Island City, I successfully sat for the exam and was made an officer of the bank and accorded the title of assistant manager in the International Corporate Banking Division (ICB), early 1980. At the time, the chairman of Citibank was Walter Wriston, a well respected figure in international banking circles. This was, for me, a period of great knowledge acquisition. I got to meet many colleagues from other banks like Chase Manhattan and Chemical Bank, and this led to enduring friendships.

At the bank, I was placed under the tutelage of one of the Vice Presidents, John Riardon. John worked me very hard. He asked for nothing but perfection from my work and said he had to drive me because he knew that if I returned to South Africa to work in the bank I would not get the training that was available from Head Office in Citibank and yet I would have to compete with the bankers at Citibank South Africa, who were mainly white, and had had the privilege of a good education and unlimited opportunities. In fact, there was a tacit understanding between the bank and me that, at some stage, I would be assigned to one of several of our African offices. Those of us who were earmarked for these international assignments were fast-tracked for intensive training. This often created tensions between us, particularly with some of our African-American colleagues, who were not only few in number at officer level, but regularly complained of neglect and marginalisation. This, perhaps, was an example of the subtle racial prejudice the Professor in Chicago had alluded to.

There was a marked scarcity of black senior bankers and role models at large US banks. One of my friends, Frank Rush, who was a rising star at Citibank at the time, constantly reminded me of their exclusion from top ranks not because of inability but rather because of other considerations. Frank, who lived in the Bronx, was a great pillar of support for me in the early days and helped to integrate me into the inner circles of high life in New York City. Like a guardian angel, he had great affinity for Africa and what he called her children in the diaspora.

In the bank, I worked with South African companies who either sought to enter the US market or were already established. One of those was a large construction company. As I recall, they had an office, at that time, somewhere in the Midwest of the USA and were trying to get their business going and we provided them with working capital. It wasn't a large account, and though they were involved in the building of railroads, the operation itself was not very extensive. In the 1980s, South African companies were just venturing into the US market. A few of them were quite large clients of the Bank.

I valued this interface with South Africans because of what it meant for me: getting to know senior businessmen and the networking opportunities that this provided. I was, however, never certain of how I would be received by the client because of my junior status in the bank and our divisions back home. In general, I was well received and created sustainable relations with all of my clients. I had not always dealt with my white compatriots at this level when I lived in South Africa as this was not possible then because of our laws. Besides, I had grown confident because of the specialised knowledge I now possessed and their appreciation of my abilities. SAMANCOR became my first large assignment in banking.

They had had a long-term relationship with Citibank and my being assigned to that account marked a huge vote of confidence for my capabilities because it was a complex account which needed to be managed sensitively. There were other large clients that conducted enormous volumes of business worldwide and conducted a multimillion US dollar account at our bank. We assisted with provision of foreign currency and other trade facilities.

With time, the intensity of the training increased. We were taught to be aggressive marketers and meticulous in credit assessment. As a consequence of where I was placed, very early in my life as a banker, I was exposed to dealing with senior people at corporate level and also in political circles.

African and Latin American clients were also a large part of our portfolio. We had branches in East, Central and West Africa. Occasionally, senior government ministers from those countries would visit the Head Office to meet some of the bank officials. Depending on the level of seniority, they would be hosted by either the President, or the Chairman himself. Since the business would be domiciled in our division I was fortunate to meet a number of ministers from various parts of the African continent that early in my career.

Working at the bank at that level was truly an inspirational experience. I was always conscious of the fact that the bank was preparing me to eventually take on a senior role in the management of its operations in South Africa, in due course.

In 1980, I made my first exploratory trip back to South Africa. I landed in Johannesburg, where I found David Msiza, a family friend, waiting for me at the airport. He drove me to the five-star Carlton Hotel on Main Street where Citibank had booked a suite for me for the duration of my stay. Those days there were only two so-called international hotels in Johannesburg, which had permission from the government to admit guests of all races.

The idea was that I would spend a few months in Johannesburg to acquaint myself with the extent of our operations at the branch there.

Since being established in South Africa, in the 1960s, Citibank was operating in a low profile but I found that the Bank was highly respected in corporate circles. From the office in Johannesburg, I went on calls, just as I did in New York, with senior managers. One late afternoon, back in the hotel, I ran into Gigi Mbere, an old schoolmate. Gigi, now a well-known physician, commanded a great deal of respect as Johannesburg's only black gynaecologist at the time. He wasted no time in introducing me to several high flyers in the city and, within days, I had caught up with some old friends I had not seen in years.

I had been at the hotel a few days when I met Winston Mosiako. Winston, like several others, was a beneficiary of Reverend Sullivan's campaign to have American companies doing business in South Africa train and fast track Africans into management positions as part of their contributions to the country's development. Leon Sullivan was a director of General Motors and a well-known American Civil Rights activist. Through what were called 'The Sullivan Principles', he single-handedly changed the face of corporate South Africa's workforce in the 1980s in a most valuable way and left this country with an enduring legacy. Many of the country's top business leaders and entrepreneurs are a direct result of his intervention, which raised the level of consciousness in the area of decent housing, education and training, and scaled up corporate social responsibility programmes. The results of his programmes were concrete and noticeable.

IBM was one of those companies that trained young Africans on the insistence of the New York shareholders' pressure coming from the growing anti-apartheid movement abroad. Several other American companies followed suit and this resulted in the accelerated promotion of black employees into positions that defied the foundations of grand apartheid. During that visit, I also met my old friend, Leslie Mampe. It turned out that he was also one of those engineers undergoing training at IBM. On many afternoons, a number of friends, old and new, would come over and join me for cocktails at the hotel. That assisted me socially, filled the gap, while I was waiting for my wife and family to arrive.

To this day, Winston still reminds me about how impressed he was the very first day he met me at the Carlton Hotel. We met at the bar, where I was chatting up a few new acquaintances. He remembers asking me what I did for a living and I said I lent money to corporations. Winston says that kept him quiet for a moment, it actually shocked him that there was a black man who could make such a bold statement. The truth of the matter was that that was my business.

At home in Mabopane, I found that not much had changed as far as the misery of township life was concerned The gravel road leading to my house at 3920 B

Section had grown larger and deeper erosions over time and no effort had been raised at improving the surroundings. The spontaneous joy and feeling of belonging remained though, and I was received with kinship warmth just for being myself. I was heartily welcomed by the people I had left behind, my neighbours and friends.

My brother, Fetsa, had married his childhood sweetheart, Phillipine, and they were blessed with a baby girl named Mongi. My sister, Semakaleng, was staying with them in our old Mabopane home, which we had handed over to them and that is where my sister still lives with her own son Tebogo. The apartheid machinery had continued to operate pretty much in the same way and had assumed a level of crude sophistication. The government still harboured hopes of consigning all black people to the barren fringes of the country where they would be governed by the government's own new crop of overzealous 'homeland' leaders.

Because of the worsened political situation, I was duly advised to adopt a low profile; I didn't want word to get around that I was back in Johannesburg. I refused press interviews, and there was just one report about my return to South Africa on a short visit. It would have been inadvisable, I told myself, to attract undue attention. I decided to use the visit to assess the prospects and timing of my return. Within a short period, I made a decision to defer my relocation out of the States. I would gain little by a premature return and would risk the security of my family as well as that of myself in the bargain.

Later on, Nana, Thabo and Amara came to join me at the hotel before we all travelled to Mabopane to visit my siblings. The reality of apartheid glared at us.

To add to our misery, I couldn't spend enough time with my family because I was trying, as hard as possible, to familiarise myself with the corporate activities and to also take a view of what would happen later on, whether we should return to South Africa, settle permanently in the US or seek some other place to go to. Our options weren't too wide; I had to weigh everything very carefully. Six weeks later, I had to return to New York where I spent a few days while waiting for a visa to Greece, for my next assignment, in Athens. I had just met Moses Marole, another South African who was an old friend of my late cousin, Simon. At the time, Moses worked for the Bell Corporation. I asked him to look after my apartment while I was gone for a few months.

A few days later, I left Manhattan for Greece. Citibank had a regional office there which was used as a training centre. I joined a group of about forty Citibank officers from Africa, Pakistan, India, and various other countries of the Middle East.

My family came from South Africa to join me. During the day, they spent their time exploring. I found them very excited every evening because they had time to explore the city, and Nana just loved the culture, the architecture and the people of Greece.

She says it was one of the few experiences she enjoyed about being the spouse of a travelling executive. The bank was taking very good care of us; we had bank drivers if Nana and the children needed any assistance. My family later left for New York while I continued to receive additional training.

Toward the end of 1980, I returned to New York. I went back to my old job at 399 Park Avenue armed with new knowledge and experiences from South Africa and Greece. I was promoted to a higher rank, which came with greater responsibilities and tasks, my lending limit was increased and I was able to make presentations to credit committees. I had learnt the business of syndicated loans. My knowledge of foreign currencies had increased significantly, especially after my return from Athens, where we dealt with what we called 'exotic currencies' of the Middle Eastern world. The Bank was at the time looking at starting operations in Saudi Arabia and there were some bank operations in the Gulf States, such as Bahrain. We met a number of officers of the bank who occasionally came to the regional office in Athens. And that exposure to the Middle East was very useful; it significantly broadened my experience.

A few years later, still in New York, we had to rethink our decision of never returning to South Africa, a decision we had made under the heat of apartheid.

I felt, if we returned, we could make a difference with the help of the people at Citibank in New York, who had demonstrated a willingness to support us. I also thought that when the country finally arrived at a political settlement, our people would need to have developed economically to support and fully enjoy their hard-earned freedom.

There were great challenges we had to consider though if we were to return; and the biggest of those was the children's schooling. African education, called Bantu education, was deliberately designed to retard the development and growth of Africans so that they would be just literate enough to understand instructions, carry out orders from white superiors, and perform menial tasks under those whites.

Also worrying was that it seemed we would have to live in a matchbox house on an unpaved street in Soweto or any other of Johannesburg's townships designated for blacks under the country's segregationist policies. The prospect was daunting especially as life in New York was particularly vibrant and attractive.

35

On Broadway with the stars

We'd discovered that New York was a complex place of startling contrasts. It was not the perfect, pretty place of blinking lights and effortless lightness of our movie-fuelled fantasies, but included the underworld of heavy narcotics whose victims roamed the streets of the city – especially in places like Brooklyn and some parts of the Bronx – their bodies and souls ravaged. That was the gritty side of life, a side we had never seen in Indiana or South Africa, before that. Despite all that, we enjoyed the company of some real New Yorkers and indulged and admired the great cultural extravaganza New York offers. We found the city a very stimulating place.

Nana was progressing extremely well at Hunter College. Even decades later, Nana maintains that it was in New York that she developed in a way in which she doesn't think she would have done in any other environment. I saw that as the Dixons had told me on my arrival, 'America is a land of boundless opportunities' and, if you assert yourself and plan your life well and you focus, you can surprise yourself and the world with the excellence you achieve, whatever your area of interest.

Our children were fairly comfortable socially. At school, the pupil-teacher ratio was low, so they received focused attention. They were active in soccer, played piano, and took art classes – both of them have had their work exhibited at a New York museum.

At the age of seven, Thabo was playing tennis and one of his coaches, Victor Geralitis, was one of America's tennis legends. Victor later gave him a tennis racket, as a gift.

We worked hard and we could see the benefits.

Homecare assistance, which we rather took for granted back in South Africa, was extremely expensive and therefore unavailable to us. Nana and I shared the household chores equally. A challenge for me, an executive, but there was an understanding that when it came to household chores there were no female or male duties. Nana was at college for twelve hours a day, from 9 am. And every night she returned exhausted from dissecting animals and the tortuous library hours. I would make her a cup of coffee as soon as she arrived. Most afternoons I fetched the children from school and after care and then prepared dinner for all of us. Nana would come home to a cooked meal. Luckily for us, there were dishwashing machines. This is a chore I have detested from my youth. Now that I live alone, with Nana working away from home; there is no one to chase after me about washing dishes!

But I am grateful for that time of real shared living, for the bond that Nana and I created between us as a couple because while she is my wife, she is a friend, a mentor and confidante I wholly trust. That time also got me to bond with the children to the extent that Saturday and Sunday mornings, notwithstanding that we might have gone out partying the whole night, in the morning the children would always find their way to me. Shouts of: 'Daddy, daddy, I'm hungry!' would wake me up.

We made friends with the legendary Hugh Masekela and his sister Barbara, a career diplomat who is currently South Africa's ambassador in Washington, DC. One Saturday, Hughie had come to visit with me and we immediately descended into our usual life pleasures. A little later, our sons, Thabo and Selema, who had been riding a bike outside, came back fazed and crying. It turned out that their bike had been forcibly taken from them by the Queens bullies, who occasionally crossed the adjoining bridge into Roosevelt Island. Hughie and I dashed down Main Street, the only street of note on Roosevelt Island, chasing the culprits. Across the bridge from the island was a block of inner city housing projects where these boys had disappeared. I knew my bounds and warned Hughie to cool it. The bicycle wasn't worth risking life or limb. The boys overcame the setback and today Selema, or Sal, as he is known on US TV, lives in California where he has made a name for himself on E! the daily show where, daily at 10, he interviews top Hollywood celebrities.

We were honoured to be Zakes Mokae's guests when he and Danny Glover won Tonys for their performances of 'Master Harold and the Boys' on Broadway, which was conceived by the South African playwright, Athol Fugard.

It was a night of magic. We celebrated the Tonys at Sardi's Restaurant with big time American stars and artists. Years after our return to South Africa, Nana and I met Glover at a surprise birthday party for Caiphus at his cousin's house Cecil Tshwaedi in Johannesburg. As I recall, this was his very first visit to South Africa. I reminded him about our get-together at Sardis, where he'd introduced us to his mother.

'Gaby,' he said, sounding (and looking) emotional, 'you're one of very few people, outside the US, who have actually met my mom.'

Other prominent artists who came into our lives and visited our home were Tony Award winners, Winston Ntshona and John Kani, icons of South African theatre, well-known elsewhere too.

Once, they visited with a bevy of top South African models, including Nakedi Ribane, Rose Francis and others who were in New York to promote South African diamonds. In typical South African style, we partied till late that night when we got a call from the doorman requesting us to 'Cool it!'

We entertained extensively from our apartment, which overlooked the skyline of Manhattan, the Triborough Bridge, the Queensborough Bridge and further down, especially at night, we could see the famous Brooklyn Bridge. We weren't that great in the selection of wines. For the most part, I used to drink the Mateus Portuguese rosé and Nana was experimenting with California's Chardonnay. Part of the reason we had the dinner parties was to meet and get to know people and it was not only South Africans who came to the house. We wanted to understand other cultures and to draw from them. I was hungry for knowledge; I was dying to broaden my scope and understanding of human life and its complexities. New York afforded us that opportunity.

I will never forget the evening when the great, late Nina Simone, in the company of playwright Duma ka Ndlovu, came for a late night dinner at our home. I had inadvertently overlooked to advise Duma of the cancellation of the dinner as it clashed with another important engagement. Needless to say, that situation brought untold embarrassment to Duma and, from reports, we gather that from her outburst, Ms Simone was definitely not amused – to put it mildly. We apologised profusely to Duma, who graciously pardoned us and we continue to be very good friends.

We continued to expand our horizons within the South African community comprised mainly of exiled freedom fighters, students and the liberation movements' representatives at the UN. Some of the people we met, from out of the City, were Caiphus Semenya and Letta Mbulu who lived in Altadena, California.

This couple (married, by the way) had made a name for themselves in the US entertainment world. Quincy Jones had composed the musical score for the epic Roots, written by Alex Haley, who has since passed on, which is arguably one of the best epic television series ever experienced on US television. It is the story of Kunta Kinte from the Mandinka tribe in West Africa. Quincy commissioned his friends, Letta and Caiphus, to write the music for the African component of the TV show. Quincy and Caiphus wrote the English lyrics for the Nigerian folk song 'Ishe Oluwa' (which literally translated means 'many rains ago' in Yoruba) and which was sung by Letta Mbulu.

One day in 1767, so the story goes, the young warrior left his village in search of good wood to make a drum. He was attacked by four men who took him captive. Kunta awakened to find himself blindfolded, gagged and prisoner to the white men. Haley describes how they humiliated the young warrior, stripping him naked, probing every orifice of his body, and branding him with hot iron. Later he and others were put on a slave ship for the nightmarish three-month journey to America. I wanted to get closer to Caiphus, or Caution, as we call him. I remembered back in the days, in Randfontein, when the vocal quartet Woodpeckers, led by the legendary Victor Ndlazilwane, used to come and perform for us at old Madubulaville Hall. There was always a group of talented singers known as the Katzenjammer Kids who toured with them. Young Caiphus was a member of the Kids. He showed promise, even then.

I can recall once, when we visited Letta and Caiphus at their lovely home in Pasadena, California, in 1981. After spending an unforgettable evening with them, we decided to accompany Caiphus to the A&M Studios where they were mixing one of their recordings. Later, we regretted having gone to that studio – the stickler for perfection wouldn't let go and we were there for long redoes, with the rest of us bored to death.

Occasionally, whenever I went to the West Coast on business, we would call them and they would spoil us with entertainment. We have since become even closer, now that they have relocated back home; and, thanks to them, we have met and dined with their friends, Quincy Jones (on a few occasions) and, once, with Harry Belafonte, here in South Africa.

Nana cannot forget the night when Letta Mbulu and Caiphus Semenya were performing in the New York area and invited her and her friend, Nonceba Lubanga, to Lena Horne's one-woman show on Broadway. After the concert, Caution and Letta invited the two backstage to meet the star. Nana told me afterwards that she was shivering – it was unbelievable to her that she was going to meet Lena Horne *herself*. Then, as though that were not enough excitement for one night (if not for a lifetime), as they were waiting in line to shake Lena Horne's hand, *there* appeared Bill Cosby, also in the queue to congratulate Ms Horne. Nana's boasting of the night she shook both Bill Cosby's and Lena Horne's hands at the same time, is something with which I still live to this day. She can never forget that. But then, who would?

Another highlight of my life in New York was assisting Hugh Masekela with the formalities when he was getting married. To follow African tradition, he asked me to be part of the delegation that would represent his interest to the Mbatha family whose daughter, Jabu, he wanted to marry.

He also requested me to officiate at the wedding ceremony.

A beautiful woman, Jabu Mbatha is the eldest daughter of the late Professor Mbatha and Mrs Mbatha. I agreed to assist Hughie and we also commissioned Uncle Collins Ramusi out of Chicago and the two of us led the delegation to the Mbatha family to plead Hughie's case and ask for the release of Jabu. That we negotiated and paid *ilobola* to the Mbatha family in an apartment on 5th Avenue in New York City just across from Central Park; that was a paradox of major proportions.

After spending two years as an account officer at Citibank, I was given another assignment to work on Wall Street, the Bank's trading operation in the business district. When I was given this news, I (literally) jumped, unable to contain my excitement. I had always wanted to have the experience of working in what can only be described as every investment banker's dream. It was something that I read about (what banker doesn't?). But, to be honest with you, it hadn't occurred to me in my wildest dreams that not only would I get that opportunity, but I would be working on one of the top floors of Citibank, overlooking the Statue of Liberty, Brooklyn and Staten Island. It was a marvellous opportunity – working in that area!

For the most part, I was trained by Menase, an Egyptian man, who knew South Africa quite well from various visits he had made to the country.

A very forceful character, he was a disciplinarian – and anyone who went through his hands knew they would get good training; they also knew he was a stickler for orderliness, accuracy and good performance. Under Menase's mentorship, I learned and got to practise the art of helping structure creative trading deals. We dealt, mainly, with trade instruments commonly used in global trading. An understanding of the complexities of a letter of credit was mandatory.

The bank's Wall Street premises weren't far from the New York Stock Exchange. I would make it my business (almost on a daily basis) to go to the Exchange, to witness equity trading, meet people who had first-hand experience. That way, I learned how people traded on the floor. The Exchange was an extremely busy place and it provided a lot of excitement for those who worked there as well as guests who went for the spectacle of wealth creation.

From Roosevelt Island, I took the tram up to 59th Street and then took the Lexington Express train to Wall Street and, within 40 minutes, I would be in my office. In the mornings, the trains were packed with throngs of people of all hues and cultures: Chinese, Africans, Europeans, Japanese, and native New Yorkers – that's New York, for you.

Three blocks from my office, stood the Twin Towers, comprising what was called the World Trade Centre. When the events of 9/11 occurred in 2001, I was greatly saddened by the loss of so many lives and I couldn't help but think of the many men and women with whom I had worked and the numerous friends in the banking fraternity I made during my time on the Street. I have fond memories of passing through the Twin Towers and the variety of restaurants we frequented during lunch and the cocktail bars we often visited after work.

The Bank was a great platform from which to launch my banking career. I was receiving excellent tuition. I rubbed shoulders with stockbrokers, investment bankers, traders and speculators. That environment assisted my growth and was good for character building. I became acutely aware of my role and responsibilities. Because of its location and its standing, Citibank was a great institution and anybody who worked as an officer of the bank felt the prestige and the glamour – so did I.

I groomed myself and dressed conservatively in pin stripe suits and white shirts. I read widely on anything to do with corporate finance, scanned the bibles of the day, *The Wall Street Journal* and *The New York Times.*

Time goes by very quickly, especially when you're having a good time. In 1982, Nana completed her Bachelor of Science degree in Nursing and had been accepted by a medical school in Canada. At the same time, it was time for me to honour my commitment to Citibank and return to South Africa. I had mixed emotions about that. Nana was adamant that she was not going back to South Africa.

She contended that the security situation continued to be volatile and South Africa offered no growth opportunities, especially for black women.

Citibank requested us to return to South Africa conditionally as 'international assignees'. We already had green cards, which gave us permanent residency in America. The green cards gave us some security. Should things not go well in South Africa we could always fall back on our permanent residency status in the US. Citibank further promised that if things became untenable for us in South Africa, they would evacuate us out of the country.

After a sustained debate, my wife and I reached a compromise: we would return to the United States the moment we felt uncomfortable and/or unsafe. Also, we had to admit that we were becoming homesick and there were Nana's parents to consider – they were getting on in years. This was a momentous decision for us and little did we realise what lay ahead as we planned our journey back to South Africa.

In retrospect would I have done it differently? No. We made the right decision even if, at the time, it seemed as arbitrary as yet another throw of the dice.

F1: Nana and I flank an ebullient Nelson Mandela at Carlton Hotel, Johannesburg, days after his release, 1990

F2: Meeting New York Mayor Dinkins who led a delegation to meet Madiba shortly after his release from prison

F3: (right) At the Carlton Hotel, Johannesburg, embraced by Publisher Earl Graves of Enterprise Magazine and Arthur Ashe, first Black Wimbledon Tennis Champ on a trip to visit Nelson Mandela shortly after his release from prison

F4: (below) Exchanging views with Tanzanian President Julius Nyerere at my home in Woodmead, Johannesburg, 1994

F5: Hosting Tanzanian President Julius Nyerere, at our home in 1994 flanked by my friends, left Khehla Mthembu and far right Baker Mogale

F6: With Professor Horace Huntley of Birmingham University after receiving the Key to the City of Birmingham, Alabama, conferred by the City Mayor

F7: With Ambassador Jerry Matjila in Tokyo, Japan, 1990. Then he was the Chief Representative for the ANC in that country

F8: Democratic US Congressman Donald Payne and myself after speaking at his election rally in New Jersey, 1988

F9: With First Lady Hillary Clinton (now US Secretary of State) and Richard Branson at HIV/AIDS Corporate Sponsor Gala Dinner at Kennedy Center, Washington DC, 2005

F10: Crusades against HIV/AIDS. With me are colleagues, Ben Plumley, Executive Director and Ambassador Richard Holbrooke, former Chair of Global Business Council on HIV/AIDS

F11: (right) Receiving
Botswana President Festus
Mogae at the HIV/AIDS
Conference where I was
guest speaker, Gabarone,
Botswana, 2004

F12: (below) President
Mogae honours me with
a framed Kente gift,
Johannesburg, 2004

F13: With my business mentor, Don Simmonds at Mayors' Conference in Philadelphia 1989, in James Mtume's limo

F14: Radio personality and R&B musician James Mtume (born James Forman) of 'Juicy Fruit' fame, attorney Ben Brown and friend, 1989. Both Ben and James had been to visit with me in South Africa

F15: Gaby and Nana dining with the legendary Quincy Jones in Johannesburg, South Africa (2008)

F16: South Africa's favourite music icons Letta Mbulu and Caiphus Semenya at my son Thabo's wedding, 2002

Part 8

1990–2009

36

A summing up: Of this and no other soil

Many people have asked me why I returned home in 1982 when apartheid was at its prime and the security situation was perhaps, at is worst. Yes, maybe, it was short-sighted of me to plunge my family into the reign of terror that prevailed during the period leading to the historic democratic elections of 1994. After all, my family were made permanent residents under the US Naturalisation and Immigration laws and we enjoyed almost full citizenship status, except the right to vote. All those who visited our residence on Roosevelt Island opposite the UN building in Manhattan, remarked on the privileged lifestyle with which we were blessed. With celebrated neighbours such as Kofi Annan, former Secretary General of the United Nations, and many other famed personalities, why did I bother coming back to face the adversity of South Africa's repression?

I have answered that question elsewhere in this book but it needs to be said that our return was a gamble, one that I believe paid off, although it was not without its losses and its tough times. I have mentioned some of these but there were others. As the country marched toward the true advent of democracy, many platforms were created for a debate about a future regime. I was fortunate to participate in several of these debates both here, at home, and abroad.

In April 1988, I was a participant in a diverse group of twenty-seven South Africans who met in Williamsburg, Virginia (USA) to discuss the future of South Africa. A book titled *Dialogue in Williamsburg* edited by Dr. Michael Briand captures the transcripts of what became a fiery discourse over a number of days. At that time, there was a sense of tense optimism that South Africans would begin negotiations to resolve our differences in a peaceful manner.

Shortly thereafter, I was invited to join another group of eminent South Africans to provide our thoughts on the future trajectory the country may take. The panel consisted of personalities from a cross section of the labour, business, academic and political spectrum. We were to meet over a number of weeks in a place known as Mt Fleur in the Helderburg Mountains, near Stellenbosch. Our mission was to create possible future scenarios to forecast without predicting what might happen in South Africa over the next decade. Facilitated by Shell International, the participants included Trevor Manuel, our present Minister in the Presidency, National Planning Commission and Tito Mboweni, the outgoing Governor of the Reserve Bank and various eminent businesses, labour, non-governmental organisations and academic representatives.

We spent several months debating possible scenarios that a new democratically elected government would pursue. Each story represented a flight path South Africa might take. After much debate, we concluded that a scenario we subsequently named "The Flight of the Flamingos" would be most suited to our country as it embraced inclusive democracy and sustained growth and was devoid of populist ideals. "Flamingos live in great numbers often scattered with separate groups. For some there's ample food, while others struggle. Some guard their privileged places from those who are marginalised. However, when conflict seems imminent, flamingos don't destroy each other. After some positioning they slowly reach agreement to better ground. They struggle to take off yet they are capable of flying high and far," the group concluded. The Mount Fleur Scenarios have, over the years, been used as a model case study at several institutions including the National University of Singapore where I later attended.

One of the great pleasures of my life has been to sit and observe how things are unfolding since 1994 when a democratic government was elected. I have been privileged to live through a difficult but well-managed transition that has attracted worldwide attention since the advent of our democracy, which installed the venerable Nelson Mandela as its first President.

I don't believe we have perfected 'The Flight of the Flamingos' scenario but the resolve exists to get there.

I cannot talk about my business activities during the turbulent 1980s and omit the name of my esteemed friend and mentor, Don Simmons from Muskogee, Oklahoma. I was highly inspired by his father, Jake, of whom the *Los Angeles Times* wrote, '... few men seem destined to shape history quite as thoroughly as did Jake Simmons, Snr.' Mr Simmons created what was perhaps the most successful African-American oil dynasty and negotiated multimillion dollar oil deals while wielding considerable influence as a political power broker. This he was able to accomplish in a very difficult time in the history of his country.

Almost single-handedly, Don transformed my perspective on doing business and very nearly, on my eating and drinking habits. An imposingly tall man with a huge frame around him, Don had mastered the art of good food. I remember once we were heading to a famous steakhouse in New York City, Smith and Wollinsky after a stormy but successful deal negotiation. As I recall, the restaurant was on the corner of 797 3rd Avenue and 49th Street in midtown Manhattan and we were some two hundreds metres away from it. Don insisted we stop over at a Wendy's to 'lay up' with a double burger. Soon thereafter we walked across to the steakhouse where he ordered us each, with his elder brother Jake, a double whisky of The Famous Grouse on ice while awaiting our sumptuous meal. After digging into what seemed like ten kilos of generously proportioned pieces of steak, he then removed the napkin from around his shirt collar. He then slowly rubbed his big tummy with satisfaction and duly declared, 'Even John Rockefeller with all his bucks, couldn't be fuller than we are!'

Don was a regular visitor to South Africa in the 1980s and 1990s, and he and I would spend long hours in his hotel suite at the Rosebank Hotel imbibing his favourite scotch, and consuming tons of his favourite prime beef steak. '*A luta continua*,' he would say and laugh out loud as he lectured me on business survival skills and the importance of leveraging on established contacts. My first visit to the US Senate and subsequent engagements with US congressmen and senators such as Paul Simon, Charles Rangel, Don Payne, Sam Nunn and others were all engineered by this master negotiator.

It was Don who led me through the doors of the Chrysler Corporation in Detroit seeking a Jeep dealership licence and into the head office of McDonald's outside Chicago, where we tried to negotiate for a South African master franchise from the giant restaurant group without knowing that they had other plans. A few months later, McDonald's entered the country on their own terms and offered me the option of acquiring a restaurant franchise. I considered that a non-starter and decided to embark on my own restaurant venture.

Around that time, I met an African-American named Harvey Lynch who told me that he had just sold his business in Swaziland and intended to settle in Johannesburg. Harvey was a native of the southern state of Louisiana and his entrepreneurial interests were in the poultry business. After getting to know each other, we decided to venture into a joint ownership of a fried chicken franchise business called Road Runner Crispy Fried Chicken.

The recipe for our product had been somewhat adapted from a well-known chicken flavour common in the southern states of America. Harvey had already made a modest start on the business model and approached me to invest in it and create a growth strategy. I relished the challenge and, after a few initial hiccups, we had established franchised restaurants in the black townships of Cape Town, Transkei, the East Rand and Johannesburg. Our recipe was a simple fried chicken served with essential nutrients that we produced from a central kitchen in our

Northcliff premises and supplied to our restaurants. Business flourished and later we invited new investors to help grow our franchise chain. Our growth plans were unfortunately hindered by the sudden return of Harvey to the US due to pressing family matters. The business was subsequently sold to third party interests.

Despite an adverse and an almost hostile trading environment, I always felt a need to support those who had novel business ideas. At the beginning of the 1990s, I helped establish the first black-owned short-term insurance company, African General Insurance Company (AFGEN). This idea came out of the genius of Khehla Mthembu who had the influence and ability as he'd worked for a large insurance company as an insurance executive. One of our mainstay clients, we hoped, would be the burgeoning taxi industry. Khehla and I subsequently collaborated with Vusi Sithole.

Vusi had worked with Khehla and both were experts in the insurance industry, particularly on the marketing side.

Realising a need for additional capital and technical expertise, we invited two large insurance companies to form a joint venture with us and this gave birth to AFGEN. I was asked to serve as chairman and Kay was appointed managing director. As we'd hoped, our business found a captive market within the burgeoning taxi industry which was an integral part of FABCOS (the Foundation of African Business and Consumer Services). Outside of that we never stopped trying to make inroads into the insurance industry despite the huge constraints with which black business was confronted. Access to credit and denial of opportunities to manage were clearly the key obstacles that stifled entrepreneurship. During that time, I also negotiated the entry of a well known pizza brand, Dominos, into South Africa. Pizza was a relatively unknown product and although we succeeded, at great cost, in promoting our franchise, we could not raise enough cash to sustain the business.

Prior to these ventures, Don and I had almost concluded our discussions with Proline Hair Cosmetics to manufacture and distribute on the sub-continent. Comer Cottrell, President of Proline was impressed with growth opportunities here although I found him somewhat inflexible in his approach. I turned my back on the deal because I had learned when to cut my losses.

A very likeable and hugely successful entrepreneur, Comer would constantly remind me during our steak lunches to 'stop nosing and tasting the wine like a Frenchman'. A native of Dallas, Texas, Comer had a private box at Cowboy Stadium where he and his guests lived high on the hog while watching football.

Meanwhile the country was heating up. We were making a name as aggressive entrepreneurs in previously unexplored areas. I had been involved with Jonty Sadler, Don Ncube, Dr Motlana, Reuel Khoza, all reputable entrepreneurs in the creation and running of a multimillion rand water-themed entertainment park, Shareworld, north east of Soweto. Regrettably, this innovative idea with impressive infrastructure, turned out to be a dismal failure. It is hard to explain the impact of a faltering business to investors and needless to say, we were crushed. A large bank loan remained outstanding and was reported as one of the biggest loans to be written off by the bank that backed us. As several people remarked, Shareworld was a damn good idea that arrived ahead of its time. The derelict infrastructure opposite the giant FNB soccer stadium remains what it was, a dream deferred!

But all this has to be put into perspective. These achievements did not make a measurable impact on a mature economy dominated by industrial conglomerates and multinational companies. I understood this. The capital markets were closed to Africans and the existing repressive laws continued to suppress black business aspirations.

Dr Sam Motsuenyane would refer to us as 'capitalists without capital'. And we were. We were trying to create capital and opportunities for our people so that they could find a way into the South African economy.

Things then weren't nearly what they are today with the advent of Black Economic Empowerment (BEE). It is important to put the introduction of this policy into perspective. I have already mentioned how tirelessly many of us worked to advocate the lifting of restrictions imposed on black business by the apartheid government. These calls date back to the founding of NAFCOC decades ago which, traditionally, had represented the interests of disenfranchised business people in the country.

Perhaps, more than anything else in recent times, it was the historic summit held in the Kruger National Park resort of Mopani that set the stage for the implementation of BEE. At Mopani Lodge from 29 to 31 October 1993 several senior members of the ANC, a government in waiting, met with their black business counterparts to debate ways and means of creating an enabling environment in which black business would be provided with tangible incentives to grow. White business, we argued, had been nurtured and allowed to thrive for over forty years under the apartheid government. In our own self-interest we needed to make a case to the incoming government to recognise our potential and sought to create a sustainable partnership under a new dispensation.

This conference was the brainchild of Willie Ramoshaba, the founder publisher of Portfolio of Black Business.

It was also partially made possible by the good offices of Deloitte and Touche (thanks to one of our members, Jeff van Rooyen). The ANC delegation was represented by the likes of top business leader and chairman of blue-chip companies, Cyril Ramaphosa, Trevor Manuel, later to be Minister of Finance, Tito Mboweni, who became Reserve Bank Governor and ex-Premier Popo Molefe, chairman of Armscor. Members of the Black Business Steering Committee that organised this indaba included publisher Willie Ramoshaba, Danisa Baloyi, Eric Mafuna, Zamani Jali, Ngila Muendane and my wife, Nana.

In the end, the historic Memorandum of Accord was signed between the newly formed National Black Business Caucus (NBBC) and the ANC. This agreement outlined the essential principles that would underpin a future relationship of mutual co-operation. We all agreed that an adherence to those principles would help to accelerate black economic empowerment. I was part of the Black Business delegation that subsequently signed this historic document at Shell House in Johannesburg where the ANC was head-quartered prior to moving to Chief Albert Luthuli House.

BEE has given rise to scores and perhaps hundreds of new entrants, mainly African, into the realm of real business in South Africa. I was one of the early beneficiaries of BEE. In 1994, I created a joint venture with a highly successful national retailer in electronics to form a cellular phone company known as Afrilink.

To add gravitas to our efforts, I invited the well-known Soweto entrepreneur, Richard Maponya as a partner. Afrilink grew to a level where Vodacom, one of our clients, considered it advantageous to buy us out in 1996.

Since then, several new entrepreneurs have successfully entered the realm of business and some have created world class enterprises. A case in point is the giant cellular company, MTN, led by Phuthuma Nhleko and ably assisted by a group of very capable technocrats. There are others who have been able to plug market gaps like true entrepreneurs. I am here reminded of the mining magnate, Patrice Motsepe, Dr Nthato Motlana, founder of the first Medical Insurance company, Sizwe, Tokyo Sexwale, chairman of the conglomerate, Mvelaphanda and many others in a variety of industries. Several others are showing great promise and have permanently transformed our economic landscape.

However, I do look forward to a day when we as African business people will graduate from purchasing equity portions of existing businesses and create a wave of new entrepreneurial undertakings from ground zero. The one sticky obstacle remains access to funding; our developmental finance institutions are going to have to transform their character and structures to help fulfil this critical mission. Most of these institutions behave as though their primary objective was to yield high returns for the shareholder who, in the main, is the government. Institutions such as the Industrial Development Corporation as well as provincial development corporations need to be re-mandated and reminded of the pressing need to bolster entrepreneurship with a view to expanding employment.

I am also confident that with time, interventionist policies such as Affirmative Action, which have assisted in accelerating some equity in the workplace, will no longer be necessary as our economy continues to mature. The record will show that I was one of the key proponents, and still am, of this policy. I have written and lectured extensively on the strategic importance of such interventionist measures as Affirmative Action and BEE but these need to be adopted with sensitivity to guard against the polarisation of the workforce.

We also have to guard against the possible loss of our institutional memory bank which was selectively placed in a relatively small pool. The evidence of deficiencies in skills and collective experience in running our towns, cities and other institutions may require some introspection.

National competitiveness in a globalising world should remain a strategic priority and, therefore, we have to guard against alienating others who may feel excluded. The country needs to retain scarce skills to raise our competitive edge and to attract foreign investors. By the same token, those who may feel alienated by these policies have to be equally cognisant of the essentiality of these policies in a workplace with the kind of inequalities as found here. I am convinced that large scale shared ownership of resources, business entities and an enlarged pool of all levels of management will, with time, remove the need for any artificial levers of change. I am indeed optimistic about the future and I know as Tennyson said, 'Tho' much is taken, much abides.'

But that is for the future. For now I am content with what I have achieved and I have had the added pleasure of watching my wife's career, both in the private and public sector where she serves, flourish beyond measure. Together, we have raised a well-knit family who regard us as role models. Returning home in the early 1980s was a bold step at the time, yet everything has evened out. I have tried, over the years, to make it my business to influence and be influenced, lead and be led, and, most importantly, bring up my children in partnership with my wife in a way that any responsible father would (or should) to instil in them the virtues of goodness, generosity and respect for others. My final word to them is: your responsibility to your families and country should remain paramount in your goals. That is the hallmark of greatness and service to mankind. To paraphrase Jake Simmons Snr in his letter of the 17th of January 1972 to his children:

'Protect your Reputation because Reputation is the Slide Rule by which History, the Public and your children will measure your worth'.

Home is where my career took off. From South Africa I draw inspiration and always will. From the island I draw strength. Which is why I recently returned the trumpet to Robben Island where it has been placed on display in the museum as part of our legacy for future generations and others visiting this place of great memories. I am of this, and no other soil.

G1: The B♭ trumpet in the Robben Island museum

G2: Mr Mlangeni and myself flanking Mr Mandela at a 86th golf birthday lunch for Mr Mlangeni

$\mathcal{G}$lossary

LANGUAGE KEY

S – Sotho
A – Afrikaans
T – Tsotsitaal
Z – Zulu
X – Xhosa

Abanumzana (X) – Misters
Abuti (S) – Elder brother
Amabhaca (X) – A Xhosa clan from Transkei
Amaqaba (X) – Non-believers
Baas (A) – Boss
Baba (Z) – Father
Basutoland – Lesotho
Bommangwane (S) – Aunts
Bontebokke (A) – Type of buck
Boggarts (T) – Blue jeans
Bouspan (A) – Building team
Bra (T) – Brother
Broer (A) – Brother
Chommie (T) – Friend
Die Blok is warm (A) –The pressure is on
Dipoko (S) – Ghosts
Dompas (A) – 'Dumb pass', name for pass book
Drie maaltye (A) – Three meals
E-kasi – Meaning 'home', used to refer to location
Fanakalo – Anglicised African languages
Greenfield de novo – A brand new operation
Haak (A) – Come on
Handlanger (A) – Handy man
Holsum – Brand of cooking lard
Huis (A) – House
Intambo (Z) – Execution by hanging
Kaboe mealies – Boiled loose kernels of maize
Kaffir – Derogatory term for black

Ka mo lokeisheneng – At the location
Katkops (A) – Cat heads, referring to quarter loaves of bread baked in prisons
Khulukhuts (X) – Solitary confinement cells
Klap (A) – Slap in the face
Knobkerrie (A) – A club or stick with a rounded head
Kolobe (S) – Pig
Kolonel, ek het jou honderd hardegatte gebring (A) – Colonel, I've brought you a hundred hard arses
Ko thabeng – At the mountain
Kuyabheda (Z) – It is bad
Kwela-kwela – Climb, climb, referring to a police van
Kyk net vir hom (A) – Just look at him
Landbouspan (A) – Agricultural team
Malaishas (T) – Loaders
Malaitas (T) – Hustlers and thugs, gang formed in the 1920s
Malome (S) – Uncle
Mfana (Z) – Boy
Mme (S) – Mother
Moegoes (T) – Country bumpkin
Moholo- Maize porridge
Mokhotsi, areye reobabontsa (S) – Friend, let's go and show them
Morabaraba – Game of stones, similar to checkers
Motoho (S) – Maize porridge
Nnake (S) – Affectionate word for my child derived from *ngoanaka* – My child

Necklaced – A form of execution for those accused of being collaborators, where a burning tyre was placed around the neck

Nkhono (S) – Grandmother

Ntate (S) – Father

Ntate Moholo (S) – Grandfather

Ons dien met trots (A) – We serve with pride

Ou Tronk (A) – Old prison

Ousie (S) – Elder sister

Outie (T) – Streetwise young man

Padkos (A) – Food for the road

Phuzamandla (Z) – Strength drink, served in South African prisons, containing nutrients compensating for deficiencies in routine starchy diet served to African prisoners

Poqo (X) – Pure

Rondavels (A) – Round mud thatched hut

Rooibos (A) – Herbal tea from rooibos (red bush) plant

Sjambok (A) – Whip

Skaftins (A) – Metal lunch boxes

Spans (A) – Teams, used for prison duty

Toyi-toyiing (T) – Dancing and singing associated with political protests

Umabhalane (Z) – Clerical employee

Uza kundishiya nabani kulo mzi wethu? (X) – Who are you leaving me with in this our home?

Val in (A) – Get in line

Volks (A) – Folks

Zinc trunk (A) – Jail made from corrugated iron sheets

Ziyabheda (Z) – Things are bad

Bibliography

Briand, Michael. 1989. *Dialogue in Williamsburg. The Turning Point for South Africa?* San Francisco, California. Institute for Contemporary Studies (ICS) Press.

Callinicos, Luli. 2000. *The World that made Mandela a Heritage Trail.* Johannesburg: STE Publishers.

Greenberg, Jonathan. 1991. *Staking a Claim.* New York: Penguin Books.

Mandela, Nelson Rolihlahla. 1994. *A Long Walk to Freedom.* Johannesburg: Macdonald Purnell.

Masekela, Hugh. 2004. *Still Grazing.* New York: Three Rivers Press.

Mercer, Derrick. 1988. *Chronicle of the 20th Century.* London: Chronicle Communications, p. 144. www.sacc.ct.org.za

Mgxashe, Mxolisi. 2006. *Are You With Us?* Houghton, Johannesburg: Mafube Publishing and Tafelberg.

Molamu, Louis. 2003. *Tsotsi-taal: A Dictionary of the Language of Sophiatown.* Pretoria: University of South Africa.

Mount Fleur Scenarios Video. 1992. Mount Fleur, Cape Town: University of the Western Cape. Pogrund, Benjamin. 1997. *How Can a Man Die Better. The Life of Robert Sobukwe.* Johannesburg: Jonathan Ball Publishers.

Zinzi Khulu Productions.1994. *A Journey Back.* Video. Johannesburg.

The author also refers to various articles from the following sources: *Bantu World, Rand Daily Mail, Sunday Times*, the National Archives of South Africa in Pretoria, the Truth and Reconciliation records available on www.doj.gov.za/trc/report as well as the Robben Island Musuem website, www.robben-island.org.za

Index

$\mathcal{I}llustrations$

C3: Taken about three months before being arrested and sent to Robben Island, a photo of a young tender-looking 18-year-old Gaby

C4: A young Gaby at home in the family front yard age 16, in 1960 Bekkersdal

C5(a): My sister, Semakaleng

C5(b): My brother, Malefetsa, on the right with a friend

PAGES 228–234. 1970–1976

D1(a): A youthful Nana shortly before our marriage

D1(b): My parents-in-law, Asaph and Machipu Matlala outside our Mabopane home, 1972

D2: Our wedding day, accepting congratulations from the presiding Officer, Soweto, November 1971

D3: Toasting the marriage with my cousin Sy Magomola on Nana's right and Matsatsi, Nana's cousin

D4: My sister-in-law, Doris Mosieleng in a warm pose, 1987

D5: An elated Gaby with Nana holding newborn baby, Dineo-Amara, at my Unisa graduation day, April 1975

D6: Family and friends came to wish me well after my Unisa graduation, 1975. Many were seeing me for the first time since my arrest in 1963. The tall heads at the back are that of my cousin Simon and Leopard Mosito, who was later killed by the apartheid police in 1989

D7: Standing outside our first 'matchbox' house in Mabopane, Pretoria, 1974

D8: Nana posing in front of our car, Mabopane, 1974

D9: My son Thabo enjoying his traditional wedding with his bride, Mosima, in the midst of family and friends, 2002

D10: Gaby and Nana's daughters Naledi and Dineo at home

D11: Our first family visit to Robben Island in 1995

D12: My granddaughters, Boitumelo and Botshelo, posing with their parents

D13: Moon Masemola, facing camera. He adopted me after the Apartheid government 'banished' me to Polokwane shortly after my release from Robben Island

D14: My childhood friend Joe Seremane to whom I was manacled en route to Robben Island. Esther, his late wife, next to him

PAGES 258–264. 1976–1982

E1: In Rio de Janeiro, Brazil (Copa Capana Beach) on my way to the USA to study, July 1976 (where I 'discovered my freedom')

E2: My first day in New York, August 8 1976

E3(a): International Student Director Kirk Robey (far left) with the 1976 intake of Ball State University foreign students

E3(b): Newby and his wife Joyce at Schidler Apartments, our student living quarters in Muncie, Indiana, 1976

E4: Joyful moment after receiving my Masters at Ball State, Muncie, Indiana, 1977